Introduction to Action Research

Social

Research

for

Social

Change

Davydd J. Greenwood
Morten Levin

SAGE Publications
International Educational and Professional Publisher
Thousand Oaks   London   New Delhi

For information:

SAGE Publications, Inc.
2455 Teller Road
Thousand Oaks, California 91320
E-mail: order@sagepub.com

SAGE Publications Ltd.
6 Bonhill Street
London EC2A 4PU
United Kingdom

SAGE Publications India Pvt. Ltd.
M-32 Market
Greater Kailash I
New Delhi 110 048 India

Printed in the United States of America

Library of Congress Cataloging-in-Publication Data

Greenwood, Davydd J.
    Introduction to action research: Social research for social change/
by Davydd J. Greenwood and Morten Levin.
      p. cm.
    Includes bibliographical references and index.
    ISBN 0-7619-1675-X (cloth: alk. paper).—ISBN 0-7619-1676-8
(pbk.: alk. paper)
    1. Action research.   I. Levin, Morten.

                 98-25539

98 99 00 01 02 03 04 10 9 8 7 6 5 4 3 2 1

Acquiring Editor:	C. Deborah Laughton
Editorial Assistant:	Eileen Carr
Production Editor:	Wendy Westgate
Editorial Assistant:	Patricia Zeman
Typesetter/Designer:	Marion Warren
Cover Designer:	Candice Harman

Contents

Foreword

Davydd Greenwood and Morten Levin met for the first time in 1986 at a planning meeting for the Einar Thorsrud Memorial Conference, and our cooperation started half a year later. Levin spent his sabbatical in 1987 at the School of Industrial and Labor Relations at Cornell, working at the Program for Employment and Workplace Systems. Greenwood was also affiliated with this group at the time, and gradually we got to know each other better. Our laughter, irony, politics, and professional interests resonated. Levin made frequent trips to Ithaca, including another sabbatical leave in 1994-95 at Cornell.

In 1986, Levin was already well established in action research (AR), whereas Greenwood was in the final year of his first major AR project in the industrial cooperatives of Mondragón in the Spanish Basque Country. For Greenwood, the planning conference was an interesting event for two reasons. He met some of the important figures in the European, American, and Australian AR movement, and he got his first dose of the process of participatory planning Scandinavian style. Levin had already been engaged in teaching AR theory and models at the Norwegian University of Science and Technology in Trondheim for some time. Greenwood would not take AR into the classroom until 1990, and had not yet thought through the teaching issues that AR would raise.

Our real collaboration began with students present, and our collaboration has been sustained by our concern with teaching. In 1989, Morten Levin and Max Elden invited Greenwood to Trondheim to give a set of seminars on the Mondragón work to the first group of doctoral students of AR in Trondheim's innovative graduate program. The opportunity and effort to explain a complex, 3-year process of AR to a group of knowledgeable students left Greenwood convinced that he had to take AR into the classroom at Cornell. He began this process in 1990 with a seminar that changed his teaching practice forever. The story of that very first seminar is documented by the participants in a coauthored monograph about the experience (Elvemo, Grant Matthews, Greenwood, Martin, Strubel, & Thomas, 1997). Levin and a group of his students visited Cornell at the end of that first seminar, and Greenwood's students and Levin's students had a spirited discussion of AR.

Subsequently, Greenwood and Levin exchanged visits frequently. Greenwood was invited regularly to advise Levin's group of doctoral students and to serve on a pair of dissertation defense committees. Then Levin appointed Greenwood to the Norwegian Enterprise 2000 Program module he directs to serve as a kind of AR consultant and provocateur for Levin's AR team. During some of those visits, we also lectured together at the university. Levin coached Greenwood carefully on the design of Greenwood's first search conference.

Greenwood and Levin served with Hans van Beinum, René van der Vlist, Kjell S. Johannessen, and Claude Faucheux as staff members in the Scandinavian Action Research Development Program, which brought about 30 professional action researchers together for additional training to improve the quality of their research and writing about AR over a 2-year period. We were stunned to learn how difficult it was for practitioners of AR both to communicate research findings in writing and to get a firm handle on epistemological issues.

These experiences led us to recognize our common commitment to teaching and our similar political and ethical views. In the process, we became close friends. But these experiences also caused us to recognize that we share many ideas that add up to a rather different view of AR from the ones we commonly read about. Although the methods we employ are not new, our concerns with the political relationship between AR and conventional social research, the passive social role of universities, and the general lack of epistemological ambition and methodological attention in much AR writing told us that we had a view of AR enough at variance with other views that it would be worth articulating in writing.

Levin proposed we write this book, using his sabbatical leave in 1994-95 as the time to plan it together. As we got into the process, we not only had a wonderful time, we deepened our conviction that our view of AR is different from the dominant views. We also had a number of chances to try out these views on both students and colleagues, including through some coauthored papers. This book emerged out of the challenges of teaching about AR and a common desire to increase the quality and reputation of AR by charting an extremely ambitious epistemological and political agenda for AR within universities.

Our students have been with us throughout in this process. They have taught us how to teach (and not to teach) about AR; they have critiqued most of the ideas in this book; they have constantly held us accountable with their tough questions deriving from the existential dilemmas they face as action researchers. We have been their colearners in the process of creating this book.

So the present book has emerged out of an 11-year dialogue between Greenwood and Levin in which students of all kinds and ages have been active participants. Our commitment to these students, combined with our belief that we have something new to say about AR, caused us to write the book. For this reason, we dedicate the book to our students.

The book is unique in a number of ways. It lays out an epistemological agenda for AR, one that reaches well beyond the aspirations of many practitioners and that issues a head-on challenge to the conventional academic social sciences on both epistemological and ethical grounds. It is also unique in trying to map out the diversity and complexity of the intellectual and political streams that feed into AR. We do not try to reduce this complexity to one ideal model. Rather, we want readers to understand something about the different approaches to AR practice.

We took this approach intentionally. We do not think there is one right way to do AR, even though we have practices that we prefer personally. AR is both context specific and linked closely to the skills, background, and interests of the practitioner. We have learned through our teaching that we cannot predict how particular students will connect to AR issues. We know that good pedagogy requires an open and diverse approach that enables students to find their own points of connection.

Though a completed book, this remains a work in progress, an invitation to dialogue and debate in a field that has not seen enough of it. Our aim and hope is that the book will encourage the reader to reflect critically on AR praxis; we invite you to join us in this project.

Acknowledgments

Our greatest thanks to our students for motivating us and helping us clarify our thinking.

This work has not received financial support from any granting agency, and so it has been carried on during moments stolen from other duties and at the expense of our free time and our families. Pilar Fernández-Cañadas Greenwood and Turid Sand Levin have not only been patient with us but have provided the space and encouragement needed to bring this large project to its completion. Such debts can be acknowledged but not repaid.

We have benefited from superb critical advice. C. Deborah Laughton, our editor at Sage, is a wonderful professional editor in every way. Our colleagues at Cornell, Larry Palmer and John Forester, also provided exceptionally helpful critical readings of the penultimate draft, and their comments helped shape the final version. We also thank Sandra Hollingsworth, David Fetterman, Kathy Whitaker, Melvin E. (Gene) Franks, and Sharon Kemp for reviewing the manuscript.

There are weaknesses in what we have written. Some arise from our stretch to incorporate so many different AR approaches; others from insufficient time to rewrite particular sections yet once again. Our students and colleagues have done their best to help us. The remaining faults belong to us.

To our students

PART 1

What Is Action Research?

The opening section of this work begins with an overview of the core elements in our own view of action research (AR). Following this is a brief and general history of the thinkers, institutions, and practices that have been key in the development of AR. We close with two AR cases designed to provide a narrative sense of the processes that go on in AR projects.

CHAPTER

1

Introduction
Action Research, Diversity, and Democracy

Action research (AR) can help us build a better, freer society. This book offers a general overview of AR, including a comprehensive philosophical justification for it, a review of some of the most commonly used methods, case examples, and a review of a variety of different approaches to AR praxis. Throughout, we advocate AR and its social change agenda vis-à-vis other forms of social research that do not contribute as actively and directly to processes of democratic social change and the simultaneous creation of valid social knowledge. Our advocacy rests on two distinct but related bases: democratic inclusion and social research quality. AR democratizes research processes through the inclusion of the local stakeholders as coresearchers. We also believe that AR can produce better research results than those arising from the professional expert social research models. And we see AR as central to the enactment of a commitment to democratic social transformation through social research.

—◄o►—

ACTION RESEARCH DEFINED

AR is social research carried out by a team encompassing a professional action researcher and members of an organization or community seeking to improve their situation. AR promotes broad participation in the research process and supports action leading to a more just or satisfying situation for the stakeholders.

Together, the professional researcher and the stakeholders define the problems to be examined, cogenerate relevant knowledge about them, learn and execute social research techniques, take actions,[1] and interpret the results of actions based on what they have learned. AR rests on the belief and experience that all people—professional action researchers included—accumulate, organize, and use complex knowledge constantly in everyday life. This belief is visible in any AR project because the first step professional action researchers and members of a community or organization take is to define a problem that they seek to resolve. They begin by pooling their knowledge. AR democratizes the relationship between the professional researcher and the local interested parties.

Because it is a research practice with a social change agenda, AR involves a critique of conventional academic practices and organizations that study social problems without trying to resolve them. Although AR views academic and professional knowledge systems that do not engage practice direction as wrongheaded, action researchers neither reject formal research methods nor ignore the epistemological issues that necessarily undergird the development of valid social knowledge. These issues are dealt with in greater detail throughout Part 2, particularly in Chapters 4, "Scientific Methods and Action Research," and 5, "An Epistemological Foundation for Action Research."

OUR ASSUMPTIONS ABOUT THE READERS OF THIS BOOK

We assume that our main audience has previous experience either in formal social research or in social change-oriented action. Thus, to be effective, our writing must present AR to readers who are seeking what they hope will be more appropriate and productive ways of conducting social research. We do not ask the reader to ignore prior experience; we encourage you to use this as a point of reference as you learn about AR approaches. As in our classrooms, we see the relationship between the reader and the authors as a collaborative one.

WHY GENERAL OVERVIEWS OF
AR ARE HARD TO FIND

We decided to write a general overview of AR because of our experience with university students and practitioners encountering the subject for the first time. They generally lack access to a sufficiently comprehensive and balanced way to learn about the diverse origins, theories, methods, motives, and problems associated with this complex field. Although there is an extensive bibliography of works on AR, including a number of introductory works that provide overviews of various approaches (we cite these throughout), we felt that another kind of general book was needed. Existing works either are compendia, focus on a particular variety of AR to the exclusion of others, or do not link the history, philosophy, and practice of AR to a sufficiently broad set of philosophical and political issues. The present book tries to overcome some of these limitations.

Gaining such an overview of AR is difficult, in part because of the organization of AR praxis. Action researchers are found in social service agencies, nongovernmental organizations, international development agencies, planning departments, and industry and spread around the disciplines in academic institutions (e.g., education, planning, communications, social services, program evaluation, sociology, anthropology, organizational behavior). Almost nowhere in academia is there a "department" of AR. Rather, networks of colleagues from diverse disciplines share an interest in AR. One result is that AR practitioners share very little common knowledge, read different journals and books, and often write in ignorance of relevant contributions of others in AR from other fields.

We do not believe that creating a university department of AR would be the answer to this dilemma. Indeed, we view the departmentalization of the social sciences as one of the ways in which the social reform agenda of the fields emerging from political economy in the 19th century was eliminated. We want the reader to understand that what follows is not an overview of a discipline in the making. It is a presentation of a diverse and often divergent set of practices centered on putting social research to use for democratic social change.

To that end, we try to include a representation of the diverse approaches to AR and offer some references to allow readers to follow their own interests. What we include is limited by our own experience, our judgements of the different approaches we know about, and our own epistemological, methodological, and political agendas. Still, our goal is to give an honest and broad-minded presentation of the field of AR from our point of view. We are fully aware that the map is not the territory, and we know that knowledgeable AR practitioners will find gaps and idiosyncrasies in our choices.

ACTION RESEARCH, APPLIED RESEARCH, AND QUALITATIVE VERSUS QUANTITATIVE RESEARCH

AR refers to the conjunction of three elements: research, action, and participation. Unless all three elements are present, the process cannot be called AR. Put another way, AR is a form of research that generates knowledge claims for the express purpose of taking action to promote social change and social analysis. But the social change we refer to is not just any kind of change. AR aims to increase the ability of the involved community or organization members to control their own destinies more effectively and to keep improving their capacity to do so.

AR is not applied research. AR explicitly rejects the separation between thought and action that underlies the pure-applied distinction that has characterized social research for a number of generations. Valid social knowledge is derived from practical reasoning engaged in through action. As action researchers, we believe that action is the only sensible way to generate and test new knowledge. We find the widespread belief that being a social scientist means not being engaged in social action so peculiar and counterintuitive that we devote a considerable amount of space to explaining the phenomenon in Part 2 of this book.

We also have noticed a tendency for people to believe that AR must be qualitative research rather than quantitative research. This unjustifiable assumption probably arises from the belief that action-oriented work cannot be scientific (precisely because it involves action) and the additional assumption (erroneous in our view) that quantitative research must be more scientific than qualitative research. Because we see no merit in these assumptions, we reject the notion that AR is qualitative research only.

Action researchers accept no a priori limits on the kinds of social research techniques they use. Surveys, statistical analyses, interviews, focus groups, ethnographies, and life histories are all acceptable, if the reason for deploying them has been agreed on by the AR collaborators and if they are used in a way that does not oppress the participants. Knowing exactly how much heavy metal is in the groundwater somewhere may be as much a part of an AR project as knowing how people make sense of the future. Formal quantitative, qualitative, and mixed methods all are appropriate to differing situations.

RESEARCH, PARTICIPATION, AND ACTION

Despite the powerful differences among AR practitioners, we believe that several important basic commitments link most of us. AR is composed of a balance of three elements. If any one of the three is absent, then the process is not AR.

- ☐ Research: We believe in research, in the power and value of knowledge, and we believe that AR is one of the most powerful ways to generate new knowledge.

- ☐ Participation: We believe in participation, placing a strong value on democracy and control over one's own life situations. These values permeate the arguments and create a strong general commitment to democratizing the knowledge generation process. AR involves trained social researchers who serve as facilitators and teachers of members of local communities or organizations. Because these people together establish the AR agenda, generate the knowledge necessary to transform the situation, and put the results to work, AR is a participatory process in which everyone involved takes some responsibility.

- ☐ Action: AR is also participatory in a second sense because AR aims to alter the initial situation of the group, organization, or community in the direction of a more self-managing, liberated state. What is defined as a liberated state varies from one practitioner to another. Some use AR to create a kind of liberation through greater self-realization. Others emphasize more political meanings of liberation, and they vary among themselves regarding how strong a political liberation agenda they advocate. Still others believe that AR occurs in any kind of research activity where there is participation by some members of the organization being studied. Although a few practitioners try to link AR and revolutionary praxis, by and large, AR practitioners are democratic reformers rather than revolutionaries.

All these different approaches are further subdivided by the kinds of topics they deal with: community development, change in educational systems, economic development and liberation in the Third World, participatory change in core institutions of society (companies, administrative bureaucracies, etc.).

Many of these different approaches to AR are incompatible. Some rest on Marxist notions of political economy and social transformation, others are rooted in pragmatic philosophy, still others build on a particular brand of social psychology, and a few simply advocate that, whatever the question, participation is the answer. We take seriously the obligation to make the reader aware of these differences, but we harbor no illusions about reconciling them.

ACTION RESEARCH, THE DISCIPLINES, AND COVERAGE

As noted earlier, AR is not a discipline. It involves practitioners from anthropology, development studies, education, engineering, gender studies, human services, psychology, human services, social work, sociology, planning, civil engineering, and many other fields, including many forms of nonacademic practice. Consequently, students will not find AR presented in introductory disciplinary courses in most departments. Academic disciplines use introductory courses to recruit neophyte disciplinarians and to enhance enrollments to satisfy the demands of university administrations. These courses generally do not aim to attract scholars and practitioners who share certain views about democracy, participation, and the creation of useful knowledge.

In a higher education environment, this is not a promising way to work because disciplinary enrollments and boundaries are the tools used in academic competition and administrative management. Despite this, we encounter increasing numbers of students from diverse fields who come to us to learn about AR. Some come in reaction to their unsatisfying experiences of the abstractions and social passivity of their home fields, others because of their rejection of the instrumentalism of many so-called applied fields, and still others because of their experiences with other approaches that are critical of "canonical" disciplinary systems (e.g., feminism, neo-Marxism, critical theory). The teaching challenge with such heterogeneous groups is how to present an introduction to people who are searching for something, to provide them with enough background to permit them to continue learning about AR independently, and, at the same time, to build as directly as possible on the experience that moved them to explore AR in the first place.

After thinking through this problem and teaching AR courses over the last decade, we decided that the best approach is for us to develop a consistent historical, philosophical, and ethical argument for AR, provide some cases of AR practice, and then introduce a variety of different AR approaches. To fulfill the conditions of this design, we develop a philosophical argument for AR as scientific activity and a view of the links of AR to many different kinds of reform movements in the sciences, engineering, and social sciences. We couple this with a political economic argument that accounts for the suppression of praxis-oriented social research in academia. Because we intend to bridge theory and praxis, we also develop discussions of AR methodologies and tools. Then, to evoke some the diverse visions among AR practitioners, we provide a general overview of some of the main AR positions (including our own). Many of these positions ignore one another in practice.

This general overview will be criticized by other AR practitioners because it is not truly comprehensive and because we express our own views about each approach we review. AR has many proponents, and several different groups would like to claim they know the "right" way to do AR, whereas others reject the name entirely, preferring (often for sensible reasons) another term (such as *participatory research, human inquiry,* or *action science*). Occasionally, some practitioners are ignorant or intolerant of each other's work. Although we are well aware that our review is not likely to win us friends in all groups, we persist in presenting our own view of the field as our intellectual and political right and invite others to present alternative views and critiques of ours.

OUR OWN PARTICULAR TAKE ON AR: PRAGMATIC ACTION RESEARCH

Our experience is predominantly, though not exclusively, in industrial settings in Europe and the United States. Greenwood is an anthropologist, and Levin is a sociologist with a background in engineering. Greenwood, a professor at Cornell University, a large combined state and private institution, served as an academic administrator of a large multidisciplinary center for over a decade and now has returned to anthropology full-time. His main research has taken place in Spain, and he has been active in a number of AR programs in Norway and Sweden. Levin is a professor at the Norwegian University for Science and Technology at Trondheim and has been the leader in the creation of combined engineering and AR programs there, as well as the leader of a number of national work-life development programs. He has also conducted AR in the United States and Canada.

We have made a good-faith effort to become knowledgeable about many different approaches, but we are aware that there are many gaps in our background. We do not intentionally slight other approaches by writing from our own knowledge base. The longer-term solution to problems of balance found here is for others to write their views of these subjects and be critical of what we have offered. We will respond, and hope thereby to open up a dialogue that broadens our collective sense of the scope of AR and enhances discourse on the democratization of knowledge creation and action. Our hope is that this book can encourage a long-needed critical discourse on the foundations and praxis of AR. Thus, our aim is to present one consistent strand of thought, integrating a philosophical, methodological, and political economic position with a consistent praxis supported by suitable methods and tools, while keeping the different kinds of AR practice and visions in sight.

As we mentioned above, we are both mostly experienced in the use of AR in industrial and community development in western industrialized countries. We share a strong commitment to the democratization of knowledge, learning, and self-managed social change. We are reformers, not revolutionaries, however, and we are social scientists, not psychoanalysts. We do not believe that we have the wisdom or the right to "lead" others to the "correct" social arrangements "for their own good," as some of the more liberationist practitioners do or as some of the more "therapeutic" approaches to AR advocate.

We believe in trying to offer, as skillfully as possible, the space and tools for democratic social change, but we refuse to guide such change unilaterally from our positions as action researchers. We consider ourselves participants in change processes where democratic rules guide decision making. We bring to the table certain skills and knowledge, and other actors do the same, bringing their own capacities and experiences to bear on the problems. This is why we call our own particular variety of AR practice *pragmatic action research.*

Our views on democracy and liberating situations are relevant, and we want to clarify them. Democracy is a concept with such a multiplicity of meanings that attempts to be clear about it are extremely controverted (see Dahl, 1989, for an excellent review). To some, especially many North Americans, the term means egalitarianism. For others, it evokes participation, whereas for others it conjures decision making by consensus, and for still others, decisions by majority rule. For some, democracy implies a homogeneous community and for others, arenas for lively debate. All these meanings have their associated genealogies, theories, politics, and ethics.

Our own view of these matters equates democracy with the creation of arenas for lively debate and for decision making that respects and enhances the diversity of groups. We explicitly reject both the distributive justice and the consensus models of democratic processes. We take the diversity of skills, experiences, ethnicities, gender, and politics as the most valuable source of potential positive changes in groups. Consequently, we reject the dominant political view of democracy as majority rule. We accept Iris Young's (1990) critique of this view of democracy as one that rests on the oppressive actions of welfare state capitalism to reduce social justice to a limited redistribution of goods to those defined as disadvantaged. Such a view of democracy neither respects diversity nor seeks to enhance the capacity of the disenfranchised to act on their own behalf. For us, AR aims to enable communities and organizations to mobilize their diverse and complex internal resources as fully as possible.

Consequently, we are suspicious of approaches to AR that seem to privilege the homogeneity of communities or consensus-based decision making, believing that such approaches open up great potentials for co-optation and coercion. One does not have to look far for documentation of these problems. At various points in recent history, such as 1968, the democratic critique of capitalist business as usual was embodied in attempts to create so-called alternative social forms. Many of these took the form of intentional communities, cooperatives, and open schools, and many tried to abolish social and cultural differences and to substitute consensus decision making for majority rule. A wonderful ethnographic portrait of such an organization is given in Jane Mansbridge's (1983) *Beyond Adversary Democracy*. To obliterate oppression of minorities by the majority, these architects of social change tried to substitute absolute consensus for majority rule. The effect, as Tocqueville saw generations ago, often was to create a tyrannical demand for consensus that eventually undermined the belief in democracy through the experience of group pressure and self-censorship.[2]

We also have a passion for diversity. We believe that diversity is one of the most important features of human societies. Diversity is a biological fact, continually reproduced in each generation, regardless of anyone's intentions. Diversity is also a cultural constant. Anyone who takes the trouble to look closely discovers that, even in the most homogeneous appearing groups, there are wide differences in knowledge, interests, experience, and capabilities. We view these differences as a rich social resource that, when effectively mobilized, gives a group or an organization a much greater capacity to transform itself. We view democracy as an open system that should be able to welcome and make humane use of these differences. From our perspective, the aim of democracy is to give rise to societies and organizations capable of emphasizing, mobilizing, and energizing the differences within them.

We view liberating situations as those in which social change is possible and can be influenced by the participants. Further, we see a group or organization as being on a liberating trajectory when it is increasingly able to tolerate, use, and reward the diversity of viewpoints, capacities, and experiences within and if it is increasingly possible for a greater and greater proportion of members to affect the future directions of the collectivity. Finally, in a liberating situation, a group increasingly welcomes change as an opportunity for group enhancement and growth.

THE PLAN OF THE BOOK

The book opens with a history of AR and two cases. Following this are chapters on the philosophical and methodological arguments for AR as a form of scientific inquiry that better meets scientific standards than what is currently called social science in academia. We provide an explanation of the marginalization of AR activities in academia through a brief historical political economy of academic institutions in advanced capitalist societies. We open the next section with four more cases drawn from our own practice, including examples of failures. From this, we move on to a set of chapters on different approaches to AR, beginning with our own approach. Throughout, we advocate our views strongly, but with the intention of encouraging the reader to consider them, not to accept them without debate.

Notes

1. Sometimes the professional action researcher is engaged in the actions deriving from the AR process and sometimes not. This depends on the situation and the needs of the stakeholders.

2. The experience appears to leave those who have been through it both alienated from forms of democracy and in limbo. In the American context, this may represent the uneven oscillation between the federalist and the puritan notions of democracy (see Miller, 1991).

2

A History of Action Research

History can be written in many ways. No one ever writes *the* history. Our intention here is to present a genealogy of action research (AR) that centers on the way we have learned to understand it during our years in the field. We make no pretense of believing that it is possible to present an objective account of the development of AR, and we are fully aware that what we present in this chapter is rooted mainly in Western industrial experience. Many other strands of thinking within AR are left out in our presentation of history in this way. The reader needs to know where we are coming from, however. In Part 3, we present the historical origins of other major approaches to AR when we introduce these approaches one by one.

The emergence of what came to be called the industrial democracy tradition or movement refers to the first systematic and reasonably large-scale AR effort in Western industrialized countries. This chapter presents a history of this tradition. Its roots trace back to Kurt Lewin's early work in the United States (first at Cornell University and later at MIT). His ideas recrossed the Atlantic and found fertile ground at the Tavistock Institute in London. Though there were a number of activities in Great Britain, the major source of large-scale AR projects turned out to be in Norway in the Industrial Democracy Project. Many of these ideas were reinvented in the form of industrial management strategies in Swedish and U.S. industrial firms; later, they reached Japan as well. This very widespread diffusion of ideas developed through AR is a success story about the dissemination of AR, but also a story about the way fairly radical ideas for social change can end up being appropriated as management tools aimed at producing more efficient, rather than more fair, organizations.

Our central claim is that the basic ideas of the industrial democracy movement are today accepted as state of the art in the organization of work. No sensible industrial leader in the West fails to take account of group-based work organization or the training of skillful and responsible workers able to engage in continuous innovation (improvement) processes at the shop-floor level. These ideas are so widely accepted now that their relatively recent origins in the industrial democracy movement are largely forgotten.

One consequence of this is that the concept of industrial democracy has lost its initial meaning. Some practitioners and companies apply the term *industrial democracy* in a co-opted form, giving the typical control strategies of management a socially euphonic name while still working in Tayloristic ways. Although we see this as a problematic situation, it is what one always sees when new ideas appear in industrialized settings. Co-optation exists alongside more genuine efforts to democratize work. The challenge for the AR community is not to retain its "purity" but to figure out strategically how to open up new ground for democratic work organization.

—◀o▶—

THE EARLY WORK OF KURT LEWIN

The spread of Nazism in Germany led Kurt Lewin to leave Europe and seek refuge in the United States. Lewin was trained as a social psychologist, and his central interest was in social change, specifically questions about how to conceptualize social change and how to promote it.

Although accounts on this matter differ, Lewin is generally thought to be the person who coined the term *action research* and gave it meanings quite close to those we use in this book. In AR, Lewin envisaged a process whereby one could construct a social experiment with the aim of achieving a certain goal. For example, in the early days of World War II, Lewin (1943) conducted a study, commissioned by U.S. authorities, on the use of tripe as part of the regular daily diet of American families. The research question was to what extent American housewives could be encouraged to use tripe rather than beef for family dinners. Beef was scarce and was destined primarily for the troops. Thus, the authorities were looking for resources to substitute for beef in domestic consumption.

Lewin's approach to this research was to conduct a study in which he trained a limited number of housewives in the art of cooking tripe for dinner. He then surveyed how this training had an effect on their daily cooking habits in their own families. In this case, AR was synonymous with a so-called natural experiment, meaning that the researchers in a real-life context invited or forced participants to take part in an experimental activity. This research approach still fell very much within the bounds of conventional applied social science with its patterns of authoritarian control, but it was aimed at producing a specific, desired social outcome.

Lewin's thinking about experimentation in natural settings became the main strategy for the Norwegian Industrial Democracy Project. Lewin was trained as a social psychologist, and thus had a strong professional concern with behavioral modification that became one of the core issues in the early stages of Norwegian efforts to improve working conditions.

Two other strands of Lewin's thinking had an important influence on the development of the industrial democracy tradition. First, Lewin conceptualized social change as a three-stage process: dismantling former structures (unfreezing), changing the structures (changing), and finally locking them back to a permanent structure (freezing). Second, his work on group dynamics, identifying factors and forces important for development, conflict, and cooperation in groups, led to the concept of T-groups, which has had a rich subsequent history.

Lewin's conceptualization of change as a three-stage process is still an influential model for social change. Lewin's major idea is that social change can be identified as sequential and discrete processes, using a thermodynamic metaphor of unfreezing, floating, and freezing matter. The core of Lewin's model is the notion of the existence of stable social states, those preceding a change and those established after the change has taken place. The action intervention (i.e., the change process) is an episode and, in the end, the social system will return to a stable state. This conceptualization of change as intermittent had a dominant influence in the early days of AR and still prevails in the conceptualizations of many U.S.-based organization development practitioners (Levin, 1994).

The model was attractive because it legitimated short-term interventions, a concept developed mainly among social psychologists in the 1970s. It also played a major role in framing the thinking behind consultation practices in the field of organizational development, that is, a planned and systematic effort to create participative change in organizations (Cummings & Worley, 1993).

In our view, this is a very limiting and mistaken position. We argue in favor of modeling AR as a continuous and participative learning process, not as a form of short-term intervention. For us, the change process has an open starting point and often no absolute final goal. Moreover, because the core idea in our own practice is to create sustainable learning capacities and to give participants the option of increasing control over their own situation, predefining the processes as short-term is inconsistent with what we take to be good AR practice. These criticisms of Lewin's view of AR do not undermine the basic idea of AR, but rather go to the limitations in his own deployment of the approach and the rather convenient use made of his concept of short-term change processes by consultants who took advantage of the early prestige of AR to turn organizational development into a profit-making enterprise. In contemporary AR, a major shift away from the Lewinian formulation can be seen in the ways change processes are now characterized. Contemporary formulations emphasize ongoing dialogue a great deal more (Gustavsen, 1992) and cogenerative learning as a vehicle for sustained change (Elden & Levin, 1991).

Kurt Lewin's work had another important effect in another area: the field of group dynamics. Group dynamics is a set of methods and praxis strongly shaped by Lewin's focus on creating groups that could withstand developmental processes, rather than breaking down as the tensions engendered by development arose. Among the most famous of these approaches is the T-group technique. The T in the name suggests the structure of the group. In this initial form, the outside facilitator plays the key social role in the group, sitting at the top of the T. The facilitator encourages practice by taking on a role of both not being in command and still being present. With such an authority figure present but not operating in the normal authoritarian way, the members of the group are put in a dilemma and forced, occasionally through painful struggles, to come to terms with their own approaches to authority, and eventually to try to make the group work in a new way.

T-group praxis began what became the road to sensitivity groups, providing experiential learning about interpersonal interaction as a path to deeper personal development. This is a much criticized approach to human development that involves high risks of creating sustained harm to participants (Filley & House, 1969). The National Training Laboratory at the University of Michigan still teaches people group dynamics by means of this methodology, but with less emphasis on the issues that were central to the initial sensitivity training model and more on group dynamics and social interaction skills needed to build teams.

Lewin is also credited with coining a couple of important slogans within AR. They are so widely known and interesting that they bear repetition here: "Nothing is as practical as a good theory" and "The best way to understand something is to try to change it." These slogans resonate with AR practitioners because they privilege praxis and value theory only insofar as it guides praxis well, clearly a position that sets them against conventional social researchers. In AR, we believe that the way to "prove" a theory is to show how it provides in-depth and thorough understanding of social structures, understanding gained through planned attempts to invoke change in particular directions. The appropriate changes are the proof.

Lewin's work is a fundamental building block of what today is called AR. He set the stage for knowledge production based on solving real-life problems. From the outset, he created a new role for researchers and redefined criteria for judging the quality of an inquiry process. Lewin shifted the researcher's role from being a distant observer to involvement in concrete problem solving. The quality criteria he developed for judging a theory to be good focused on its ability to support practical problem solving in real-life situations.

THE TAVISTOCK INSTITUTE
OF HUMAN RELATIONS

In Great Britain after World War II, rebuilding the industrial base was a major political goal. During the years of the war, this industrial base had been severely damaged, and national efforts were launched immediately to revitalize the economy. The Tavistock Institute of Human Relations in London was called on by the British government to support various parts of this effort.

The Tavistock Institute (called "the Clinic" by its members) was an intellectual environment shaped by psychoanalytic thinking and an action orientation. Its rise to importance began with a path-breaking study done in the English coal mines, where the introduction of new mechanized equipment had not led to the expected increase in productivity. The board overseeing the coal mines commissioned research on this issue, and Tavistock got the contract. The resulting, and now famous, study by Trist and Bamforth (1951) shows how production technology and work organization are linked inextricably. These authors show that the lack of improved performance can be explained by the incompatibility between the demands created by the technology and what is beneficial for the workers as a group of interacting human beings. Breaking up the work cycle in fragments on each shift caused suboptimization on the shifts and lessened overall productivity.

The insight based on Trist and Bamforth (1951) represents a break with the conventional Tayloristic approach to work, where research is always focused on finding the most technically efficient way to organize workers into separate, responsible groups dealing only with a clearly identifiable and bounded element of the production cycle. These insights shaped the emergence of the industrial democracy movement.

Tavistock brought Lewin's work on the concept of natural experiments and AR (Gustavsen, 1992) back from the United States, and Tavistock committed itself to doing direct experiments in work life. The relationship between employers and trade unions in Great Britain was such that it did not allow for experimentation on the organization of industrial work there, however. At this very moment, a Norwegian scholar was in the process of creating a link to Tavistock. Einar Thorsrud, a psychologist and former human resource manager of a Norwegian industrial company, made the link with Tavistock, and this link eventually led to the hoped-for real-life experimentation in industrial democracy in Norway. In cooperation with key Tavistock researchers Eric Trist and Fred Emery, Thorsrud sketched out a Norwegian program very much in line with Lewin's approach (Gustavsen, 1992). The major strategy was to begin several experiments at the same time, all focusing on improving democracy at the shop-floor level. Through what was called the sociotechnical reorganization of work, semiautonomous groups were created to provide increased motivation for the workers and to open up participation in decision making at the shop-floor level.

Thorsrud and the Tavistock professionals managed to convince the Norwegian Confederation of Employers and the Trade Union Council to support the Industrial Democracy Project. The first stage of the activity was a European study of industrial democracy in general, focusing on whether representative or participative models of democracy really gave a high degree of employee control over work (Emery & Thorsrud, 1976). Not unexpectedly, the conclusion was that participative approaches to work organization are necessary for increasing industrial democracy.

The Norwegian Industrial Democracy Project was contracted out as a set of experiments in different companies engaged in different types of production and located in both rural and urban areas. Of the six field sites in this project, probably only one can now be identified as a long-term success, in the sense of there still being a clear effect on the company. The other experiments gave rise to short-term successes, proving that group-based production is both feasible and efficient in industrial settings. These altered work systems clearly outperformed conventional Tayloristic organizational systems.

Three major conceptual schemes emerged through this work. The first is sociotechnical thinking, that is, building direct links between technology and work organization. The sociotechnical approach became a design criterion for all interventions. Second, the design of work was done according to concepts called psychological job demands. Third, by linking sociotechnical thinking with fulfillment of psychological job demands, the idea of semiautonomous groups was created. The psychological job demands could be fulfilled if a group of workers took on the responsibility for production. Learning, the needed variation, and self-control could be achieved within such groups. Modern industrial technology could be reorganized to give greater freedom to workers and to offer greater possibilities for both human and industrial development by linking more jobs together.

We will provide some brief examples of the central concepts. The sociotechnical interrelationship argument (sometimes called "joint optimization") affirms the possibility that the adjustment process can move in either direction, from social organization to technology or vice versa. Given a specific technology to be used, one would have to recruit or train workers with the necessary skills for operating in that technical environment or design the technology with particular kinds of behaviors and group organizational features in mind.

The core principle in sociotechnical design is to make these two adjustments at the same time, seeing technological and organizational design as inseparable elements of the same web of relationships. It is impossible for a worker to operate a lathe unless the worker has skills to understand how to set the piece in the chuck, how to choose the appropriate cutting speed, and how to match the cutting depth. The skill requirement could be further specified, but it is enough to point out that a lathe creates requirements for operational skills. A worker without the necessary skills would certainly be a catastrophe in grinding any product.

A parallel example from the organizational side is a conveyer belt production system. An ordinary work cycle in a car assembly line is usually less than 1 minute. Under these conditions, it is hard to conceive how work can create learning opportunities and personal freedom. Unless the conveyer belt system is totally redesigned, there are few possibilities for organizational change. It is possible to produce cars through group-based work, using long work cycles and providing relatively high degrees of freedom to the workers. Volvo, in both the Kalmar and the Thorslanda factories, created such systems. In both examples, it is obvious that a joint social and technological design created an effective production system.

Psychological job demands turned out to be a central design criterion in the sociotechnical tradition. Emery and Thorsrud (1976) formulate them as in Figure 2.1.

The criteria suggested in Figure 2.1 guide the design of work. Another important aspect of sociotechnical design is the application of Philip Herbst's (1976) concept of minimum critical specification. His idea is that we should shape technology and organizational structures

Optimum variety of tasks within the job:

- A meaningful pattern of tasks that gives to each job the sense of a single overall task

- Optimum length of work cycle

- Some scope for setting standards of quantity and quality of production and suitable feedback of knowledge about results

- The inclusion in the job of some of the auxiliary and preparatory tasks

- The task included in the job should entail some degree of care, skill, knowledge, or effort that is worthy of respect in the community

- The job should make some perceivable contribution to the utility of the product for the consumer

- Provision for interlocking tasks, job rotation, or physical proximity where there is a necessary interdependence of jobs

- Provision for interlocking tasks, job rotation, or physical proximity where the individual jobs do not make an obvious perceivable contribution to the utility of the end-product

- Where a number of jobs are linked together by interlocking tasks or job rotation, they should be grouped

- Provision of channels of communication so that the minimum requirements of the workers can be fed into the design of new jobs at an early stage

- Provision of channels of promotion to supervisor rank that are sanctioned by the workers

Figure 2.1. Psychological Job Demands
SOURCE: Emery and Thorsrud (1976), pp. 103-105.

in a way that they render as much choice in organizational design as possible. By introducing as few constraints as possible in modes of operating tools and machines or in organizational structures, more freedom can be given to the workers to design their own working conditions. Thus, by specifying the minimum conditions for operation, one can achieve a higher degree of participative control at the shop-floor level.

Another important concept applied in sociotechnical design is Emery and Trist's (1973) *redundancy of functions* and *redundancy of tasks*. In a system with redundancy of functions, a worker is able to handle more than one job, whereas in a system designed according to redundancy of tasks, the organization is built on having workers easily substitute for each other because they all have such limited and narrow competencies. Here the aim in following the principle of redundancy of functions is to design work in such a way that every member of the organization is able to handle more than his or her own immediate work task. If problems occur at any stage in the production system, someone else will be capable of stepping in to help. This creates greater flexibility and potential freedom for the people responsible for production. It also enhances the workers' opportunities for learning because they are trained to manage more than one job. This, in turn, gives them increased understanding of the total production system.

The Norwegian Industrial Democracy Project had a strong democratic and idealistic dimension. Participation at the shop-floor level was a value in its own right. Labor leaders and action researchers advocated this position. A remarkable example is the blunt and unconditional statement from one of the lead researchers, Philip Herbst (1976), that democratizing workplaces is the first step to enhancing democracy in society at large. This ideological element gradually dissipated over the years in Norway and was also lost from view in most of the process of diffusion of the ideas beyond Norway.

It is important to note that the ideas from the Industrial Democracy Project did not immediately spread in Norway. To the contrary, the ideas were treated as interesting, but most of Norwegian industry was not willing to act on them. Initially, these ideas had more effect outside the country.

THE DIFFUSION ROUTE: FIRST EAST AND THEN WEST

The core ideas in industrial democracy—semiautonomous working groups and work designed according to psychological demands—were picked up by key industrial enterprises in Sweden. Volvo, Saab-Scania, and Alfa Laval saw the potential in these ideas and soon redesigned some of their production systems around these concepts. The Saab engine assembly plant in Skøvde and the Volvo car assembly factory in Kalmar soon won international reputations for their ingenious ways of redesigning work. But efficiency was emphasized in praising and justifying these projects and the rhetoric about democracy as a goal in itself was left out.

An organization that emerged from the ranks of the Swedish Confederation of Employers became the leading change agent working near the border between AR-based approaches and conventional consulting. It did a respectable job of communicating the ideas and practices and convincing Swedish industry to take on ideas produced through the Industrial Democracy Project. But one consequence was that industrial democracy gained a reputation in industry more as an efficient way of organizing work in assembly line production than as the path to a more just system. It certainly outdid conventional Fordist ways of organizing work in economic terms, but the motivation that led to its creation involved a broader social change program than this.

The transfer of sociotechnical thinking to the North American continent was almost equally fast. Louis Davis, a professor at the University of California in Los Angeles (UCLA), picked up the ideas and soon set up a teaching and consultation program in sociotechnical design (Davis & Taylor, 1972). Davis's thinking was completely separated from any ideological connection to the value of democracy in itself. Instead, sociotechnical design was converted into a design tool for high-performance industrial production. The design concept focused on joint optimization of technology and social systems, indicating that the only way to generate a really effective production system was when technology and people were properly matched.

Morten Levin participated in one of the workshops held by the UCLA group. In 1980, the UCLA group organized a 14-day training program in Toronto, bringing together people both from Canada and the United States. Levin was amazed to learn that the social system dimensions of work were described and analyzed according to Talcott Parsons' (1951) role pattern variables. Because the Parsonian model is one of the most abstract constructions in the field of role theory, it was a singularly inappropriate bridge between technology and social systems analysis. More fruitful was the use of social psychological models and analysis of psychological job demands but, even then, Levin noticed that the joint optimization of technology and work was simply ignored as a concept.

As an interesting coincidence and perhaps relevant to the above, Levin noticed that a union-busting firm also was running a 14-day workshop at the same hotel to train managers how to keep the union out of their companies. Clearly these counterposed training programs highlighted the difference in the political and economic context between Scandinavia and North America.

In the Scandinavian context, union busting is not a conceivable strategy for running any business. On the contrary, the change projects in Scandinavian work life have almost always been joint ventures between trade unions and management. Thus, the lack of attention to many of the internal social justice dimensions of sociotechnical systems work in North America appears to reflect clearly the broader and more adversarial political economy of industry there.

The industrial democracy thinking also inspired other national movements. Japan was looking for ways to organize its industrial production that would secure both high productivity and excellent quality. Two U.S. scholars who specialized in quality control, J. M. Juran (1980) and W. E. Deming (1983), played an important role in the Japanese reindustrialization process. Their models for obtaining quality production were easily picked up by Japanese companies. In fact, the Japanese were much more receptive to them than their U.S. counterparts. "American" ideas (even though some were imported from Great Britain and Scandinavia) helped make the Japanese production miracle work. This story might appear to be a sideline but, in fact, it runs parallel to the industrial democracy movement. The central themes of industrial democracy found fertile ground in Japan because collective work had a strong cultural base in Japan and the ideas of groups taking on joint problem-solving and operational responsibility were easily picked up.

In Japan, these activities first emerged in the form of quality circles, problem-solving groups created to handle emergent problems in the production system (Ishikawa, 1976). The aim was to have workers and engineers work together to solve production problems. These quality circles were mostly organized separately from daily work routines. The groups often met on unpaid time in the evenings, working for free to solve company problems. In the Japanese cultural context, this made sense.

Later, new concepts of production control as *Kanban* (the Toyota system of production management, see Monden, 1983) and *just-in-time* (production without unnecessary waste and temporary storage, see Womack et al., 1990) demanded a different approach to the organization of work. A high degree of autonomy and local responsibility, combined with the ability to learn ways to improve performance systematically, became a core element in the mode of organization. These efforts were in line with the major sociotechnical design principles emanating from the industrial democracy tradition. The diffusion route was from Norway to Sweden, then to the United States, and finally worldwide.

The diffusion trail is itself an interesting phenomenon because research networks also play an important role. The diffusion to Sweden and then subsequently to the United States was made possible by communication between researchers. Part of the mission of academics is to play with ideas. In the case of industrial democracy, ideas created within academic circles soon gained a foothold in industrial praxis. In the early phases of the Norwegian Industrial Democracy Project, the effort was located at the Norwegian Institute of Technology (later renamed the Norwegian University of Science and Technology) in Trondheim, creating a locus for links to the international scholarly networks. Tavistock was not a university-based institution, but it had a high profile among work researchers interested in organizational change, and thus was well-known internationally. This facilitated the fairly rapid diffusion of sociotechnical ideas in academic contexts. It makes no sense to overestimate the academic role. The widespread proliferation of this thinking must ultimately be attributed to the success of the design principles grounded in industrial democracy in shaping effective and profitable production systems.

THE INTELLECTUAL CONTENT OF THE INDUSTRIAL DEMOCRACY TRADITION

The major reason for attaching the label *industrial democracy* to the tradition starting with AR efforts in the United States, intellectually extended during the Tavistock period, and fully emerging in the Norwegian Industrial Democracy Project is the focus on shaping an alternative to conventional hierarchical organizations. As noted earlier, only a thin strand within all this activity really claims democracy as a major concern. Still, it does not make sense to overlook the participatory dimensions of these changes.

Industrial democracy focused on the ways research results manifested through redesigned organizations would improve the participants' ability to control their own situations. Industrial democracy also began the first reflections about designing research processes that redefined the relationship between participants and researchers. The second generation of research practice within the Norwegian Industrial Democracy Project opened up even greater possibilities for participant control (Elden, 1979).

Carole Pateman's (1970) book, *Participation and Democratic Theory*, forcefully presents the democratic argument; it played a major role in creating a theoretical backdrop for participatory industrial democracy efforts. Pateman draws a genealogy between Rousseau and Mill's thinking and the modern debate on democracy at the shop-floor level. Her work offers a well-argued model of democracy, with a point of departure in the ability of workers to control their own working situation. In her argument, immediate control over the work situation replaces numerical (i.e., representative) models of democracy as the key to shaping a successful democratic society.

Despite this, the strongly idealistic democratic content of the first decade of the industrial democracy tradition within AR gradually lost ground. Initially, the dominant argument of democracy was an ideological imperative. It was gradually replaced by pragmatic arguments that domesticated the broader political economy issues that industrial democracy raises. In this process, the rhetoric shifted from a focus on democracy to an emphasis on empowerment, from participation as the key to democracy to participation as a necessary move to motivate workers to shape a more effective organization. Indeed, it seems to us that *empowerment* is a term that substitutes for the more ambitious and clearer concepts of participation and democracy. This point is illustrated in one of the standard textbooks on organizational development (Cummings & Worley, 1993), where empowerment as an ill-defined concept was substituted for democracy. The first edition, published in 1975, took a stronger position.

Another dimension of the link between industrial democracy and the early work of Kurt Lewin is reliance on an oversimple change model (unfreezing-change-freezing) and the notion of the experimental design of change processes. Both elements were prominent in the early development of the industrial democracy tradition in AR. Experimental design, drawn from the Lewinian tradition, became the way ideas were acted on. The researchers made their analyses, recommended new organizational designs, and structured processes by which changes were implemented. The core idea was to make the changes and then let the organization develop a stable state incorporating the changes. Consultation with the participants was not to be found.

Another point deserving emphasis is that, in the early stages, researchers within the tradition of industrial democracy played a clear-cut expert role. They made their analysis of a situation in the specific context and they worked out their recommendations for a new design. The next step in their activity was to have these ideas implemented in a way that involved workers who were affected by the changes. In this way, the researchers created an experimental situation in a natural setting to test whether their ideas were fruitful or not. They did not become collaborative researchers in any broader sense, however.

Sociotechnical thinking is the major conceptual outcome of the industrial democracy tradition. In Trist and Bamforth's (1951) study of coal mining, interrelationships between technology and work organization were already articulated. This represents a major shift from Tayloristic thinking, where technology and management control are totally dominant, or from human relations thinking, where organizational, social, and psychological factors are considered independent of technological influence (Herzberg, 1966; Maslow, 1943; Mayo, 1933). In these approaches, organization and technology are considered two distinct and separate spheres, whereas the sociotechnical view argues that no technological or social design could be done independently of the other.

Trist (1981) summarizes the relationship between old paradigms of work organizations with new (sociotechnical) paradigms, as shown in Table 2.1.

There seems to be little doubt that sociotechnical thinking has had a major effect on organizing industrial work. Sociotechnical design has

TABLE 2.1 Old and New Paradigms of Work Organization

Old Paradigm (Scientific Management)	New Paradigm (Sociotechnical Design)
The technological imperative	Joint optimization
Man as an extension of the machine	Man as complementary to the machine
Man as an expendable spare part	Man as a resource to be developed
Maximum task breakdown, simple narrow skills	Optimum task grouping, multiple broad skills
External controls (supervisors, specialist staff)	Internal controls (self-regulating subsystems, procedures)
Tall organization chart, autocratic style	Flat organization chart, participative style
Competition, gamesmanship	Collaboration, collegiality
Organization's purposes only	Members' and society's purposes
Alienation	Commitment
Low risk taking	Innovation

SOURCE: Trist (1981), p. 42.

involved efforts to break away from Tayloristic modes of organizing work and has been important in pinpointing the interrelationship between technology and social life. It has argued effectively that an exclusive concentration on technological change or on the social organization of work will not create good work systems. Yet the proponents of the sociotechnical approach certainly overestimate its influence (e.g., Van Eijnatten's, 1993, book with the bombastic title *The Paradigm That Changed the Work Place*).

CONCLUSION

This partial history of AR provides the background of the perspectives that have influenced the writing of this book. Other histories underlie other AR practices and they are given in Parts 2 and 3. Our aim here is clarify the historical and theoretical underpinnings that influenced us when we began our initial AR work. Over the years, we have found it necessary to develop and expand our thinking, eventually resulting in a new epistemological and practical position of our own. We have anchored it in this history, but the main "project" of this book is to present where we hope AR will go, not merely to recount where it has been.

3

Action Research
Cases From Practice I

*The Stories of Stongfjorden
and Mondragón*

This chapter provides the two first evocations of action research (AR) processes, one in a small community and the other in a group of industrial organizations. These portraits precede the more abstract and detailed discussion of AR. After the detailed discussion of the epistemological foundations of AR, we will present four more cases. Our aim is to convey the complexity and challenges of doing AR. It is important to show that even projects failing to reach desired action goals create rich learning opportunities. We believe the reader can best start with a concrete, overall sense of AR activities. The two cases present AR in two very different contexts. The Stongfjorden project was aimed at supporting local community development in a small rural community in Norway, whereas the work in Mondragón was focused on organizational problems in industrial cooperatives in the Spanish Basque Country. Both cases are based on the authors' long-time involvement in these local settings. AR is about specific action-reflection processes in particular contexts, and so the cases are an appropriate starting point. Our aim is for these two cases to shed some

light on what AR work is like. We emphasize presenting how
projects develop and change over time and how the reflection processes involved follow, to different degrees, the
unique patterns of the emerging projects.

◄○►

STONGFJORDEN—VILLAGE DEVELOPMENT
IN WESTERN NORWAY

Sailing south along the Norwegian coast and passing the western-
most reach of the mainland, one sees a narrow, short fjord reaching 3
miles inland. Stongfjorden is surrounded by low mountains cascading
straight down to the water. At the shoreline, some scattered houses can
be seen, along with an industrial building, a small school, a grocery
store, a tennis court, and a waterfall, partly dried up by the hydropower
plant that channels the water into turbines. Small farms encircle the
fjord. In all, 217 people inhabit this village, most of them over the age
of 40.

The village was isolated from inland Norway until the early 1960s.
Although a road linked residents to a community center, besides that,
going on the main road required the use of various ferries. Sea-based
communication was dominant. In the mid-1960s, the inhabitants decided to improve their road links, and, through collective action, they
built several miles of road over difficult mountain terrain, linking the
village to the mainland highway system. The "people's road," as it was
named, illustrates the community's solidarity and ability to solve problems of common interest. This activity caught national attention as an
illustration of how a small community could reverse public decisions
simply by making things happen on its own.

Stongfjorden was "discovered" by an English fisherman in the late
19th century. One day in early summer, this man, who also was the
chairman of the board of British Aluminum, was impressed by the sight
of the local waterfall found at the base of the fjord. As an industrial
entrepreneur, he immediately saw an energy potential, and the process
leading to the creation of the first aluminum smelter in Norway began.
He bought the rights to use the waterfall, built a hydroelectric power

station, and started on the construction of the aluminum smelter. The power station was finished in 1908, and the smelter was finished in 1913. A company town was created on the model of English industrial communities. A tennis court nicely completed the picture of a class-divided town. Management built their houses on the sunny side of the fjord, whereas the workers' quarters rested in the shadows. Infrastructure, such as schools, doctors, and technical support, was created by the company, and soon the village had one of the best public schools and health care systems in the whole of western Norway.

The industrialization of Stongfjorden met with several obstacles. The first challenge came during the first winter the smelter was in operation. The waterfall did not deliver enough power to keep the smelter going. Consequently, the first high-voltage transport line was constructed to link the community to the mainland power distribution system. The smelter produced aluminum until the end of World War II. The end of the war also meant the closing of the aluminum smelter, and the workers were offered jobs in a smelter some 300 miles north of Stongfjorden. There is a very moving and powerful story of how families left the village on the same boat to settle and work at this new aluminum smelter. Some years later, when a local knife producer took over the facilities and started production of knives and cutlery for home use and the food processing industry, the downturn of the fortunes of Stongfjorden had begun. Great numbers of industrial jobs were lost, and houses and public facilities in the village deteriorated. In many ways, the village seemed to be preparing for its own funeral as the social structure dissolved.

In late 1970s, the Norwegian Ministry for Environmental Protection and Land Use launched a program to support municipal activities aimed at increasing local participation in and control over community affairs. Towns, neighborhoods, or municipalities could apply to the program. A group of "burning souls" (Philips, 1988), under leadership of a very capable woman, applied for money through this program. This local task force sent in the application without following the formal procedure of sending it through the municipal government. Even so, Stongfjorden was accepted as one of 60 sites that participated in this revitalization program.

As outside consultants, Morten Levin and a group of collaborators from Trondheim were linked up with this task force in Stongfjorden through the administrator of the national program. Sociologists Levin and Tore Nilssen made up the AR team leaders. In addition, two students were engaged the first year. The project involved the Department of Organization and Work Life Science and the Institute for Social Research in Industry at the Norwegian University of Science and Technology.

Getting to Stongfjorden from our office location in Trondheim was complicated. Flying there required the use of at least three different planes and the rental of a car. The time spent in air transport matched the 12 hours spent driving the whole distance, but the driving also involved crossing three mountain passes and driving on roads cut in the steep slopes that drop straight into the fjords. At first we flew in, but later we turned to cars as our major form of transportation.

The first meeting with the task force was productive. Task force members presented their view of the situation and articulated their interest in preserving their home village. We suggested running a search conference (see Chapter 9, "Pragmatic Action Research") to initiate the development process. We had several reasons for suggesting the search conference as the first move. At that time, we were ideologically committed to this kind of consensus model for local community development. We also saw a need to mobilize the village as broadly as possible. We believed that a development effort would never succeed if only a handful of people became involved. It was easy to convince the task force that a search conference was a good idea.

Planning the conference brought us back to the community a couple of times over the next 1 1/2 months. In planning the conference, we wanted to get acquainted with as many of the potential participants as possible, and, at the same time, we wanted to convey what a search conference was. A new task force was established, incorporating more people than the original applicants for the grant. The search conference staff consisted of three researchers from Morten Levin's home institution and one from the National Institute for City and Regional Planning, an overstaffed situation that inadvertently led to internal staff conflicts. The person running the conference refused to cooperate with other staff members. Still, the search conference worked out very well, which tells us a lot about the robustness of the design itself.

Several new task groups were formed. One took on the responsibility of building new road lights, another focused attention on constructing a new sheltered harbor for small craft. The third group planned the reconstruction of houses and roads. One of the old houses, formerly inhabited by several working-class families, was given to the local activists, and the task force organized the work to restore it and then used it for community purposes. A kindergarten was established and a workshop for textile production was created.

In the first year after the search conference, we organized two follow-up conferences. The goal was for the participants in the different task forces to present their work and thereby share possibilities, successes, and problems with the other participants. Thus, the follow-up meetings functioned as tools for sustaining the group elements of the developmental effort, encouraged collective reflection, and supported mutual learning between researchers and activists. In addition, the follow-up meetings forced the task forces to make clear commitments to their own aims and to revise their plans for further activities. These follow-up meetings were invaluable in creating feedback loops. It was advantageous to start a reflection process on the previously stated goals and to identify what had been achieved and what remained to be done.

The task forces generally were quite successful in achieving their goals. The group aiming at rebuilding the road lighting made a series of smart moves in applying for municipal, county, and power company money. Most of the expenses for the lighting hardware were covered by these funds, whereas the work itself was done collectively. This built on a strong tradition of collective work in Stongfjorden that relates to the Norwegian concept of *dugnad,* which is inherited from early farming and fishing cultures where people had to cooperate to resolve issues of mutual interest that could not be dealt with in households alone. In the beginning, the work was done fast and effectively, with good support from many people. The task turned out to be quite extensive and demanded a lot of individual commitment; as time passed, the group was reduced in size to some of the original burning souls.

Other tasks were dealt with quickly. The tennis court, a symbol of former wealth, was soon fixed up. A few people played tennis there, but mostly it was used as a children's play area. The clean-up activities were generally very successful. Roads and houses were restored, and the general look of the village was improved.

One task that did not turn out to be so successful was the construction of a harbor for small craft. To be able to finance it, the task force had to establish a nonprofit company. Everyone who wanted a slip for a boat had to pay the money up front. The task force then signed a contract with an entrepreneur, but this person was unable to deliver the harbor. His machines were not suitable for the work, and he could not finish the job without buying new equipment. Because he was living in the village, this created tension. Some thought the entrepreneur had cheated the boat owners, but others saw and understood his miscalculations. The task force wanted to take the matter to court, but the problem was settled before it came to that.

We continued our work in the community until 1986. In the later stages of the process, activity focused more on entrepreneurial efforts and on relationships with political and administrative bodies of the municipalities. The central local woman who had moved the project along over the years gradually burned out. She had devoted enormous time and energy to it, but because she felt her energy was no longer sufficient, leadership was handed over to a very creative local entrepreneur. He initiated a fishing venture centering on sea crawfish, developing the technology and a fishing strategy and creating a market. He started building high-tech wooden boats using state-of-the-art gluing and mantling techniques. He started farming black grouse. In addition, he successfully created his own tourism business, running his own campground and renting out several cabins.

Every activity was high risk, but always with the promise of making a lot of money. Through the project, he also developed the marketing ability and initiated cooperation with other campgrounds in the neighborhood to enable the development of a foothold in the German market. To a high degree, this turned out to be a successful activity. Over the later years of the project, we cooperated closely with him, and we were kept informed about his entrepreneurial work, but we did not become directly involved in it.

Another major issue we were involved in over the last year of the project was an effort by the village to convince the municipal government to support the reconstruction of roads and the public quay in Stongfjorden. The local activists had long been interested in rebuilding the public quay in the fjord because the old quay had almost fallen down, and there was no money available for building a new one. The municipal government resisted spending money on this refurbishing project, arguing that there would not be enough traffic over the quay to make it profitable. Ship berthing had been reduced drastically over those years, a process that the municipal administration felt was caused by a structural transportation change from ships to trucks. The Stongfjorden people argued that a reduction of transportation volume at the quay was because the quay itself was in such bad shape. Thus, they were stalemated.

Local people had contacted the Ministry of Environment for help and had received all kinds of support. Through the contact person in the ministry, we were asked to help the local group negotiate a solution with the municipal authorities. We traveled to the community, set up meetings with the municipal administration, and ran roughshod over them because we had the requisite skills in framing arguments and the explicit support of the ministry. The money was granted, and the quay was refurbished.

After this, our relationship with the local community slowly wound down. The grants from the ministry ceased, and we pulled out after 3½ years in Stongfjorden.

Over time, our roles shifted a great deal. We started as facilitators for the fairly narrow task of running a search conference, and we worked on that for some months. As the project shifted, our roles changed to supporting particular efforts and to encouraging collective reflection on the ongoing activity. During this period, we also brought in two students both to support the activity and to give them an opportunity to learn about AR based on direct involvement in the field. Through their work, we were able to describe and analyze the social structure of the village, learning about the 13 different local missionary groups consisting of women knitting for a Christmas auction, thereby making money for missionary work domestically and abroad. We also learned about family structures, kin relationships, and how the inhabitants were linked through other kinds of networks. This middle phase involved a lot of analytical work, though that was coupled with facilitating the ongoing change activity. During this period, we also took on the task of running a search conference for the local knife factory. This company was clearly the dominant employer in the municipality, and the search aimed to develop new markets for knife-related products. This was a reasonably successful activity, even though a great economic market breakthrough did not emerge for the company.

In the later part of our work, we took on a much more direct and active role. We played the activist role, being the ones that nearly dominated local activity in handling external interest groups. This was an unpleasant role, and involved many serious ethical questions. In retrospect, we should never have taken on the power role in the negotiations with the municipal government. We entered the scene as resourceful foreigners able to mobilize our professional networks to support the Stongfjorden activists. We should have taken on a conflict handling role in at least an initial effort to make the conflicting parties find solutions by themselves.

In Stongfjorden, we had a very powerful partner in burning souls. Some of them burned out in the process, but mostly they stayed through the whole project period. These people, four men and one woman, had the inner strength and ability for concentrated work on important goals. This group operated as a fairly closed unit. Only the campground entrepreneur and the local knife factory manager eventually entered that group. The manager was active over a couple of years, but when his company demanded greater attention, he dropped out. The entrepreneur became the lead person during the later phase of our engagement. Although we occasionally had contact with other members of the local community, these persons never became central and key activists. Still, it seems reasonable to believe that the core group had the backing of a large proportion of the village population. When *dugnad* was called for, people showed up.

Over the course of the project, several different arenas for communication were constructed. We started with the search conference. This activity was followed up by a series of meetings where stock taking and collective reflections on the process development were central. These meetings created knowledge both for the local people on how to reengineer their activity to reach desired goals better and for the outside researchers to understand more about the challenges in local community development.

Two issues became cornerstones in our intellectual research efforts. The first major question was related to understanding the complex social structure. We were struck by how fast information spread in the community. Basically the whole village knew everything, even though we were sure that we had communicated with only a few people. The initial research question then focused on the integrating factors in the social structure. Through the students' work, we eventually spotted the effect of the 13 missionary clubs, the choir, the boat harbor, and all the kitchen table, coffee-drinking groups. These closely nested networks created the possibility for the very efficient distribution of information. These findings were published in the students' work.

The most important published research resulting from this work focused on understanding why certain inhabitants become burning souls. How could it be explained that a person gets up from in front of the TV set and takes on the work load and the responsibility for leading local development activity? The initial framing of this question was done during the work in Stongfjorden. Several discussions with local activists created some preliminary understanding of the mobilization question. This preliminary insight shaped the research question for a masters thesis (by one of the students) focusing on the early phases of local community development. Eventually this work was published by Morten Levin (1988), carrying the title *Local Mobilization*.

AR IN MONDRAGÓN

The Mondragón Cooperatives in Spain are one of the most successful examples of industrial democracy anywhere and the subject of worldwide attention and debate. As a group of labor-managed businesses, the cooperatives have been at the center of a great deal of debate centering on the ability of democratic organizations to compete successfully in advanced capitalist societies (Bradley & Gelb, 1983; Kasmir, 1996; Thomas & Logan, 1982; Whyte & Whyte, 1991). The project described briefly here involved 4 years of AR by a team drawn from the cooperatives and a number of professional researchers from outside, and resulted in a number of reforms in the cooperatives and the book about the research by members of the research team (Greenwood et al., 1992).

Mondragón is located in the Spanish Basque Country, one of the most densely populated and highly industrialized parts of Spain. The region is known because of the Basque nationalist political movement and because the Basques speak a language unrelated to any other language currently spoken in the world. As a focus of Spanish industrialization since the 19th century, the Basque Country has been a major destination for internal migration and has a non-Basque population drawn from the rest of Spain of over 24%. After a long period of growth,

the region experienced industrial decline due to the aging infrastructure, the high costs of doing business, and increased national and
international competition. At the time the project began, the overall
unemployment rate in the region hovered around 25%. Mondragón
itself is an industrial town of about 27,000 with a much lower unemployment rate. The Mondragón Cooperatives employ about 50% of the
active population of the zone and account for this radically lower rate
of unemployment.

The cooperatives were founded as a single cooperative, Ulgor, in
1956 by 5 leaders and 13 coworkers. There are now nearly 200
cooperatives employing more than 30,000 worker-owners. Through
worldwide recessions, the cooperatives have remained generally sol-
vent, and they have successfully managed the transition to competing
effectively in the European Union.

They manufacture industrial robots, machine tools, semiconduc-
tors, computer circuit boards, refrigerators, dishwashers, stoves, micro-
wave ovens, electrical and plumbing supplies, and also retail food and
have a variety of service cooperatives such as janitorial and cooking.
They export in excess of 30% of their production.

The cooperatives were founded on principles of industrial democracy and embody the principles of worker ownership and participation.
To join, a person must pay an entrance fee that is the equivalent of a
year's wages. This becomes the basis of one's own capital account and
part of a personal stake in the cooperative's success. As pay, members
receive a distribution of the profits and increments to their capital
accounts. The amount distributed back to the members depends on
anticipated economic performance and future capital requirements
based on the cooperative's business plan. These distributions and plans
are voted on annually by all the members. The pay distribution is made
according to the functional classification of the job the member holds.
At the time of the study, the pay differential was 1:6, the lowest-paying
jobs receiving one sixth the compensation of the highest paying jobs.[1]

Cooperative management, who because of this compensation
scheme receive much less income than they would in a private company,
is elected from among the membership for 4 years and is subject to
recall. Elaborate internal governance structures provide freedom of
information and strong checks and balances in decision making. The
cooperative system also has its own health and retirement system, a

major research and development cooperative, a major cooperative bank, and a wide variety of schools, ranging from primary to university level.

Within this system, until a recent reorganization realigned the entire structure and created a single overall Mondragón Cooperative Corporation, the Fagor Cooperative Group was the largest and best-known cooperative group and contained the founding cooperative, Ulgor. The AR project took place within the then Fagor Group.[2]

The project began when William Foote Whyte, a well-known professor of industrial and labor relations at Cornell University, decided to write a comprehensive history and structural analysis of the cooperatives. After a research visit in 1982 to complete gathering data for the book, he offered a seminar on what he had seen to his hosts. He made a number of critical observations about certain practices within the system and, to his surprise, the Fagor director of personnel, José Luis González, stood up, thanked him, and then asked how Whyte would propose to help them solve the problems he had identified.

Whyte returned to the United States and involved Davydd Greenwood, a Cornell anthropologist with years of fieldwork and historical research experience in the Basque Country, in the project. Together with González, the three developed proposals for funding that lasted 2 years.

As González stated the aims of the collaboration, and he took the lead in doing so, the goal was to develop the internal social research capacity of the Fagor Group, bringing it to a level of sophistication comparable to that already achieved in internal economic research. This kind of thinking embodied González's own understanding of the necessary equilibrium that the cooperatives have to maintain between their economic and social dimensions. Nevertheless, the underlying motives for the research, the identities of the local partners, and the actual agenda of activities were not clear to the outsiders.

The AR process began with mutual visits, followed by a 1985 summer course in AR taught by Greenwood to about 15 members of the Fagor Group. This course ended with the cowriting of a preliminary monograph on crises in the history of Fagor. On the basis of this monograph, the group and the Fagor management decided to continue the project. Then followed an extensive interviewing project, another summer course, a series of focus groups, and a lengthy cowriting process by which two books about the project's findings were written (Greenwood et al., 1990, 1992).

The cooperative participants were primarily drawn from the central personnel department of the Fagor Group. They did not represent the founding generation, but rather the next generation of cooperative management. These people expressed a deep and authentic concern that the future of the cooperatives was by no means assured. In particular, they worried that the many new members being recruited were not committed to cooperative values and that, under stress, the system would not be able to adapt.

To address these concerns, the AR team developed an analytical perspective that stressed understanding cultural systems as dynamic webs of meanings that generate both contested meanings and complex and often contradictory practices. We read the books written by outsiders and insiders to the cooperatives and articulated our critiques of them. We explored the constant use of dichotomies to stereotype desired and disapproved behavior in the cooperatives and to contrast the cooperatives with ordinary businesses.

Over time and through training, we developed a team attitude and set of techniques that permitted the coresearchers to get into more direct touch with reality as conceived and experienced by cooperative members and to link abstract cultural formulations back to institutional structures in their organizational and historical contexts. The aim became to gain a differentiated, dynamic understanding of the state of the cooperatives and to do so by means of research processes that were, like the cooperatives, self-managed, open ended, and practically useful. The project began in an analysis of the feared loss of cooperative values, but gradually evolved into a full-scale AR project touching on the members' deepest fears and hopes about their collective future.

The research process that took place was unusual. The beginning July 1985 seminar opened with a colossal mismatch of expectations. The Fagor Group members clearly expected and thought they wanted academic lectures on organizational culture. Greenwood came believing that most social research fails to produce useful new knowledge and that a successful self-managing group like this, if the cooperatives really were the self-managing organizations they seemed to be, should also be able to self-manage research processes and learning. Greenwood therefore refused to prepare a neat course and relieve members' anxieties by providing a set of tools for them to use. Rather, his goal was to develop a research mindset through which members could learn new things about themselves, find counterintuitive information, and develop action plans that linked these findings to appropriate actions. Greenwood was unwilling to teach social research tools until the group was willing to define the problems and concerns that brought it together. Greenwood believed that standard social research, with its parametric assumptions and shallow positivism, would produce no useful outcomes and that no cooperative resources should be wasted in this way. He believed that the members of the Fagor Group were already researchers, but that he might be able to help them to learn counterintuitive nonparametric approaches to social research and learn to be "falsificationist" researchers. He was particularly concerned that they be alive to the complexity and diversity of the scene because he was aware that members intended to act on their findings.

As a result of these beliefs, Greenwood came to the seminar with no prepared lectures, and the members of the Fagor Group were duly upset. The effect of this mismatch of expectations was to create a T-group atmosphere.[3] Greenwood was not willing to teach research techniques until the group had taken responsibility for identifying the issues that should be studied and considering the ethical dimensions of collaborative research within the cooperatives, where all members, in principle, are equal.

After struggling for a period with the authority dynamics this created, Greenwood suggested that the group could begin to discover what it wanted to know by finding out how others viewed the cooperatives. The group engaged in a critical reading of the professional social science literature and insider books on Mondragón. The coresearchers disliked this literature a great deal because they felt it misrepresented them and their experiences. Building on this notion of misrepresentation, Greenwood argued that they had to take control of and responsibility for the development of a view of themselves if they intended to have an ongoing social research effort that met their objectives. The project developed from there.

As time went by, the group did learn many techniques of social research and developed its own view of the cooperatives. Central to this view is a vision of culture as complex and dynamic. In particular, the team came to believe that organizational culture in Fagor set the terms of conflict and contradiction in the group, and that the strength of the system was not found in absence of conflict but in commitment to broad goals and a set of rules of debate. There was no absence of prolonged disagreement about how to achieve strongly desired goals.

As the team developed its own research and interpretations, each new view was subjected to reality testing through continued research and feedback sessions with other cooperative members. Greenwood and González insisted on keeping open the possibility of terminating the project at any time it ceased to be deemed useful.

Because the cooperatives are a success story and these successes are well-known, the team decided to concentrate its attention on diversity, dissension, debate, and disagreement within the cooperative system. Throughout the process of conducting surveys, through a long series of interviews with members who were felt to be the most alienated in the system, and through focus groups, the research team stressed paying attention to the heterogeneity of viewpoints, sought out conflict and contradiction within the system, and tried not to flinch in dealing with the most threatening questions about the possible future of the cooperative system. The formal research process closed with a series of focus groups in which the team members subjected their most important values about cooperative life to open questioning: participation, solidarity, and freedom of information.

This research process sought and found conflict and contradiction, but we also discovered a great deal of strength within the system, including among newly recruited members. Gradually, it became clear that there was no fundamental crisis of cooperative values, that the initial premise of the research itself had been wrong, and that the most common explanation for perceived problems in the cooperatives was simply wrong. Yet the sense of anxiety about the future remained, and the research had produced lots of information about dissatisfaction with many dimensions of cooperative operation. The coresearchers thus began to look for other factors that could help understand the evident tensions within the system. In particular, they began reflecting on their own role and practices as part of the cooperatives' personnel system in creating negative conditions.

The cooperative members recognized that their initial formulation of the problems of the cooperatives as a lack of commitment by new members to cooperative values was self-serving. It became clear that they had developed a distrust of new members, who they did not feel were as committed to the cooperatives as this group of long-time members was.

Because of the decision to do extensive interviewing of disaffected members, the team began to notice that many of the complaints were about the practices of personnel departments themselves. They gave examples of situations in which personnel departments were guilty of applying rules impersonally to cooperative members rather than embodying cooperative principles and direct personal treatment of affected parties in their work. Thus, they began to see themselves as part of the problem that they wanted to solve.

Reflections also proceeded at a broader level. The coresearchers had enough case material and enough sense by this time that there were significant negative dynamics in the system to begin to reflect on larger processes in the system. They noticed that when some kind of problem surfaced in a workplace and a complaint was lodged, the local managers and the personnel departments often took the matter directly to the cooperative governance apparatus, rather than trying to find a solution in the workplace. As this view was developed, the coresearchers came to recognize a dangerous institutional dynamic within the cooperative system. Rather than struggling to democratize the workplace, the cooperative system had developed a strong tendency to extract all conflicts from work relations and treat them as matters of governance, to be dealt with by the governance system (rules, statutes, procedures). This made the cooperatives both unresponsive to individual claims about justice and increasingly bureaucratic. It is a beautiful example of Argyris and Schön's (1996) Model O-I organizational behavior that responds to error by reproducing the conditions that make the error recur. One result was the truncation of the ongoing growth and development of workplace democracy.

Support for this view was found in one interview after another. The coresearchers began to understand better the complaints heard from members about the tension that existed between operating in a largely undemocratic work environment while simultaneously voting on the annual business plan, being able to recall management, and participating in general assemblies of the cooperative group that often restructured the whole cooperative system in fundamental ways. To put it another way, the members articulated an existential contradiction between their lives as workers and their lives as managers. The insider members of the research team found this result to be quite convincing because they were able to recount numerous episodes from their own experience in which these very contradictions were augmented by their actions as personnel managers.

Another, more abstract, dimension of reflection also characterized this phase of the research. One of the main ways the literature on Mondragón explains the success of the cooperatives is to attribute it to strongly shared values that unite the members. Either elements of Basque culture (solidarity, egalitarianism, etc.) or simply a strong organizational culture imposed by the priest-founder of the system and his collaborators is used to explain how, in a capitalist world, successful democratic industrial organizations can prosper in Northern Spain but not in London, Detroit, or Singapore. The coresearchers' close reading of these analyses, coupled with their own experiences and the research process they had undertaken, invalidated these viewpoints.

The AR carried out in the cooperatives showed that every core value in the system was contested and that existential tensions abounded. Though it became clear that cooperative members shared high levels of agreement about what an ideal cooperative would be like and the kind of process rules that should govern cooperative life, they suffered significant tensions and disappointments over the daily failure of the system to live up to these values. They also had very different takes on the ways to solve these problems. Thus, the organizational culture of these cooperatives was indeed a strong one, but its strength was not to be found in its uniformity. The culture of these cooperatives is a culture of contestation, debate, and dialogue about a certain basic set of organizational principles and ethical ideals. Thus, the coresearchers came to formulate their own conception of a strong organizational culture as one that does not glue individuals together in a uniform matrix but that creates ongoing dialogue and debate over the ways to embody certain important and shared values. This view of organizational culture was quite novel in the academic and consulting literature on the subject at the time, and was a direct result of this AR project.

Having reached this point, Greenwood suggested to the team that it should write a book to tell others about its results. This was a long and arduous process, both because team writing is difficult and because writing a book initially was a very threatening notion for most of the team members. Despite their gains in competence and confidence as social researchers, the insider members of the team initially did not feel qualified to write for an outside audience. At the very end of the process, during a final session of reflections, the coauthors agreed that the process of reflection that writing demanded was the richest part of the whole learning experience.

Parallel to the writing, AR as an approach to problem solving was also institutionalized in a limited way within the Fagor Group. Some 40 people had received training in these approaches over the 3 years of the project. Five pilot projects had been undertaken in particular cooperatives, with members of the AR team serving as AR team leaders in the new venues. A number of the team members quickly were given major management responsibilities within the system, three becoming general managers of cooperatives in the years immediately following the project and another two becoming central figures in the cooperative training system for new members and retraining for existing members. The book emerging from the project (Greenwood et al., 1990) is now used in training courses. One of the pilot projects resulted in a fundamental reorganization of one cooperative that is now among the most successful in the system.

All in all, this case shows how AR can be linked to organizational reflection, training of organizational insiders, and organizational development efforts, while also reaching intellectual goals that go well beyond the limits of the particular case.

CONCLUSION

Though the richness of the two experiences cannot be evoked in such brief presentations, we have aimed to characterize what we have in mind when we use the term *action research*. These two cases shed light on some of the potential diversity of AR. There are clear differences in the focus of the AR in these cases. The Stongfjorden case started from an action point, whereas the Mondragón case was rooted in a more abstractly analytical research design. The important point is how the discourse between researchers and local group members gradually shapes a mutual learning situation, affecting both research and actions. Stongfjorden moved from an activist community to one that learned how to research issues related to the mobilization of resources effectively, whereas Mondragón shifted from a strong research focus on organizational culture to inclusion of actions to solve important challenges for the Fagor Group.

AR is a complex, dynamic activity involving the best efforts of both members of communities or organizations and professional researchers. It simultaneously involves the cogeneration of new information and analysis together with actions aimed at transforming the situation in democratic directions. AR is holistic and also context bound, producing practical solutions and new knowledge as part of an integrated set of activities. We hope that we have conveyed an understanding that AR is not a method as it is conventionally understood. AR is a way of producing tangible and desired results for the people involved, and it is a knowledge-generation process that produces insights both for researchers and the participants. It is a complex action-knowledge generation process. In both cases, the immense importance of insider knowledge and initiatives is evident, marking a clear distinction from orthodox research that systematically distrusts insider knowledge as co-opted.

Notes

1. It is difficult to characterize this dimension of the cooperatives accurately now. For many years, the differential was 1 to 3 and it was gradually expanded to 1 to 6, though it is one of the thorniest subjects the members debate. More recently, different cooperatives have adopted different scales, a few permitting as much as a 1 to 20 differential and others holding the line at 1 to 6.

2. The story of this research is told in detail in Greenwood et al. (1992).

3. The T-group technique was developed to enhance group dynamic learning. The idea is to train the members to take responsibility for their own learning and development of social relationships. The concept of T groups is presented in Chapter 2, "A History of Action Research."

Science, Epistemology, and Practice in Action Research

Part 2 introduces the main epistemological and methodological arguments that govern our views on action research (AR). We take on the question of the scientific status of AR, ground AR in a longer history of pragmatist thought, and present a variety of methods and forms of practice we believe are key to successful AR.

4

Scientific Methods
and Action Research

The mantle of science is highly prized in contemporary social research.[1] For those seeking it, being "scientific" confers ideological support and social prestige on theories, conclusions, and recommendations. If action research (AR) can be categorized as unscientific or "soft," then power holders both in academia and in society at large feel free to ignore our results, which is convenient when our findings are critical of existing power relations.

In this work, we take the social and cultural conditions awarding this prestige to science for granted. Although the hegemony of the idea of science itself requires an explanation, addressing it would take us beyond the purposes of this chapter and book.[2] We do need to clarify that, for us, science is not a dirty word; science can be carried on as an activity aimed at generating new knowledge and can serve as the basis for emancipatory processes. Whether or not this is true depends on how science is socially embedded and deployed.

In this chapter and the next, our intentions are quite specific. We make a simple but bold claim: AR is much closer to the practices of physical and biological sciences than any of the mainstream varieties of academic social research. We affirm this not because we want to sanctify AR with the name of science, but because we insist that AR is far more likely than conventional forms of social research to produce reliable and useful information and interpretations of social phenomena. The conventional social sciences (economics, psychology, sociology, political science, and, to a lesser degree anthropology) have situated themselves in academia as *the* social sciences. This logically makes it appear that other practices, such as AR, must therefore depart from science. We agree that the praxis of AR is fundamentally different from that found in most conventional social research, but we argue that AR proceeds by methods quite likely to produce valid research results, whereas conventional social research rarely produces results whose validity can be tested in action.[3] In the following chapters, we will explain why the current structure of conventional social research exists and marginalizes AR in academic institutions.

◄o►

CAN AR PRODUCE SCIENTIFICALLY MEANINGFUL RESULTS?

We begin with a review of the standard criticism that AR is unscientific. Some of our AR colleagues address this issue by accepting the idea that science itself is necessarily inhumane and alienating. They are proud to be called unscientific. We disagree and thus make an argument that AR can and does produce valid and meaningful social research results.

In academic circles, AR, applied research, and qualitative research are generally denigrated as unscientific. Although conventional social science researchers occasionally admit that some AR is useful, they generally argue that AR findings are anecdotal, based on telling stories rather than on doing science. Indeed, most conventional researchers behave as if they believe that useful work is, by definition, scientifically trivial. In these circles, doing science is equated with being objective and rigorous, using statistical tests, using at least quasi-experimental controls, and staying away from the world of application. Because we think this notion is wrongheaded, we examine in detail what science and social science can mean.

It is not as if we are inventing criticisms that have never been leveled at the social sciences. The conventional social sciences have been criticized over the years for their often-questionable scientific practices. Critics of the contemporary social sciences often claim that these fields erred in accepting classical physics and chemistry as the model of science (see Clifford & Marcus, 1985; Geertz, 1973; Rabinow & Sullivan, 1987). For some of these critics, the proper response is to repudiate science and to advocate some perspective that challenges the very existence of generalizable knowledge. Others argue for various reforms in social science practice, such as doing more "relevant" research.

Many critics say that the social sciences have been captured by some kind of mechanistic and ritualistic error in conceptualization, to be remedied by a variety of cures ranging from hermeneutics to structuralism to deconstruction. According to this view, the social sciences have become derailed from methods appropriate to them. This tragic narrative usually argues that the social sciences have not paid sufficient attention to the dimensions of social phenomenon that do not exist in the sciences (e.g., intersubjective understandings, language). A different academic agenda emerges from these criticisms, including a struggle for power and influence in the academy.

We do not dispute the need for a changed agenda, but this attractive history of the social sciences does not correspond to the situations we have experienced. The problem is that research in the physical and biological sciences does not match the stereotype of scientific research that these critics unknowingly (we suppose) use. Rather, we believe that much research in the sciences can best be understood as a successful and disciplined form of repeated cycles of testing the relationship between thought and action. In other words, the sciences indeed are radically different from the contemporary social sciences, but not for the reasons conventional critiques give.

In particular, the conventional social scientists' disengagement (actual and intended) from the phenomena they study is virtually complete. Equating this disengagement with objectivity, impartiality, and the requirements of scientific practice, these practitioners systematically distance themselves from their objects. Then, by separating science from action, they sever the connection between thought and action that permits the testing of results both in the physical and biological sciences and in AR.

We will not take on the larger issues about the meaning of science itself. We will simply assume that it is useful to consider the physical sciences to be scientific in some meaningful sense.[4]

We make the argument that AR's pursuit of constant interactions between thought and action resembles research in the physical sciences far more closely than the practices of conventional social science. We then conclude that AR is more capable of producing scientific results (in a positive sense) than conventional social science.

At the heart of this problem is the tremendous emphasis social scientists place on their claim that being scientific requires researchers to sever all relations with the observed and to avoid being co-opted by the seduction of their own prejudices. Such social scientists equate objectivity with disengagement from the phenomena under study. Yet this belief undermines the argument that conventional social science can be scientific precisely because biological and physical scientists do not disengage themselves from the phenomena they study to be objective. The experimental method requires just the opposite. The scientific method and its experimental apparatus are a form of praxis on and in the world, though certainly not one oriented around democratic social change.

Viewing social research this way is not a new idea, but it has been ignored as conventional social scientists and the social interests their work serves have turned away from social engagement and social reform. Kurt Lewin, the social psychologist and an early proponent of AR, operated with a view of social research as both scientific and socially engaged. As we indicated in Chapter 2, "A History of Action Research," his view of the matter is summed up in two often-repeated statements attributed to him: "Nothing is as practical as a good theory" and "The best way to understand something is to try to change it." He articulated these views in the 1930s and 1940s, echoing the earlier ideas of the famous pragmatist philosopher of democracy and education, John Dewey. We will make a fuller presentation of these arguments in the next chapter.

What is important about Lewin and Dewey in the present context is that their approaches to social research are in concert with the way contemporary scientists think and behave. Lewin understood clearly the link between AR and the scientific method.

Rather than pursing the contention about AR and scientific method in the typical manner of such discussions (i.e., through more broad generalities), we will make the case by narrating an episode that illustrates our claim.[5] Our purpose is to clarify the implications of our argument that AR is more capable of producing valid results than conventional social science[6] and then to examine in subsequent chapters why conventional social science has deviated from this course.

PHYSICAL AND BIOLOGICAL SCIENCE AS ITERATIVE CYCLES OF THOUGHT AND ACTION

The episode that we recount happened to Greenwood 15 years ago. He has retold the story often enough that, in the way of narratives, his recollection of it is as much tied up with the retellings as with the original episode. He did not document the episode with anything other than lecture notes because only on reflection over the years did the larger meanings become clearer. Still, Greenwood feels that he is being true to the episode that he participated in.

At the time this occurred, Greenwood was the chair of the Biology and Society major at Cornell University. A program for students in their first 4 university years in the U.S. higher education system, this multidisciplinary, multicollege major was designed to link the basic biological and physical sciences with the social sciences and the humanities. It provided opportunities for students with a strong interest in the basic sciences to explore the social sciences and the humanities systematically. Greenwood was responsible for the core, upper-level course that included an overview of the relationship between biology and society, as well as discussions of science and scientific method.

Having taught this course several times, Greenwood discovered that good, advanced undergraduates with strong backgrounds in mathematics, physics, chemistry, and biology had very little in the way of concrete, behavioral understanding of the scientific method. They were sophisticated enough at using the appropriate language to describe the rules of the scientific method, but they did not understand the scientific method as a form of behavior. Instead, they used their notions about the scientific method mainly as a way of talking about scientific values.

On reflection, Greenwood realized that it was not really surprising because, by their third year at the university, most students had done only rote science work in the introductory courses they had taken. They had very little experience of science as a form of discovery and interpretation in a laboratory setting.

Although this situation was understandable, Greenwood found it unacceptable for the Biology and Society major. Many of the majors were preparing for careers in medicine or in other branches of health care where their understanding of the scientific method as a form of behavior would have direct consequences for thousands of patients. He cast around to find some way to deal with the problem. He knew that, despite his good relations with the students, as a cultural anthropologist, his views about the scientific method would have little credibility to them. He thus decided to invite a Nobel Prize winning chemist from Cornell to come to the class and lecture on the scientific method. He made this choice partially because he knew the scientist and partly because this professor was known to be an extraordinarily good and committed teacher of science.

The lecture given by the chemist lasted the standard 50 minutes, and the students were on the edge of their seats throughout. The prestige of this individual, combined with his congenial and down-to-earth manner, made the lesson effective for most present. It was clear at the outset that the students expected a very abstract and theoretical lecture from this eminent scientific intellectual. They apparently equated great science with great abstractions, very general laws, and big theories. What they got was something different. The chemist chose to describe his activities as a scientist and to bring the students into his world through a behavioral perspective, particularly through the perspective of the principal investigator in charge of a scientific research project.

He began by pointing out to the students that the first issue in any scientific inquiry is to generate a problem to study. He explained that this is not a simple process. It was evident from the students' reaction that they had not been asked previously to think about how scientists come up with questions to ask. Probably this was because students are generally given a set of predigested questions to address in their class work. The chemist pointed out that there are many problems in the world and many more suggested in the scientific literature. Some of these are interesting to the researchers in question; some are not. What is interesting, he argued, is partly a matter of personal preferences and histories. Also, some problems require equipment and funding that are not available; others touch on elements of previous experience that make them attractive or unattractive. Occasionally, an anomaly picked up through observation generates a questioning process and a review of the literature that eventually causes a group of people to decide it has a problem worth studying.

It was already clear at this point that the students were hearing ideas new to them. Most had not considered the matrix of ideas, experiences, organizational structures, and histories that provide the context in which scientists ask questions. Yet the chemist's statements accord well with studies carried out in the philosophy of science (Kuhn, 1962) and the social studies of science (Barnes, 1977; Barnes & Shapin, 1979; Latour & Woolgar, 1979; Rabinow, 1996; Zabusky, 1995). There are few convincing accounts of the scientific problem generation process. The exception is a study by Paul Rabinow (1996) that addresses this issue to good effect for one discovery in recombinant DNA work. This subject is now a central concern of the field of science and technology studies.

Problem selection tends to be bracketed under the headings of "individual creativity," "genius," and so on, converting science into a story of individual heroes that, we note, is a story with a hierarchical and authoritarian moral to it. The lecture pointed out that this process turns on the creativity of an individual or team in thinking up and defining problems well enough so they can be studied. The individual and team operate in a social context locally, through the scientific literature, and through their ongoing contacts around the world that place problems in a complex social, intellectual, and spatial web.

The chemist then asked the class how anyone could know that a selected problem is worth studying. Again the students were puzzled. He pointed out that there are many rational tests of the consequences arising from particular subjects, but none guarantees that the problem itself is worth the effort. Whether or not a researcher or a team becomes committed to the study of a problem is a matter of individual preference, intuition, insight, and the availability of the required resources, including money. It often is also the result of a chain of previous work in which this particular activity forms a link.

Having defined a problem and decided it is important enough to pursue, the next issue for researchers is to figure out how to study it. The group must ask itself what would be potentially relevant data for the study of the selected problem. The professor problematized this deliberately by showing that it is often not obvious what relevant data might be for a particular problem. In his view, much valuable effort often goes into trying to decide what data could bear some reasonable relationship to the problem and other researchers would find convincing.

Again the students were surprised. The ambiguity of what constitutes data, the amount of social processing that goes on in a scientific research team, and the dependence of local researchers on their wider networks and on the limitations of local equipment and funding were all dimensions of science that their introductory science courses had not revealed to them. They had been given a view of scientific method primarily as an individual encounter with a world of facts and individualistic formulations of hypotheses, research strategies, experiments, and reports. That is, they had been given the heroic view of science, and they were listening to a scientific hero who was giving them an anti-heroic narrative of science, yet one that was filled with a profound respect for the activity of scientists.

They seemed particularly bewildered by the notion that the data also are determined, to an extent, by the kind of equipment available at the research site. What is at hand plays some role in what data are thought to be relevant and the way data might be collected. Greenwood could see the students were uncomfortable with this, as if it was a form of cheating because of the idealization of scientific processes they were familiar with.

The chemist also emphasized the large number of decisions about how to document the information being collected and organizing the activity among a team of researchers to make it efficient and reasonable. The notions that a Nobel Prize chemist would have to be a team leader, an accomplished grant writer, and a social actor skilled in organizing and motivating groups were surprising to the class. That compromises would be made to design an activity that would not cause the research group to run out of resources before the data collection was completed was also new. Of course, this is not the students' fault, because few had ever faced the need to write grants, collect resources, and conduct experiments within a budget.

Having emphasized the intellectual and social embeddedness of all the elements in the scientific process, the chemist then argued that it is difficult to decide when data collection is complete. He pointed out that deciding how much data are enough often is a pragmatic matter, not always justifiable in abstract terms. It may be a decision based on fatigue; the exhaustion of financial, physical, or temporal resources; or the sense that there are enough data to say something others will believe about the problem in question. The students realized that this was a much more indeterminate view of the closure of the data collection phase of a scientific process than they had expected.

At this point, the chemist moved on to the second phase of hypothesis or question formulation. He pointed out that, although the activity is initially guided by a sense of a particular problem and possibly by a hypothesis, once a body of data has been collected and is examined, the issue becomes how to account for the array, or the distribution, or the structure of the sort of data at hand. In the physical and natural sciences, this part of the process often is a group activity. A variety of hypotheses is often formulated by a brainstorming activity though interaction influenced by a reading of the literature, flurries of e-mail, interpersonal and interunit relationships, and other interactions.

The chemist then asked the class members how they would know when they had formulated enough hypotheses. The students were mystified because hypothesis formulation as a form of behavior is apparently not often discussed in science courses. His sober answer was that hypothesis formulation is over when you cannot think of any more hypotheses or when you are too tired to go on. The students initially thought he was joking, but it became clear that he was not. He wanted the students to understand that science is not an activity that takes place in some idealized metaphysical space with perfect information, infinite resources to spend, and perfectly rational human beings in attendance. Science is a form of human activity that combines a set of pragmatic compromises between all the elements present at any given moment.

Beyond the pragmatics of the situation, the chemist also wanted to make a deeper point. We believe he was arguing that there is no rational way to know when one has formed enough alternative kinds of explanations for the array of data in question. The world is more complex than our apprehension of it can be, and thus we will always be approaching this complexity through a series of imperfect compromises. Being trained in a particular institution with a particular group of scientists is likely to have a powerful effect on judgements about how many hypotheses are sufficient. The appetites for complexity and other characteristics of these groups will, probably, socialize a young scientist to a particular standard. However this occurs, the chemist was pointing out that one can never know that all the relevant, possible ways of accounting for the data have been formulated. Science, as powerful as it is, is not a means for transcending the human condition.

Having completely perplexed his audience, the chemist then moved on to the next step: the process of testing questions or hypotheses against the data. Doing prestructured experiments with finite solutions in laboratory exercises did not prepare the students very well for what he said. In the students' experience, all the puzzles had specific answers, and they would receive grades for solving the puzzles with a specific set of resources and in a limited amount of time. They knew the answers were there, and they simply had to uncover them. These scientific training practices did not prepare them for the chemist's much less determinate view.

He pointed out that translating hypotheses into testable propositions and matching data to hypotheses are complex, ambiguous, and creative activities. Chains of assumptions and definitions are required to link data and hypotheses, and these chains have to be built so they are capable of convincing others that the reasoning and research process gone through is sensible and, therefore, that the results are acceptable. Doing this in laboratory situations is often a group process with rapid brainstorming and much trial and error, eminently social activities.[7]

Once the group has inventoried all the questions or hypotheses it can think of against the data collected and organized, the lecturer said that the best possible outcome is that the group has not invalidated all the explanations that it initially developed. The hope is that it would have at least one left. Quite often, this does not happen, and the group must return to the process of hypothesis formulation because none of the hypotheses is left standing. Alternatively, the data may not provide the basis for choosing among alternative explanations, and the experiment has to be redesigned.

At this point, the students were relieved because this began to sound like the sort of science that they could identify with. At the end of the process, the group has a validated explanation. But the chemist was not through. He explained that, having not invalidated all the hypotheses did not mean that the remaining hypotheses had been proved true. He insisted that one could only say that the group had not invalidated all the hypotheses that it had been able to think of.

In making this argument, he was not being perverse. Having pointed out that the initial process of hypothesis formulation is indeterminate, in the sense that there always exists the possibility of hypotheses that the group did not think of and that financial and human resources are finite, he was being consistent. If a single hypothesis were left after the testing procedures were complete, one could only say that, of the hypotheses thought of, at least one had not yet been invalidated. It might be invalidated in the future, but other better hypotheses might be formulated to account for the data in the future. Thus, the remaining explanation could not be said to be correct. It is simply the only one left of those thought of.

The 50 minutes were over. Greenwood's class seemed stunned, though appreciative. Rather than making the usual quick and noisy exodus, they wandered out of the room silently.

The chemist had given a master class, but more important, he had conveyed a view of science as a form of human action involving complexity, ambiguity, creativity, group dynamics, and many pragmatic concessions to the limitations imposed by the time and resources available. Rather than diminishing or demystifying science, this view helps us understand that science is a way of behaving, a way of acting in relation to the nonhuman and human worlds that has resulted in remarkable improvements in our understanding of how those worlds work and our ability to change the state of those worlds. Good scientific practice centers on constant cycles of thought and action.

Something the chemist did not mention at any point was prediction. Although it was clear that a good explanation could be used to generate a prior idea of the way the data should be arrayed if the explanation were to hold, he did not stress prediction itself as a core element in science. Rather, he emphasized explanation. Yet, commonsense views of science almost always equate science with prediction. We believe the chemist was right to deemphasize prediction as a fundamental criterion for science.

Scientists seek to explain arrays of data. Predicting the expected array of data under given conditions is a powerful way of testing explanations, but the goal is having an explanation that makes sense. Prediction is a tool to be used in this effort, and its use varies a great deal with the conditions. Under some conditions, prediction, in the ordinary sense, is out of the question, as in the historical studies of evolution.[8] Under other conditions, predictions take the form of statistical generalizations about huge populations and cannot accurately capture what is happening in particular segments of those populations. In other situations, predictive activity takes the form of intervening in the phenomenon under study to change its state in a desired direction. This is precisely what the experimental method in science does and what AR aims to achieve in the social world.

The chemist's view matches closely with our experiences of scientists and engineers at work. It puts them, as human actors, at the center of the combined social-research activity that is science. He made it clear that scientists and engineers are not the enactors of some abstract, perfect, determinate system. The chemist conveyed to the students that scientific method is a form of social behavior, a form that is not foolproof, but one that uses human capabilities to pose questions and attempts to examine those questions through rational but fully social inquiry. He stressed the need to recognize the significant gaps and imperfections in any process of this sort, and he affirmed that human judgement, creativity, and social interaction are an intrinsic part of the process.

Repeatedly, he emphasized that science is a collective activity carried out by members of research teams within a larger scientific community. The larger community provides the literature on which the research is built to some degree, as well as the resources used to carry out the research. The research team and the laboratory form a complex, dynamic social system of people acting on phenomena and sharing their thoughts within the pragmatic limitations set by the availability of key resources and the dynamics of the human relationships involved.

SCIENCE IS HUMANS IN ACTION

There is much to learn from this story, but we want to stress the social and cultural dimensions of scientific activity that are revealed by this way of presenting the scientific method. Not only do the scientists go out and get grants, often writing collaboratively to do so, but the laboratories in which they work are social systems involving teamwork and divisions of labor (see Latour, 1987; Latour & Woolgar, 1979; Zabusky, 1995). Their activities are often characterized by cogenerative problem solving because they work in groups and use both present records that they create themselves as well as written records of data from others. Brainstorming is a common activity in these settings, and data collection is often also a product of teamwork. Question formulation often takes place in groups, with people interrogating one another. Good science is an eminently social activity, as the field of science and technology studies has clearly shown.

Science is also a highly iterative and dynamic activity involving repeated action-reflection-action cycles. The amount of time spent cross-referencing resulting data with expectations, checking and rechecking for fit, and acting on the data to assess the effects of particular actions in relation to expectations about how the data will behave is a dominant characteristic of science. Thought and action cycle around each other repeatedly, as they necessarily do in any kind of AR.

AR is very similar in its use of thought-action cycles and the testing of understandings collaboratively generated through actions that then become part of the next cycle of thought and planning. By contrast, conventional social science, which is purposely separated from the world of action, is not like this.

This matters, not as an exposé, but as a call to reconsider the history and development of social research in the 20th century. Our experience of collaborative cycles of thought and action in AR corresponds well to the chemist's presentation of his experiences as a scientist. We encourage you to pause and wonder why conventional social science is hegemonic in our societies, has claimed the mantle of science, and yet does not resemble what scientists do.

In this chapter, we have developed a systematic comparison between the way the scientific method is deployed in the physical and biological sciences and the iterative cycles of reflection and action characteristic of AR, using a narrative of a lecture on science as the centerpiece. We have pointed out that the conventional social sciences resemble neither the physical or biological sciences nor AR because they sever the relationship between reflection and action. In the next chapter, we turn to more detailed philosophical arguments about AR as a form of social science.

Notes

1. One may object that deconstructive and other postmodern approaches to social research in the current generation have turned their backs on the prestige of science. We think, rather, that most such endeavors are built on a poor and stereotypic understanding of science and therefore constitute a retreat that is portrayed as an advance. Some exceptions are Latour and Woolgar (1979), Zabusky, (1995), and Rabinow (1996).

2. There is an ample literature on this subject under the general heading of the social studies of science. In addition to the works cited in Note 1, there are the works of Sharon Traweek (1992), Barry Barnes and Steve Shapin (1979), and Dorothy Nelkin (1982; Nelkin & Lindee, 1995; Nelkin & Tancredi, 1987).

3. One common reaction to our argument from readers interested in AR as been to view this as bad news. Apparently, as part of the process of becoming alienated from conventional social science, many practitioners become alienated from the idea of science as well. We believe this is an error. Being scientific is not tantamount to being inhumane. Social action is more likely to be inhumane when it is based on poor research practices and a weak understanding of local situations. We believe that many of the inhumane and authoritarian trappings of conventional social research are elements that prevent it from discovering the causes of most social problems.

4. Readers who reject this point need read no farther because we reject the radical relativist position that all knowledge is equally flawed.

5. Because one of the main criticisms of AR by conventional social researchers is that we are just storytellers, we think that narrating a story with a very sharp moral for conventional social scientists is appropriate here.

6. This claim closely echoes the view espoused by Chris Argyris, Robert Putnam, and Diana McClain Smith (1985) in *Action Science.* For those interested in a view of these issues deriving from a very different approach, see our Chapter 11, "Action Science and Organizational Learning," and the extensive writings of Chris Argyris.

7. One relevant dimension of science as a form of action that was not touched on in the lecture is the sheer amount of trial-and-error experimentation and troubleshooting that goes on in any scientific work. Most experienced scientists know that science is composed of a few insights and discoveries and a vast amount of routine, tiresome, and often frustrating laboratory work. Troubleshooting, false positives, false negatives, and confusion are all part of the daily routine of scientific work.

8. Occasionally the term *retrodiction* is used to refer to an attempt to build a prediction about past processes out of a theoretical formulation and then compare the predicted result with what happened historically. This seems to us simply another meaning of prediction, albeit a useful one.

5

An Epistemological Foundation
for Action Research

How scientific can and should social research be? What does it mean for social research to be scientific? In this chapter, we present our reasons for believing that action research (AR) is a powerfully scientific approach to social research. To do this, we touch on some issues from the general philosophy of science and then contrast positivistic views of science with contemporary versions of pragmatism and hermeneutic philosophy. What follows is a very modest map of a broad and challenging set of issues. Our aim is to provide enough perspective on them to stake out the positions that are the axis of our approach.

We begin by reviewing the connections between AR and general systems theory. Following this, we examine the contributions of pragmatic philosophy to AR and make some links to Wittgensteinian philosophy as well. We conclude by setting our arguments in the context of political economy, and return to our original claims that AR has the potential to be the most scientific form of social research and that conventional social research does not resemble scientific research in most important particulars.

◄◦►

DEFINING SCIENTIFIC RESEARCH

To anchor our discussion, we define scientific research as investigative activity capable of discovering that the world is or is not organized as our preconceptions lead us to expect and suggesting grounded ways of understanding it. Scientific research documents both the investigative processes and conclusions arising from them in sufficient detail for other interested parties to be able to evaluate the information and interpretations offered.

In the following discussion we use the terms *logical positivism* and *hermeneutics*. For the sake of clarity, it is important to define what we mean by these two concepts.

- Logical positivism is based on the ontological argument that the world is objectively given; the epistemological effort is to apply objective methods to acquire the truth.

- Hermeneutics is based on the ontological position that the world is subjective and the epistemological project is to make interpretations of this subjective world.

A central strategic problem we face in making this exposition is that introductory instruction in most fields (including the sciences, social sciences, and humanities) does not reflect accurately the best practices or the most thoughtful views in those fields. In the often misguided effort to simplify perspectives to make them suitable for introductory students, classroom presentations often distort the frameworks and practices of our fields. Few practicing social scientists would turn to an introductory textbook for guidance about the practices in their own field, partly because the books are too elementary, but mainly because the books rarely reflect the best practices in their fields.

This problem is not unique to the social sciences; it afflicts the basic sciences as well. Generally, introductory instruction in the sciences gives students an idealized, ahistorical, nonbehavioral view of science either as a set of truths or as a set of rather unproblematic methods. Science's diversity and confusions, its human face, its social and historical dimensions, and, consequently, its behavioral and human excitement are often lost from view. Scientists are portrayed as disembodied seekers of the truth behind the confusing world of appearances, with much of the complexity and excitement of their tasks washed out.

Doing scientific work is not copying methodological blueprints written up in textbooks, but applying research methods in the complex politics of the social world (Latour, 1987). In addition, formulas and principles are presented as achieved truths. Laboratory exercises and problem sets all have one or two "correct" solutions. All puzzles have a definite answer. Scientists know these answers, and the students, to become scientists, must come to know them also.

This is not all nonsense. Respect for systematic work with principles, handling and reporting of materials, and understanding of laws whose consequences are reasonably well understood are all meaningful parts of science. But practicing scientists generally do not live science in this way. As our chemist from the previous chapter pointed out, scientists live in a socially complex world, chasing dynamic phenomena with limited and imperfect instruments and finite energies and budgets. For this exposition, we assume that many readers with an interest in AR may not have an experience-based understanding of science as a form of practice. This limits their tools for dealing with the arguments for and against AR as a form of scientific inquiry. There is no simple solution to this socially produced dilemma.

SCIENTIFIC RESEARCH DEFINED

We have defined scientific research as investigative activity capable of discovering that the world is not organized as our preconceptions lead us to expect and suggesting alternative ways of understanding it. Scientific research documents both the investigative processes and conclusions arising from them in sufficient detail for other interested parties to be able to evaluate the information and interpretations offered. The institutional edifices of what is called science today do not necessarily bear a close relationship to this definition of scientific research.

GENERAL SYSTEMS THEORY

One stream of scientific ideas and concepts directly relevant to AR comes from a loosely integrated field that is known as *general systems theory* (GST), a field little taught to university students outside of the sciences and engineering. Having its origins in physics, chemistry, biology, and engineering in the 1920s and linked at that time to the development of self-correcting guidance systems for military use, GST has had an immense influence on the world around us. Despite this, GST is not a household word. Partly this is because, like AR, GST is not a single discipline anchored in a particular academic department. It is a set of perspectives shared by a wide array of scientists and social reformers with diverse backgrounds and divergent political ideas.

At the core of GST is a set of holistic concepts about the way the world is organized. Rather than accepting the notion of a particulate universe made up of separate atoms, molecules, and higher combinations, GST views the world (inorganic, organic, and sociocultural) as composed of interacting systems whose processes differently integrate the same basic matter of the universe to produce the immense array of things we encounter in the world of experience. The GST view argues that the differences between an inorganic, an organic, and a sociocultural system are to be understood as the product of the differences in the way these systems are organized: the kind and sequences of processes that take place within them.

Though GST contains complexly differentiated concepts, practitioners make a fundamental distinction between *closed* and *open* systems. These two broad classes of systems operate quite differently. Equilibria in a closed and open system are maintained by different kinds of processes, and these systems react very differently to perturbations from the environment. In GST, a system is largely understood by a combination of its open or closed properties and then by the history of the processes occurring within it or affecting it from the outside.

This view is radically different from the particulate view of the world that has been central to Western thought until recently. In GST, the units of analysis are systems, not individuals—systems, not separate institutions. Individuals operate within systems that create process environments that affect the outcomes of behavior in complex ways. The world is not a neat stratigraphic map beginning with inorganic matter, passing to organic matter, and then being transcended by sociocultural forces. Rather, the world is a complex, interacting array of systems and system processes, bumping into each other in a variety of ways. The only hope of understanding any particular thing is by placing it in the appropriate system context and following the processes by which it acts. This is what Senge (1990) argues for as the "fifth discipline"—the ability to understand how elements and subsystems interact, forming a total situation.

GST has been applied to the ancient riddle of explaining the relationship between inorganic matter and organic matter and the evolution of life. Here the work of Ludwig von Bertalanffy (1966, 1968) has been fundamental. In applying these perspectives to social systems, a variety of theories of international conflict (Rapoport, 1974) and a whole tradition in the analysis of organizational behavior (see Argyris, 1985; Argyris & Schön, 1996; Flood & Romm, 1996) have been built around these notions. Finally, the path-breaking work of Gregory Bateson (1979) on the relationship between mind and nature relies on this approach. Bateson persuasively shows that the nature-culture problem is radically transformed when we understand the relationship as an expression of processes found everywhere in nature. For Bateson, the mind is part of nature and necessarily works according to a set of organizational processes found in nature but combined in particular ways in mental activity. Thus, mind is both fully part of nature and unique as a system.

Why is GST relevant to AR? To begin with, the GST account of the world is at odds with much of what is currently called social science. Orthodox social science is still largely carried out in the stratigraphic, particulate world, based on images of social facts that stand on their own. Thus, GST is a profound critique of the scientific pretensions of orthodox social researchers.

More important, the systems approach necessarily underlies AR in all its manifestations. Both rely heavily on a holistic view of the world. Humans are understood to exist only within social systems, and these systems have properties and processes that condition human behavior and are in turn conditioned by that behavior. Social systems are not mere structures, but are processes in continual motion. They are dynamic and historical. They are also interlinked, entwining the individual social structures and the larger ecology of systems into complex interacting macrosystems.

The relevance of GST to AR can be seen because AR can be understood as an effort to transform society into ever more open systems. Indeed, some AR practitioners equate increased openness with democratization (Flood & Romm, 1996). So, one thread leading in the direction of or supporting the development of AR is GST. Another is the considerably broader philosophical movements of pragmatism and neopragmatism.

PRAGMATIC PHILOSOPHY AND AR

That a stereotypical view of science prevails among nonscientists does not mean that the world is or has been unaware of the perspectives we articulate here. All the elements in a more complex and humanly meaningful view of science are well-known and have been articulated effectively by John Dewey (1976), Charles Peirce (1950), William James (1948, 1995), Kurt Lewin (1935, 1948), and more recently, Stephen Toulmin and Björn Gustavsen (1996), all writing in the pragmatist tradition.

John Dewey is particularly important for our exposition because his pragmatic philosophy laid out an action approach to science as a form of human inquiry and underscored its connections to democracy in a way in concert with our views on AR. Dewey was born in 1859 and died in 1952. His intellectual production dates from the 1880s and continued to the end of his life. Dewey is generally viewed as having been a key influence on public education in the United States and as having been the prime mover behind one of the few rather uniquely American contributions to Western philosophy. Nevertheless, a recent intellectual biographer, Robert Westbrook (1991), shows that Dewey's was always and remains a minority view. There is little evidence that those who cite Dewey approvingly have acted on his ideas.

What, then, are his ideas? To render 70 years of intellectual work (his complete works run to over 30 volumes) in a few paragraphs is impossible. We outline only a few of the key points of his approach that relate to AR and to the relationship between social research and social reform.

Dewey was a staunch believer in democracy as an ongoing, collective process of social improvement in which all levels of society had to participate. These arguments are put forward in *The Public and Its Problems* (1927/1991). In his view, the role of public education was to permit everyone in society enough training so that they could contribute their own views and experiences to the collective democratic process. In *The School and Society* (1900) and *The Child and the Curriculum*

(1902), Dewey presents his arguments on the connection between democratic theory and pedagogical ideas.

Perhaps the most characteristic feature of Dewey's approach is his steadfast refusal to separate thought from action. For Dewey, everything is forged in action. He sees democracy itself as an ongoing form of social action, a combination of institutional forms and ethical commitments that works toward the increasing ability of all members of society to contribute their intelligence to the whole. He believes that the only real sources of knowledge are to be found in action, not in armchair speculation. For him, all knowledge testing and proofs are experimental activities. This position is clear in his views on logic, which he treats as a theory of inquiry (Dewey, 1927/1991).

One consequence is that schools should create environments where the students can safely confront problems that can be resolved only by using skills gained from studying the sciences, history, and the arts. Schools should not be locations where the students, seen as empty vessels, are filled with knowledge bits. This is consistent with Dewey's view that scientific judgement is not a form of esoteric knowledge. Dewey believes that all humans are capable of scientific judgement and that society could be improved to the extent these capacities are increased among all of society's members. Consistent with this, he strongly opposes the division of public education into vocational and academic tracks, seeing this as the preservation of inequality and ultimately the weakening of democracy as a whole. He believes that limiting the learning of any individual ultimately limits society as a whole.

These ideas connect to Dewey's view of schools as environments and learning as a process of action in which the student must be an active learner and not a passive listener. Though many connect these ideas to Dewey, few students would describe the bulk of their educational experiences in these terms. Dewey is a figure simultaneously lionized and ignored. The best way to blunt a reform is to co-opt it, to state approval of it, and to act in the opposite way.

One of the hallmarks of Dewey's thought is his resolute focus on diversity and conflict as essential elements in a democratic society. He views democracy as a process of working through conflicts, not to a final resolution but toward an improved situation. He does not hunger for the elimination of conflict in society because he respects the diversity of people and their experiences. His aim was to build momentum for democratic social reform by bringing together these conflicting experiences and by working democratically to ameliorate intolerable situations. He believes that communities (including community schools) are central to this process precisely because communities are divided and diverse. Their common stake in solutions can permit them to work through problems together.

Dewey's views on science are in no way separate from the above. For Dewey, scientific research is not a process separate from democratic social action. Scientific knowing, like all other forms of knowledge, is a product of continuous cycles of action and reflection (Dewey, 1927/ 1991). The center of gravity is always the learner's active pursuit of understanding through puzzle solving activity with the materials at hand. The solutions achieved are only the best possible at that moment with materials at hand, hence the denomination of his philosophy as *pragmatism.*

Dewey remained politically engaged in a variety of democratic movements throughout his life. He was realistic about the situation he faced. He understood that the existing power structures favored having a ruling class and a duty-bound, vocationally educated populace to work for them in unreflective harmony. He was aware of the radical separation between academic institutions and the human situations he wished to change. Although he asserted that experience was an organic whole, he knew that educational practice divided it up into tiny, specialized parcels and that this process weakened the ability of the citizenry to take control of democracy in the way he advocated. Above all, he knew that academic social science was radically opposed to his action orientation. Because it separates thought from action, it creates social researchers who offer no threat to existing power arrangements.

To summarize, Dewey believed that all humans are scientists, that thought must not be separated from action, that the diversity of human communities is one of their most powerful features (if harnessed to democratic processes), and that academic institutions in general and academic social research in particular promotes neither science nor democratic social action. Nearly his entire corpus of work can be seen as consistent with the premises of general systems theory as well, because he focused on the individual in society and society in their environments as dynamic and open systems. His resolute emphasis on processes rather than on outcomes and the way in which society can be made responsive to the continual changes from within and from without also link him to GST. Dewey's pragmatism, with its linkage of knowledge and action, its connections between knowledge, action, community, and democracy, remain important for AR.

EPISTEMOLOGICAL FOUNDATIONS OF AR

The presentations of GST and pragmatism connect directly to AR. AR aims to solve pertinent problems in a given context through a democratic inquiry where professional researchers collaborate with participants in the effort to seek and enact solutions to problems of major importance to the local people. In doing this, AR specifically engages in systems-informed, pragmatic social science. Indeed, AR is challenged to practice leading-edge science, combining the best in scientific practice with a commitment to the democratic transformation of society. Yet AR is almost universally viewed with Olympian disrespect by conventional social scientists, who see it as unsystematic, atheoretical storytelling. We, of course, believe these criticisms to be ill founded.

One point that needs to be made here is that AR generally takes on much more complex problems than the conventional social sciences. AR focuses on specific contexts and demands that theory and action not be separated, and is committed to the idea that the test of any theory is its capacity to resolve problems in real-life situations. This focus on the world of experience, with its complexity, historicity, and dynamism, means that AR distances itself from the often purified world of conventional social research with its friction-free, perfect information and "other things being equal" assumptions. Academic social researchers seem content to chop up reality to make it simpler to handle, more suited to theoretical manipulation, and to make the social scientist's life easier to manage. AR does not accept these compromises.

As a result, and consistent with our presentations of GST and pragmatism, AR as a form of research has the following core characteristics:

- AR is context bound and addresses real-life problems.

- AR is inquiry where participants and researchers cogenerate knowledge through collaborative communicative processes in which all participants' contributions are taken seriously.

- AR treats the diversity of experience and capacities within the local group as an opportunity for the enrichment of the research-action process.

- The meanings constructed in the inquiry process lead to social action, or these reflections on action lead to the construction of new meanings.

- The credibility-validity of AR knowledge is measured according to whether actions that arise from it solve problems (workability) and increase participants' control over their own situation.

Given this conceptualization of AR, several important questions emerge. What is the logic of inquiry constructed this way? What are reasonable criteria for judging knowledge to be credible in AR? How can strongly context-bound knowledge be communicated effectively to academics and other potential recipient groups? The aim of the following discussion is to present an epistemological position that supports our arguments for the value of AR.

Context-Bound Inquiry on
Important Local Problems

AR focuses on solving real-life problems. The focus of the inquiry is determined by what the participants consider important, what affects their daily lives.

The inquiry process is thus linked to actions taken to provide a solution to the problem being examined. Inquiry can precede actions. In this case, it is a way of acquiring necessary knowledge to design actions that will resolve the pertinent issue. Inquiry can also be a way of developing reflections based on experiences drawn from prior actions that can be understood in new ways. Of course, in most real-life situations, any attempt to solve important problems involves a priori and a posteriori meaning construction.

We emphasize that the inquiry process is linked to solving practical problems. But practical problems are not necessarily simple ones. Community economic development, developing new organizational structures in an organization, building a house where inhabitants in a neighborhood can meet, or collective efforts to reduce violence in the local community are all practical problems, but they are often extremely complex.

Whether the problem is a social-organizational or a material one, the results of AR must be tangible in the sense that participants can figure out whether the solution they have developed actually resolves the problem they set themselves. Here we connect directly back to pragmatic philosophy. The results of an AR process must be judged in terms of the workability of the solutions arrived at. Workability means whether or not a solution resolves the initial problem. This is not a matter of double-blind experimentation, stratified random samples, and significance levels. It is a matter of collective social judgement about the outcomes of a collective social action. Social judgement is itself the result of a kind of democratic conversation in which the professional researcher has only one vote.

Democratic Inquiry Processes Linking Participants and Professionals

We frame AR as democratic processes supporting the creation of new knowledge that potentially can be liberating. Obviously, then, the inquiry process has to aim at the solution of problems important to the local participants, and the knowledge produced by the inquiry process must increase participants' control over their own situation. This is consistent with Freire's (1970) concept of *conscientization,* which identifies the inquiry process as aimed at shaping knowledge relevant to action built on a critical understanding of historical and political contexts within which the participants act. The participants must be able to use the knowledge that emerges, and this knowledge must support the enhancement of the participants' goals.

The democratic element in the inquiry process indicates that mutualism between outside researchers and inside participants must exist. AR is a communication process where the best of both sides can merge through the inquiry process. Local knowledge, historical consciousness, and everyday experience of the insiders complements the outsider's skills in facilitating learning processes, technical skills in research procedures, and comparative knowledge of the subject under investigation. At the same time, we agree with Dewey (1976) that "in all this, there is no difference of kind between the methods of science and those of the plain man. The difference is the greater control by science of the statement of the problem, and of relevant material, both sensible and conceptual" (p. 305).

Linking the outside researcher with insiders in a joint inquiry process eliminates the possibility of believing in Fregian (1918/1956) and Russellian (1903) logic as some kind of objective outside standard for what can be considered true or relevant knowledge. The logic of inquiry is linked to the inquiry process itself, in the struggle to make an indeterminate situation into a more positively controlled one through an inquiry process where action and reflection are directly linked. The outside researcher inevitably becomes a participant in collaboration with the insiders.

Years ago, a Norwegian philosopher titled his masters thesis "Objectivity and the Study of Man" (Skjervheim, 1974). It deals with the foundations of social science. According to Skjervheim's (1974) view, in AR there is no doubt that the researcher is an active participant in the inquiry process. The acceptance and the active and conscious use of this position contrasts AR with conventional social science that purposely obfuscates the researcher's social role. The obvious participant status that any social scientist must take in any research is fully acknowledged in AR and is treated as a resource for the process, and the construction of new knowledge is built on the premise of this mutual engagement.

Diversity as an Opportunity

The involvement of participants in the research process creates a genuine opportunity to use individual capacities. We have argued that research involves human creativity in developing potential solutions to and explanations for the problem at issue. A purely rational argument in favor of having a diverse group of coresearchers is that the broader set of experiences and attitudes the participants bring to the research process can permit more creative solutions to develop. Lessons from research on creativity illustrate this point.

A second and equally important argument is the ethical position that it is important to sustain diversity as a political right in itself. AR must be constructed to gain force from the creative potential in the diversity of the participant group, not to create solutions to problems that unnecessarily reduce diversity.

The AR Inquiry Process Is Thus
Inevitably Linked to Action

Knowledge emerges and is evaluated through acting or as a consequence of actions. The discovery process is not purely mental, receding into the intellectual sphere at a distance from human actions. With Dewey, we argue for understanding inquiry as a process linking reflection and action in a unified process for the creation of new knowledge. This means that the logic of the inquiry process itself is the real basis that underlies human knowledge (Burke, 1994).

By linking inquiry to actions in a given context, AR understands human inquirers to be acting subjects in a holistic situation. Inquiry is not fragmented and separated; it is treated as a coherent social field. Dewey (1976) identifies this as an organism-environment system that configures the holistic situation. In this view, the inquirer is also always a subject in the processes of acquiring new knowledge. AR rules out conventional positions that imagine the inquirer taking on a neutral and objective stance to the question under study.

AR processes do not make claims for context-free knowledge. The conventional concept of generalizability equates the general with what is universally true, context notwithstanding. Because AR is built on the notion of context-bound inquiry, it offers a very different concept of general knowledge, one that we believe is more powerful and certainly much more useful.

We argue that AR-developed knowledge can be valuable in contexts other than those where it is developed, but we reject the notion that the transferability of knowledge from one location to another is achieved by abstract generalizations about that knowledge. Transferring knowledge from one context to another relies on understanding the contextual factors in the situation where the inquiry took place, judging the new context where the knowledge is supposed to be applied, and making a critical assessment of whether the two contexts have sufficient processes in common to make it worthwhile to link them. We will return to this issue later.

In AR, insiders and outsiders join in a mutual learning process. The enabling mechanism for this is communication. New understandings are created through discourses between people engaged in the inquiry process. For this to occur, a mutually understandable discourse is required, and this is achieved through living together over time, sharing experiences, and taking actions together. This discourse that enables communication is much like what Wittgenstein (1953) describes as practice. Language creates meaning because it identifies actions that are meaningful for the actors. New knowledge, which we have identified as emerging from an action-reflection process, accordingly shapes a language that is relevant for describing actions, and the learning arising from them. The AR process thus creates a language shared between insiders and outsiders that identifies the meaning constructed through the inquiry process.

This argument leads us not only to an understanding of the way communication processes create meanings supportive of action but also to an understanding of the reverse process. In some situations, outcomes or experiences arising from actions initiate collective reflection processes that subsequently create new meanings.

Credibility and Validity in AR Inquiry

Credibility, validity, and reliability in conventional social science research function as the researchers' amulet. In a world of confusing information, these practitioners seem to find comfort in an elaborate methodological (and ritual) apparatus that purports to resolve these thorny problems cleanly. By focusing on methodological rules as a substitute for facing the question of whether a specific understanding is worth believing enough to act on it, it permits conventional social science to bypass the challenge of workability.

It is important to understand what the prerequisites for someone believing in meanings constructed through AR are. We define credibility as the arguments and the processes necessary for having someone trust research results. We can distinguish two different types of credible knowledge. First, there is knowledge that has *internal credibility* to the group generating it. This kind of knowledge is fundamentally important to AR because of the collaborative character of the research process. Its direct consequences in altered patterns of social action constitute a clear test of credibility, one that many abstract social science frameworks lack. Members of communities or organizations are unlikely to accept as credible the "objective" theories of outsiders if they cannot recognize the connection to the local situation, or because local knowledge makes it clear that the frameworks are either too abstract or simply wrong for the specific context.

A second kind of credibility involves external judgements. *External credibility* is knowledge capable of convincing someone who did not participate in the inquiry that the results are believable. This is a complex matter. Because AR depends on the conjugation of reflection and action and the cogeneration of new knowledge in specific contexts, conveying effectively the credibility of this knowledge to outsiders is a difficult challenge.

Often AR reports are called mere storytelling, an insulting attempt to disqualify the general knowledge gained in a specific AR case. A great deal is at stake in understanding that the stories of individual cases can and should have powerful general effects. The logic of scientific reasoning requires that any individual AR case that contradicts a general social theory thereby invalidates that theory and requires that a new theory be developed to take account of the case. Viable theories do not have exceptions; they must be reformulated to include the exceptions in a coherent way. Thus, individual cases and stories, the stuff of most AR, have immense power to alter theories.

This is the crux of the credibility-validity issue in AR. The conventional social research community believes that credibility is created through generalizing and universalizing propositions of the universal hypothetical, universal disjunctive, and generic types, whereas AR believes that only knowledge generated and tested in practice is credible.

CREDIBILITY IN AR

Workability

In AR processes, a first credibility challenge relates to the solution of the AR question under examination locally. Here the workability test is central. We must figure out whether the actions taken in the AR process result in a solution to the problem. This is in line with Dewey's (1976) thinking on the inquiry process, where knowledge is created or meaning is constructed through acting on the environment. Johannesen (1996) develops a similar conception when he addresses the validity standard of AR. Thus, borrowing from pragmatist thought directly (Diggins,1994), we understand the inquiry process as an integration of action and reflection and the test of the tangible outcome as workability.

Making Sense

The second and complementary process in inquiry is making sense out of these tangible results. How can the outcome be integrated in a meaning construction process that creates new knowledge? Here we focus on how meaning is constructed through deliberative processes. Berger and Luckmann (1966) represent an early line in the argument that all knowledge is socially constructed. Their constructivist position does not reflect sufficiently on the quality of the socially constructed knowledge, however, because they do not attempt to scrutinize the quality of the constructed outcomes. For them, any construction is as right or wrong as any other possible one, a position antithetical to AR.

In AR, we need a process where chains of arguments can undergo some kind of testing procedure. We can describe two possible processes for such deliberations: Habermas's (1984) ideal speech situation and Gadamer's (1982) hermeneutics, though many more formulations exist.

The Habermasian (1984) ideal speech situation counterfactually characterizes a process free from domination, where the actors involved in meaning construction exchange arguments without coercion. In this idealized situation, each participant seriously and honestly judges the arguments presented to him or her and comes back with the best judgement he or she can make. This process will lead to an understanding that is characterized as a legitimate truth when no further arguments are able to overturn those already stated.

The credibility of the line of argumentation emerges out of this ideal situation when no better explanation can be offered. This is not a one-shot affair; it is a continuous process where new experiences or new arguments continually challenge what is already thought of as credible knowledge. The Habermasian (1984) ideal speech situation is appealing and alluring in its strict logical and rational reasoning, but it leaves out emotions, power, and inequality as key determinants of all communication processes, a critique that has been widely made (see, e.g., Flood & Romm, 1996).

Gadamer's (1982) *Truth and Method* resists facile synthesis. He treats Habermas's (1984) ideal speech situation as a piece of naive idealism, advocating instead a more complex combination of dialogue, mutual interpretation, and eventual (but never final) "fusion of horizons." Gadamer respects the historicity of the knowledge, interpretations, and experiences the participants bring. Gadamer, unlike those who have tried to convert hermeneutics into an academic parlor game, insists that hermeneutics is a form of acting, not merely a method for thinking.

Transcontextual Credibility

At a still broader level, there exists the possibility of transcontextual modeling of situations, and this can be explained historically and causally. This is vitally important because it is precisely here that conventional social scientists usually invoke the canon of generalizability and try to move social research toward what they view as objectivity and away from what we understand as scientific research.

Our view, paralleling that of François Jacob (1982) on the possible and the actual, sees every situation containing more possibilities than those that are acted on. We understand that all current situations could have been different but were not. A particular outcome was realized through the intersection of environmental conditions, a group of people, and a variety of historical events, including the actions of the participants.

From this perspective, all explanations of present situations are actually accounts of historical moments and particular causes acting on particular organizations in specific contexts. In this way of thinking, theory does not predict the outcomes of a particular situation. The roles of theory are to explain how what happened was possible and took place and to lay out possible scenarios for the future and give good reasons for the ones that seem to be probable outcomes. This latter move, of course, relies precisely on analogizing outcomes from other cases and contexts in a coherent way.

These practices are science at its best, and our example is drawn from evolutionary biology. Are there examples in the social sciences? We believe there are, but that they are generally ignored. One such example is the structure of thinking underlying the work of Max Weber. He built a wide variety of ideal types to deal with the diversity and complexity of the issues he studied: bureaucracy, charisma, legitimacy, authority, religion, urbanization. In every case, he created an abstracted list of transcontextual characteristics after the painstaking study of many historical cases. He then used these characteristics to develop explanatory strategies.

Weber's (1958) rarely cited work on cities presents a particularly clear example. He gathered all the evidence he could from all over the world about the phenomenon of cities. On the basis of this broad reading, he developed a synthesis of the traits he found in each major example of cities in different places. He then took this list of traits and arrayed the traits together until he had a list of all the major features that he could find in the cities of the world. The total list of major traits made up the basis of his ideal type[1] of city. This was only the beginning, however.

Armed with this list, Weber returned to each world area, to each context, to examine what traits were present or absent in each situation. When he found particular complexes of traits present or absent in a location, he reexamined the history of that area to explain the presence or the absence. Gradually, he developed what he calls a "causal interpretation of history" that helped him understand why particular features were present or absent in particular situations, built over the backdrop of a general knowledge of the phenomenon of urbanization.

Weber's way of examining particular situations and environments closely—gathering traits from those situations, listing and analyzing those traits, and then returning to the particular situations—helped him understand why particular features were present or absent. This is how knowledge developed in one AR situation is to be transferred to other situations. AR does not generalize through abstraction and the loss of history and context. Meanings created in one context are examined for their credibility in another situation through a conscious reflection on similarities and differences between contextual features and historical factors. They are moved from the context where the understanding was created through a collaborative analysis of the situation where this knowledge might be applied. Based on the historical and contextual analysis, AR judgements are made about the possibility of applying knowledge from one situation in another.

Thus, we believe that detailed attention to cases, context, and history is essential to the development of science, and that it is the most meaningful way to proceed in developing a social science that respects the diversity of situations while also developing an understanding of the processes found in many situations and that can be used to explain what happened in each case.

READDRESSING THE AR PROCESSES

We argued that relevant actions to solve the problem at hand are the first outcome of an AR process. We also argued that the meaning construction process linked to solving practical problems is the major knowledge generation element in AR. Finally, we discussed the situations that transfer learning from one context to another and how to develop historical and causal interpretations of what has happened in each particular situation.

To reflect on why all this is not so obvious as to be banal, we have to return to the broader epistemological debate that forms the backdrop. Though we have concentrated on Dewey, it is important to recognize that Dewey's ideas developed in discourse with many colleagues, including Charles Peirce and William James, who were also at work on the pragmatist framework for philosophy. They were very well-known and respected for a long time, and then eclipsed almost completely. This eclipse of pragmatism is the subject of a controversial and important work, Richard Rorty's (1980) *Philosophy and the Mirror of Nature*. A broader meta-commentary on these issues is found in John Diggins's (1994) *The Promise of Pragmatism*. These works deserve attention from anyone interested in AR because their analyses provide an analytical and historiographical structure into which the vicissitudes suffered by AR can be fitted.

For Rorty (1980), the pragmatists, contemporary hermeneuticians (e.g., Gadamer, 1982; Taylor, 1985), linguistic philosophers such as

Quine, the Frankfurt School, Wittgenstein, Heidegger, some existential-ists, and some of Rorty's colleagues aim at the repudiation of what he calls "the epistemological project." Though Rorty defines this project in a variety of ways, at base, he means to criticize modern philosophy's pretensions of creating a system of analysis that would permit philoso-phers to distinguish between "correct" and "incorrect" knowledge, to become a kind of supreme court of knowledge to which everyone would have to submit.

Rorty (1980) counters the epistemological project by distinguishing between systematic philosophy as the search for an absolute reality determined by philosophical experts and edifying philosophy, which he views as an ongoing conversation involving methods and debates that attempt to bring people into some kind of state of communicative clarity. Rorty clearly advocates the latter but notes that the edifying philoso-phers are peripheral to contemporary philosophy. He specifically men-tions Dewey, Wittgenstein, and Heidegger (pp. 367-368).

In praising Dewey, Wittgenstein, Heidegger, and others like them, Rorty (1980) points out that

> they make fun of the classic picture of man, the picture which contains systematic philosophy and the search for universal commensuration in a final vocabulary. They hammer away at the holistic point that words take their meanings from other words rather than by virtue of their representative character, and the corollary that vocabularies acquire their privileges from the men who use them rather than from their transparency to the real. (p. 368) . . . The point of edifying philosophy is to keep the conversation going rather than to find objective truth. Such truth . . . is the normal result of normal discourse. (p. 377)

These arguments are central to the structure of AR as we view it. AR is, first and foremost, a way of "keeping the conversation going." AR's methods aim to open horizons of discussion, to create spaces for collective reflection in which new descriptions and analyses of impor-tant situations may be developed as the basis for new actions. This is what we mean by *cogenerative learning*.

This is directly relevant to the intellectual and social project an-nounced by Gadamer (1982) as well. His emphasis on the interpretive, dialogical, and practice-oriented character of all human knowledge includes a powerful argument that these dimensions are present in all the sciences: the physical, biological, and social sciences, and, of course, the humanities and the arts. He emphasizes the ongoing, ever-provisional character of interpretations and points out that hermeneutics is a form of action, to use Rorty's (1980) language, a way of keeping the conversation going. That AR practitioners have not examined the work of Gadamer and other contemporary hermeneuticians is hard to understand and contributes to their vulnerability to improper but energetic criticism from conventional social researchers.

Elements of pragmatism and democratic political critiques of existing social arrangements are also closely connected. One of the most interesting points emerging from Diggins's (1994) analysis is his linkage of Henry Adams and John Dewey's scathing critiques of education. Quoting a letter from Adams to R. Cunliffe written August 31, 1875, Diggins reproduces Adam's words describing the Harvard professorate and their students:

> They cram themselves with secondhand facts and theories till they burst, and then they lecture at Harvard College and think they are the aristocracy of intellect and are doing true heroic work by exploding themselves all over a younger generation and forcing up a new set of simpleminded, honest, harmless, intellectual prigs. (p. 307)

Academic institutions are seen as centers for the promotion of knowledge without action, reflection without commitment. This directly parallels Adams and Dewey's critique and links back to the common ground between pragmatism and AR in asserting that the truth is not a thing to be acquired but rather an aim of an endless process of collaborative social inquiry.

Diggins (1994) also makes persuasive links between pragmatism, hermeneutics, linguistic philosophy, the Frankfurt school, and deconstruction. Although these seem like odd bedfellows, if one takes the critique of the epistemological project as the centerpiece, they all contribute key elements to it. More important for our purposes is that these schools are also the inspiration for a significant amount of AR thinking.

Thus, AR is not on some side road. AR is neopragmatism in social research, an attempt to keep the conversation going and to democratize our society further. Like pragmatism, AR has met with the unflinching resistance of the epistemological project and positivist social science for whom taking pragmatism seriously would bring about the end of the academic world as they know (and profit from) it.

POLITICAL ECONOMY AND THE SOCIAL STRUCTURE OF SCIENCE

Underlying what we have said is a set of ideas about power relationships in our society. AR is about the transformation of power relationships in the direction of greater democracy. Yet most of the experience we have of the world is of authoritarianism, command and control systems, bureaucracies, narrow specializations, separation of reflection and action, and sanctions against those who oppose these systems. John Dewey posed the issue well when he affirmed that life, thought, and action are all part of one larger whole, but everyday experience makes it appear that the world is composed of a pile of independent, self-serving atoms that continually crash into each other.

What makes an integrated whole system appear to be a set of independent bits and pieces? The answer AR gives is that the cause is power relationships. Without an analysis of power relationships, AR is impossible. The political economy of capitalist societies, of science as an activity, and of academic institutions are all necessary elements in any attempt to understand the dilemmas that AR seeks to overcome and the continual effort by power elites to marginalize AR activities in all social arenas.

AR explicitly seeks to disrupt existing power relationships for the purpose of democratizing society. It also instrumentally seeks to incorporate the great diversity of knowledge and experience of all society's members in the solution of collective problems. AR asserts that societies, because of authoritarianism, use only a tiny portion of their knowledge and capacities to confront important problems. The reasons for this are the desires of the few who currently control key resources to retain that control and the fundamental lack of respect that elites have for the capacities of nonelite members of society. Given these interests and the resources at their disposal, these elites create and maintain reasonably loyal bureaucracies that operate by categorizing the citizenry in infinite ways (deserving-undeserving, criminal-good, heterosexual-homosexual, male-female, black-white-yellow-red, etc.). According to these classifications, the resources controlled by elites are then doled out to the categories, who in accepting them, are accepting the elite's definition of them. This kind of bureaucratic distribution in the pseudoname of welfare creates a dyadic relationship between the subordinate individual and power structures, discouraging rebellion and collaboration among the receivers of this largesse.

This political economy affects science and the academy. Science is largely paid for by the governments and by large corporations. As the funders, they decide the topics and methods of the research and create a policing process of peer review that guarantees that, like welfare recipients, scientists are unlikely to be very collaborative among themselves. In the social sciences, this kind of funding has created socially disengaged, statistically oriented "disciplines." As a result, these disciplines end up mainly documenting the workings of bureaucratic control structures. They rarely promote or envision an active process of social change, and they assuage their consciences by affirming the self-serving notion that they are doing science and that social action or even modest application of their knowledge is not their responsibility.

Thus, social research and social reform are definitively separated, and each new generation of students, who arrives at universities after having competed ferociously with others like them, is quickly taught to accept this separation. As an ideology to retain power in the hands of the powerful while employing a vast number of bureaucrats and their academic extensions, this has been notably successful. The participants discipline each other, and the hand of power is rarely seen.

In this context, AR is branded unscientific because of its social and ethical engagements, and thus it is deprived of funding and institutional support. It is also cut to ribbons in academic and other bureaucratic structures because AR is inherently a system activity, with the fundamental multidisciplinarity this implies. By dividing the disciplines and creating structured interests that guard against any territorial incursions, schools, universities, and other bureaucracies strangle the social project of democratization that is the heart of AR. In the end, the answer to the question of why AR is currently so marginal is to be found in the general lack of commitment to democratic social change in our societies, not in AR's inherent weaknesses as a form of scientific inquiry.

CONCLUSIONS

In subsequent chapters, we spell out the details of the various methods AR uses to keep the conversation going. In Figure 5.1, we summarize in very general terms of our overview of the map on which AR fits.

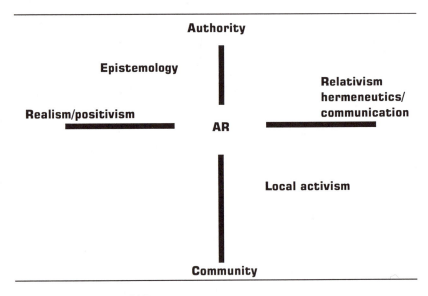

Figure. 5.1. The Map of AR

In our perspective, AR lies at the very center of human life. It is constituted by a series of communicative actions that take place in dialogical environments created by communities or other organizations for the purpose of the cogeneration of new knowledge, the development and implementation of plans of action, and the democratization of society. Unlike the epistemological project, it rejects both unquestioned authority and realism-positivism as reasonable approaches to social learning and social change. Unlike local activism, it also rejects pure relativism and an uncritical commitment to the group it serves. It is a form of discussion, of critical communication that generates new, and often painful knowledge. AR processes create an arena in which the forces of authority and community, realism and relativism, meet in communicative situations that are structured to open up all positions for scrutiny as well as for positive contributions. AR is open to all and aims to keep the conversation going.

Note

1. The concept of ideal type is stupidly treated in most social science literature. According to the dominant view, ideal types are a form of primitive modeling in which variables are not formulated in dynamic relationship to each other. A major contribution of current social science has supposedly been to get beyond ideal types to create models of dynamically connected variables that then yield predictions that can be tested. Not only do we see no evidence for the superiority of this method, we believe that the destruction of social science connections to context and history is part of the contemporary domestication of social science analysis.

6

The Friendly Outsider
Knowledge and Skills in Action Research

Action research (AR) is a cogenerative process through which professional researchers and interested members of a local organization, community, or a specially created organization collaborate to research, understand, and resolve problems of mutual interest. AR is a social process in which professional knowledge, local knowledge, process skills, research skills, and democratic values are the basis for cocreated knowledge and social change.

AR differs starkly from conventional social research because action researchers insist that research processes, research outcomes, and the application of results to problem solving are inextricably linked. Conventional researchers make a radical separation between the research process that they determine in advance of initiating the research and endeavor to control tightly throughout the research and the results of the research, which are analyzed and reported after the research actions are completed. Conventional researchers seldom take on responsibility to produce socially applicable research results or to be involved in the application of their research. Some do claim that their research is useful because all improvements in knowledge are useful.

For conventional researchers, the world seems to be an unruly place that attempts to fool them into believing what is not true. Their response to this unruly world is to do all they can to gain control through reliance on impersonal techniques of data generation and manipulation and through self-discipline. Research techniques are important insofar as they impart so much control, distance, and objectivity to the researcher that any other similarly motivated researcher can reproduce the same results using the same techniques.

Action researchers reject this position on a variety of grounds. Although many action researchers recognize how easy it is to believe what we prefer about the world, we do not accept that it is possible to separate the research process from its human dimensions or to separate the process from the results. AR seeks to bring the process and the results into the closest possible relationship, and builds research on fundamental respect for and trust in human capacities. AR also emphasizes democratic values and processes by cocreating knowledge applicable by the researched in efforts to increase control over their own situation.

The research process and the results are adjusted to each other at every point to ensure the continued relevance of the research process to the needs and interests of the local partners and to keep the broader research questions being addressed fully in view. As the research process continues and the research partners gain understanding, the goals of the process are constantly being redefined, refined, and even altered completely. The goal is not an a priori definition of a problem that is then studied by an objective outsider; it is the ongoing collaborative definition of problems relevant to the research partners and the development of information and analyses that enable them to address the defined problems effectively and democratically.

◄O►

AR AIMS AT CREATING POSSIBILITIES

The dominant imagery in conventional social research comes, for very good reason, from the language of bureaucratic organizations. These organizations write constantly about controls, objectivity, classification, and replicability, all essential features of a bureaucratic mindset. Bureaucracy, despite supposedly fashionable antibureaucratic ideologies in academia, is, among other things, an embodiment of attempts to build public structures and decision-making criteria on an abstract notion of social justice. Rather than making decisions about allocation of public resources on personalistic grounds, bureaucrats supposedly develop criteria for classifying clients and problems in such a way that the allocation of public resources is beyond the reach of personal choice. By developing and employing "impartial" norms and methods, bureaucrats are supposed to make fair and unbiased decisions on important issues and allocate social resources justly.

Underlying the ideology and practices of bureaucracy are notions that humans are strongly given to self-deception and that the unruly world has to be brought under rational control. Bureaucrats are taught to set themselves apart from other people, using their rational minds to solve problems that others react to personally and emotionally. They also accept radical differences in social power and intellectual ability, bureaucrats having all the power and resources, their clients being active only insofar as pressing their claims for assistance. This bureaucratic ideology provides the basic belief system for conventional social research.

Action researchers reject this framework on theoretical, methodological, political, and moral grounds. On theoretical grounds, action researchers believe that those who face social problems have much of the information and analytical capacity needed to solve them. Action researchers weigh the knowledge of local people much more heavily than do orthodox researchers. Action researchers are deeply skeptical about the transcendence of professional knowledge over all other forms of knowing.

Methodologically, action researchers believe that shared decision making about methods, collaborative case analysis, and teaching analytical techniques to a group of research partners produces superior research results in the quality and amount of information gathered and in the depth and quality of the analyses made.

Politically, action researchers believe that research results should be useful for the local partners in gaining increased control over their own situation and that the research questions should be influenced by all parties involved in the research.

Morally, action researchers reject the imposition of research on other human beings. We do not believe that social research is a professional right. We promote research methods that enable nonprofessional researchers to enhance their own control over their lives and their social situations.

AR thus is a process comanaged by the interested parties, not a technique applied by a professional researcher to other people. This means that action researchers visualize research processes in unique ways, and use these visualizations to help keep the processes moving in useful directions without imposing an overall direction from above. One of the visualizations of this kind of process that best captures our collective experience of AR is that provided by the French biologist, François Jacob (1982), in his book, *The Possible and the Actual*.

Jacob (1982), one the foremost evolutionary biologists of the contemporary generation, is not writing about AR. He is trying to communicate to a general audience a clear sense of the open-ended, dynamic, and diversifying character of evolutionary processes and is criticizing the ever-present tendency to try to reduce evolution to some kind of preordained and directed optimal process. To this end, he writes about evolution as a process built on a constant dialogue between the possible and the actual.

Jacob's (1982) analysis of the physicochemical and biotic universe is built on the view that what exists at any moment in history is always much less than could possibly have existed. Although this may sound odd, it is quite logical. Jacob observes that physicochemical and organic matter are capable of yielding an immense number of possible combinations, all those that have existed and that currently exist plus many more that are possible but have never existed.

The reasons why certain combinations exist or do not exist are fundamentally historical. History intervenes because, at each point in the earth's history, particular conditions exist. At those moments and under those conditions, only certain of the physicochemical or biotic capabilities of matter are acted on, leaving the other possibilities forever untouched in ongoing evolutionary processes. In other words, what happened simply is what happened, not everything that could have happened. As time goes on, only some of the new possibilities generated are acted on at the next turning points (or selective events, in biological parlance).

This perspective (Jacob, 1982) argues that the relationship between the possible and the actual is a historical and contingent relationship and that the history of the process itself is a causal agent. According to Jacob and the evolutionary biologists, this is not Pangloss's best of all possible worlds, but rather a possible world that was actualized historically, leaving others unrealized. This is precisely what the concept of evolution means, despite repeated attempts to domesticate the notion by making it a directed, teleological process (see Greenwood, 1985).

Thus far, we have been discussing so-called blind evolutionary processes, that is, those in which self-aware beings have not intervened. When dealing with humans, the situation becomes more complicated because the dialogue between the possible and the actual continues to operate, but the human ability to conceptualize alternative pasts and futures opens up a much wider range of possible-actual relationships. Thus, the relationship between the past and the future in human affairs is a combination of the physicochemical and biotic possibilities and historical conditions and the variety of visions of the past and the potential futures that humans conceive as they determine the actions they will take.

Like other teleological, antievolutionary forces, bureaucratic control systems and existing power holders expressly attempt to gain control over the way the relationships between the past and future are conceptualized to determine themselves the direction the future will take. Against this, AR specifically aims to reopen the dialogue between the possible and the actual and to counter attempts by power holders and their bureaucratic agents to predetermine the future. Thus, a core belief in AR is that there are always more possible futures than appear at first to be open, and there is a significant effort in all AR processes to reanalyze the past, projecting what happened against other possible outcomes, and a consequent division of the future into what is likely to come about if no self-conscious action is taken and what other, possibly more desirable, futures may be available.

Action researchers aim to reopen the possibilities for change, enhance a sense of responsibility for the direction of the future, and emphasize the sense that human agency, not impartial control systems, is the centerpiece of social change. One consequence of this perspective is that action researchers do not apply techniques to a situation. Rather, we bring knowledge and skills to a group of people who collaboratively open up the possibilities for self-managed social change. Nearly all the AR approaches we discuss in this book, in one way or another and in very different languages, center on this basic vision.

KNOWLEDGE IN AR—LINKING THEORY AND LOCAL UNDERSTANDING

In conventional social research, expert knowledge is the basis of the high status of the researcher and his or her ability to impose controls and methods on a research situation. Action researchers obviously must have expert knowledge, but this knowledge is not treated as a source of unilateral power but rather as their contribution to a social situation in which they participate as contributing human agents.

The knowledge demands on an action researcher are heavy and keenly felt. To assist a group of collaborators in resolving some kind of important social problem, the action researcher must have some kind of substantive appreciation of the particular issues involved. If the problem is a polluting industry, the action researcher must know or learn about the industry, the pollution, and some of the possible solutions. Unlike the case of the conventional social researcher who systematically distrusts local knowledge, however, this contextual knowledge is not a unilateral responsibility of the professional expert. The action researcher can and must rely on local knowledge to a considerable degree.

The local interested parties have a great deal of information (or access to such information) about what is going on and long experience with the situation. Action researchers actively seek out this knowledge as an element in the research process. This contrasts strongly with conventional researchers' claim that the universal applicability of their research methods and techniques makes such substantive knowledge minor and considered an unreliable and co-opted source of information.

Precisely because the outcomes of an AR project are likely to be applied in specific human situations, the action researcher must master the scientific method. Perhaps AR has an even higher ethical standard to meet here because conventional social research rarely entertains responsibility for the application of its results to human situations.

Professional action researchers must be adept in the use of the scientific method, with its insistence on the systematic attempt to discover the unexpected and counterintuitive explanations often hidden from view by assumptions and other elements in cultural training and social systems. This is one fundamental contribution that the action researcher makes to a research situation. The ability to ask counterintuitive questions, to approach issues from the "outside," and to question pet explanations is a role that the action researcher must know how to play well.

The action researcher must also bring a set of analytical frameworks to the process, among them, views on political economy, social structure, change processes, and ideology. These analytical frameworks are important to the conceptualization of the relationships between the past and the possible futures. Some work in the social sciences has developed perspectives and methods that can assist in make these structures clear, and action researchers must be knowledgeable about them.

Humans have views on political economy, social structure, and ideology. These are necessary equipment for living, and they form part of local knowledge. Social science research adds some analytical techniques and comparative frameworks generally unavailable, or often not entertained in local knowledge. Having analyzed political economies, social structures, and ideological systems from around the world and over long periods of time, professional researchers develop a sense of where the local systems fit into a larger range of variation. This broader contextualization is useful in AR because many groups suffering from acute problems feel stuck in a particular view of the situation and have a difficult time developing a sense of alternative courses of action. By setting the local situation in the context of these broader comparisons, the professional action researcher can assist the local group in opening up its sense of the situation and some options for the future.

Though we strongly believe that the views on political economy, social structure, and ideological systems that professional action researchers bring to local situations are of critical importance, we do not believe that there is one correct approach to each of these subjects. We have our own views on these matters, but we recognize that there are many different kinds of analyses of political economy (Marxist, neo-Marxist, Gramscian, neoclassical, reformist, revolutionary, trade union-ist, etc.), just as there are of social structures (Parsonian, constructivist, etc.) and ideational systems (structuralist, deconstructivist, construc-tivist, etc.).

Though no one system of analysis is correct, some approaches can make no meaningful contribution to AR. Frameworks that are blind to the play of economic and social power or triumphalist about the overall beneficent direction of history have no place in AR. The analysis of power relations and the direction of history necessarily animate all AR projects and must be on any research agenda as problematic phenomena to be dealt with.

PRACTICE AND SKILLS IN AR

Academia generally merchandises a narrow notion of competence and expertise that limits intellectual capacities and training. AR challenges this position, building on a long tradition of philosophical discourse about skills, competence, and knowing. Gilbert Ryle (1949) argues for an important distinction between *knowing what* and *knowing how*. Knowing what is the main activity of conventional intellectual life in academia, and stresses the ability to know why a certain issue exists and what its definition is. A competent expert is defined as one who verbally can argue in favor of what he or she thinks, not one who knows how to do anything in particular.

Ryle (1949) rejects this framework by arguing that intelligence is more manifest in the way we act than in the way we think. Knowing how is manifest in intelligent actions that apply whatever capacities and knowledge a person has; it emerges through the application of knowl-edge in a given context. The definition of competence and expertise is knowing how to do something appropriately.

Framing the issue this way, Ryle (1949) anticipated and laid the groundwork for later efforts on the subject of competence. For example, the philosopher Michael Polanyi (1964, 1966) argues that competence is gained through the tacit dimensions of human behavior. Human beings know a great deal more than we can put into words, and unspoken (tacit) knowledge is a key component in competent human action.

Polanyi's (1964, 1966) most powerful illustration focuses on how children are able to learn to speak. If we limit ourselves to a view of knowledge as only expressible in language, then, by definition, children would be unable to learn to speak. Polanyi resolves this problem by arguing that language conveys only part of what we perceive and know and that another, major part of our knowledge is expressed in our actions. Thus, children learn initially from tacit knowledge, which eventually permits them to join the community of language speakers, though they always retain the tacit dimension as well.

Building on this framework, we conceptualize the complex activities underlying intelligent actions as human skills, complex combinations of knowing how, tacit knowledge, and other kinds of knowledge (knowing what, language, etc.). We believe that conventional academic knowledge (knowing what) about AR is important for future practitioners, but we assert that such knowledge is never sufficient to train an AR practitioner.

Given this framework, we argue that skills are a fundamentally necessary component of AR and that they emerge only through intelligent actions, not merely from abstract and passive intellectualization. At the same time, we emphasize that skills can and must be developed. We do not believe that such skills are inherited human traits. Throughout life, all humans develop new and enhanced skills. A central aim of this book is to support the development of skills for AR practitioners. Skills in AR are certainly based on intellectual mastery of concepts (called by some "theory"), but skills express themselves in actions taken to facilitate AR processes, and the process and skills focus is an essential part of learning about AR.

In this regard, we strongly support the perspectives on reflective practice developed by Donald Schön (1983, 1987, 1991). In his work, Schön introduces the concept of reflective practice to analyze the way in which professional competence is developed through training. Focusing on the analysis of a number of master-student interactions, he develops a conceptual apparatus that highlights the role of linked reflection and praxis in the development of professional skills. Knowledge is not imparted simply through the passage of concepts from a teacher to a student, but rather through the interactions between them and their collaborative efforts to solve certain problems together through their actions.

Schön's (1983, 1987, 1991) argument is directly in line with Ryle's (1949) knowing how and Polanyi's (1964, 1966) notions about tacit knowledge, but he takes the issue farther because he is concerned with how to educate these reflective practitioners. These concerns are stimulated both by his readings of John Dewey and psychoanalytic theory and by his long experience in organizational consulting.

Schön's (1983, 1987, 1991) response is to identify two reflective processes. The first is reflection-in-action, the ability to mirror a reflective process in the action itself that is a way of assessing actions in the process of acting. The second is reflection-on-action, consisting of working through experiences gained from actions after the fact. Both of these processes are greatly enhanced when the professional is engaged with other people in interactions in which mutual reflections are used to enhance understanding. As a result, in developing and presenting his framework, Schön privileges the master-apprentice relationship as a key means of improving the professional's skills. Working with an experienced master, following him or her through daily work processes, and engaging together in reflective processes, the apprentice accesses the master's skills as they are embodied and explicated in actions. This is accompanied by the dialogical processes of reflection between master and apprentice.

One consequence is that skillful actions are not developed in isolation. We agree that a logical first step in acquiring skills can be the gathering of intellectual knowledge by reading texts and taking classes, the road usually open to university students. But this is only a beginning phase in a much longer process. The development of expert AR skills is a process involving many stages.

Over the years, Levin has run several PhD programs training graduate students to do AR. The main idea in all this training has been to combine theoretical knowing with practical skills in knowing how. The way to achieve this has been to have students work with experienced researchers. Projects are run with students working with senior faculty. They share the responsibility for the project and engage the research issues together. These professor-student dyads are further combined in a group structure that creates a community of action researchers colearning and developing skills together. These relationships are more complex than a master-apprentice dyad.

Dreyfus and Dreyfus (1986) suggest five stages in the development of expert skills: novice, advanced beginner, competent, proficient, and expert. Skillful human activity gradually reaches different levels, and practitioners operate differently on each of these levels. The novice follows analytical rules applied without much recognition of context and, like the orthodox researcher, feels detached from the process. Gradually, the ability to read a context and to understand possible implications for actions moves the novice practitioner to the level of advanced beginner. Building on one's own experience is key to this development; a history of actions taken is much more important as a source of learning than the forms of explicit and analytical communication so prized in academia.

A competent practitioner has the ability to shift between context-free (e.g., analytical) and contextual components in a particular intervention situation, but her or his involvement in the activity is limited to trying to influence the outcome. Finally, an expert bases professional activity on full involvement in the local situation and makes many suggestions on the basis of experientially informed intuitions about reasonable options drawn from previous experiences. "Intuition or know-how, as we understand it, is neither wild guessing nor supernatural inspiration, but the sort of ability we all use all the time as we go about our everyday task" (Dreyfus & Dreyfus, 1986, p. 29). Dreyfus and Dreyfus's (1986) developmental schema is summarized in Table 6.1.

Whether or not you accept the particular models of skill development in Schön (1983, 1987, 1991) or Dreyfus and Dreyfus (1986), we want to be clear that skills are a major component in the competence necessary to become a good AR practitioner. Professional practice involves more than explicit rules imparted abstractly in academic settings. Knowledge is context bound, intuition and tacit knowledge play important roles, and the acquisition of skill is mainly achieved through refection in and on action. Learning from one's own experience is a core element in the development of AR practitioner skills, and there is no substitute for it.

TABLE 6.1 Stages of Skills Acquisition

Skill Level	Components	Perspective	Decision	Commitment
Novice	Context-free	None	Analytical	Detached
Advanced beginner	Context-free and situational	None	Analytical	Detached
Competent	Context-free and situational	Chosen	Analytical	Detached understanding and deciding. Involved in outcome
Proficient	Context-free and situational	Experienced	Analytical	Involved understanding. Detached deciding
Expert	Context-free and situational	Experienced	Intuitive	Involved

SOURCE: Reprinted with the permission of The Free Press, a Division of Simon & Schuster, from *Mind Over Machine: The Power of Human Intuition and Expertise in the Era of the Computer* by Hubert L. Dreyfus and Stuart E. Dreyfus. Copyright © 1986 by Hubert L. Dreyfus and Stuart E. Dreyfus.

THE FRIENDLY OUTSIDER

In addition to the general orientation to skills we have articulated, we wish to point briefly to certain specific skills that AR practitioners must master to be effective. A professional action researcher must know how to be the "the friendly outsider." This complex role is vital in AR because the external perspective is a key element in opening up local group processes for change. But this outsider is friendly in a special sense. He or she must be able to reflect back to the local group things about them, including criticism of their own perspectives or habits, in a way that is experienced as supportive rather than negatively critical or domineering. Good professional action researchers achieve a balance of critique and support through a variety of actions, including direct feedback, written reflections, pointing to comparable cases, and citing cases from the professional literature where similar problems, opportunities, or processes have occurred.

The friendly outsider must also be expert at opening up lines of discussion. Often local organizations or groups are either stuck in positions that have hardened or have become pessimistic about the possibilities for change. A variety of methods, discussed in subsequent chapters, is used to reopen the possibilities for change. Flexibility and opportunities for change are pointed out to local people, along with encouragement in the form of moral support and information from other cases where similar problems existed but change turned out to be possible.

Another key role of the friendly outsider is to make evident the tacit knowledge that guides local conduct. This can be in the form of critical reflections or supportive comments about the extent of local capabilities. The outsider, who is not used to the group and to the local scene, is ideally placed to notice this kind of tacit knowledge, whereas it is often invisible to insiders.

Often this takes the form of encouraging local people to realize that they have a valuable store of knowledge that is relevant to solving the problems they face. Occasionally, it takes the form of criticism of particular local modes of thinking that cause groups to shut down or to cycle unproductively over issues without resolving them.

Related to this is the role of speaking the locally unspeakable. Local people, because of their history together, because of local social structure and economic relationships, or simply because of decorum, often are unable to tell each other uncomfortable things that they clearly are aware of. Human groups are like this everywhere (Argyris & Schön, 1996). No human group operates with every member giving every other member absolutely honest feedback, but social change processes require the development of more open feedback to generate possibilities for action.

In this context, the friendly outsider does not speak up on every unspeakable matter. The effort is to seek out and examine those tacit agreements, not to discuss certain things, local silences, that constitute obstacles to positive change for the issues at hand. This is a judgement the action researcher must make carefully. Too much feedback can block a group; too little can prevent the group from moving ahead.

Another role of the friendly outsider is to help local people inventory and assess the local resources available for a change project. Although local people are far more expert about the local scene than the outsider will ever be, their history together can lead them to overlook some important resources for change. This may simply be a matter of not appreciating that they have a store of knowledge somewhere that they are not thinking about using. It may be the matter of insisting that a particular local person or group must be included in the process, despite a history of either bad relations or distrust. Sometimes this takes the form of the outsider insisting on the presence of representatives of opposed political factions or other kinds of ideological groups. Or it may require the outsider to insist on a better gender, class, or ethnic balance in the working group.

One of the outsider's principal resources in doing all this is precisely being from the outside. The outsider's links to the outside world—universities; state, national, and international agencies; unions; philanthropic groups; professional consultants—may be of considerable practical value to the local project. In this regard, the outsider is also a resource for the local project and must be able to deliver on these relationships effectively. These outside links also lend a certain legitimacy to the views of the friendly outsider, however, and this legitimacy has to be managed carefully to enhance the possibilities for local change.

THE PROCESS SKILLS OF
THE FRIENDLY OUTSIDER

The friendly outsider is a coach, not a director or a boss. The last thing most local groups who are stuck in difficult situations need is someone else telling them what to do. The coach counts on local people to be the talented players and helps them improve their skills and strategies. The boss takes over the direction, management, and control of subordinate local groups and acts for them, further disempowering them in most cases and usually guaranteeing that whatever changes are produced will not continue to produce locally initiated changes over the long run.

The outsider must be self-confident in social situations. The outsider can and may need to express doubts about what to do and how to do it; the outsider should have a kind of basic optimism about herself or himself and about the collaborators. Not a form of arrogance, this confidence is expressed in openmindedness, a lack of concern with maintaining rituals of status superiority over local people, a willingness to celebrate the capacities and actions of local people, and an active appreciation of the possibilities for change that exist locally. This also involves an ability to appreciate the skills of others and to articulate this appreciation tactfully. The outsider's interest in the success of a local project and community must be authentic. Local people are very good at sensing the sincerity of those who come to them from the outside.

The outsider must also be a risk taker. Unless the outsider is willing and able to risk personal failure by supporting a local group that may or may not succeed, she or he will not provide the necessary moral support and confidence to people who are trying to persuade themselves to take risks as well. Most academics and bureaucrats are trained to avoid risks at all costs and to always try to look good, no matter what happens. The friendly outsider must be willing to be implicated in the success or failure of local projects, as a professional and as a human being who is taking some responsibility for the lives of other human beings.

Finally, a kind of playfulness and irony[1] is an indispensable tool for the professional action researcher. Someone who is unremittingly serious and dour and carries the burdens of the world on his or her shoulders energizes no one. Humor and playfulness have an important role in social change processes. This is because AR projects attempt to suspend business as usual and try to produce unlikely but positive outcomes. In these contexts, the powers of irony, absurdity, and humor are considerable precisely because they cause ordinary thought to stop momentarily, creating juxtapositions that can provoke both amusement and openness to change.

Strictly speaking, the trope of irony centers on affirming in words facts or situations that are precisely the opposite of what the listener understands them to be. Irony is a kind of displacement, a viewing of the world in reverse that often provokes humor but also is capable of opening up patterns of thought to new possibilities.

Humor also evokes tacit knowledge—it provokes people to respond and to become active themselves. It can also equalize statuses by turning many participants into commentators on the local scene rather than reserving the right to definitive judgements to the professional outsider and powerful insiders.

There is a strong connection between irony, humor, and achieving a sense of Jacob's (1982) world of the possible versus the actual. Irony and humor look at the world from the vantage point of the possible, making the actual only one of the possible outcomes. The outsider's use of irony and other forms of displacing humor and commentary can induce local participants to do the same, opening up groups to brainstorming and the play of ideas that is a necessary part of prefiguring a possible new future.

Note

1. Irony is increasingly recognized as a key element in thoughtful action. See Rorty (1980) and Flood and Romm (1996).

7

Local Knowledge, Cogenerative Research, and Narrativity

In action research (AR), professional social researchers and insider community or organization members are cosubjects and coresearchers in the research process. Both contribute many kinds of knowledge and actions to their joint enterprise. The conventional social sciences have no difficulty with the idea of expert social researchers, but they reject the idea that local people, untrained in the theories and methods of academic social science, can make valuable contributions to both the form and the substance of a social research process.

AR is based on the affirmation that all human beings have detailed, complex, and valuable knowledge about their lives, environments, and goals. This knowledge is different from scholarly knowledge because everyday knowledge is embodied in people's actions and the way they reflect on them. This kind of knowing is different from conventional scientific knowledge because practical wisdom and practical reasoning are its central characteristics (Carr & Kemmis, 1985; Schwandt, 1997).

AR centers on an encounter between the worlds of practical reasoning and the worlds of scientifically constructed knowledge. We do not assert the superiority of either type of knowledge. AR processes bridge these worlds by integrating practitioners and professionals in the same knowledge generation process. We call this *cogenerative learning.* Through these collaborative processes, the quality of the research can be enhanced because the insiders are able to contribute crucial local knowledge and analysis to the research, and can comment effectively on external interpretive frameworks as well. By the same token, the practical reasoning guiding the insiders' actions can be enhanced and reformulated through accessing and transforming scientific knowledge for use in dealing with everyday problems.

We believe that local people often act skillfully on the basis of appropriate valid knowledge. We believe that local knowledge systems are complex, differentiated, and dynamic, and we believe that, without formal training, it is possible for people to develop warrants for action based on good analyses. We therefore believe that local people are essential partners in any social research activity. Action researchers do not believe in the idea of scientific, cosmopolitan knowledge that is valid everywhere, and we reject the notion that valid knowledge can be produced only by "objective" outsiders using formal methods that supposedly eliminate bias and error.

Further, we know that when local people act in the world, they prefer to produce their desired outcomes skillfully. Precisely because they take action in their own environments, the consequences of errors are both significant to them and rapidly apparent, in most cases. By contrast, conventional social researchers, who have severed the connection between research and action, rarely know whether they are right or not, and any application of their ideas has very few direct consequences for them.

—◦—

LOCAL KNOWLEDGE AND PROFESSIONAL SOCIAL RESEARCH KNOWLEDGE

Despite the importance of local knowledge, the AR literature does not offer many clear statements about it. For some action researchers, local knowledge is chanted like a mantra rather than evaluated critically. For others, local knowledge is treated as a mixed bag of analyses and information, some useful, some useless, some helpful, some actually dangerous. The choice of positions is not based only on empirical analysis; it seems to depend partly on the action researcher's system of beliefs and views of human nature and the human condition—views that generally exist prior to any action research activity. It also depends on the action researcher's experience in the field where she or he has experienced local knowledge in action and the consequences of its deployment in change processes.

For some action researchers, local knowledge simply means insider knowledge, the knowledge that people in the community or organization have. For others, local knowledge is understood to be detailed knowledge of local situations. In the second view, local knowledge belongs to insiders, but outsiders can also develop varieties of local knowledge through ethnographic research based on participant observation. Probably the most common view of local knowledge is that it is true knowledge, in opposition to the false and class-interested knowledge imposed by hegemonic outsiders. Each of these views carries very different consequences, both ideologically and methodologically.

Our own understanding of local knowledge centers on viewing it as practical reasoning in action and local reflections by participants on their actions. This conception of knowledge can be traced back to Aristotle's concept of *phronesis*: "the ability to spot the action called for in any situation" (Toulmin, 1996, p. 207). As Eikeland (1992) and Schwandt (1997) point out, this is a different type of knowledge from that used to develop scientific theories. For us, one of the aims of AR is to create a research process that reveals the combination of practical reasoning and socially constructed meaning (Berger & Luckmann, 1966) held by local people. AR becomes the process of bridging local knowledge and scientific knowledge, a process that will create both new local knowledge and new scientific understandings. For us, AR centers on the communication between locals and professionals in cogenerating new knowledge.

No matter which view of local knowledge an action researcher has, it is clear that local knowledge in AR is generally understood differently from the same knowledge in conventional social science. Although there have been a number of recent moves toward constructivism and discourse analysis, and there is a gradual return to qualitative research approaches, the dominant social science traditions still generally reserve to the researcher the right and power to create the structures into which knowledge is put, ostensibly to create separable units of objective knowledge that can be intercorrelated, subjected to formal manipulations and comparison, hypothesized, and synthesized outside of the local context. Even when the conventional social scientist is not a positivist of this sort, he or she generally reserves the right to formulate and express what the subjects think, how they think it, and what import it has. What is valid, interesting, important, and trivial is treated as the professional researcher's decision.

This conception of the generation of social research knowledge makes social science research production and local knowledge production antithetical to each other because local knowledge is built in and conveyed through a wide variety of context-bound formats and often has a complex narrative structure. From ethnographic fieldwork and from AR experiences, we know that the narrative structures of local knowledge are often key components in the way it is constructed, learned, conveyed, and applied. Because AR privileges local knowledge, AR necessarily works with the role of narrative in the research process, as well as in the write up of the results.

A key question in dealing with local knowledge is validity, an issue we discuss in Chapter 5, "An Epistemological Foundation for Action Research." This validity question is capable of generating some very extreme and unproductive positions. Many conventional social scientists equate local knowledge with invalid or at least subjective information. They want to believe that untrained people cannot produce valid knowledge because they lack the methods, training, and commitment to transcend bias and self-interest in their interpretive processes. By contrast, a few action researchers equate local knowledge with valid information, believing that only those natives uncontaminated by the capitalist system are able to see things clearly.

We find neither position persuasive. If one believes that local people are always right or never right, there is no need for theories, methods, or much else. We think it is more important to examine the extent and ways local knowledge can be mobilized, relied on, acted on, and interpreted, and to learn how research results based in part on local knowledge can be communicated and contextualized effectively beyond the local situations where it was generated.

Co-Researchers

We argue that AR, in addition to generating valid knowledge and effective social action, embodies democratic ideals in its core practices. This democracy is involved in both the research process and the outcomes of the research. In AR, the research process must be democratic in the sense that it is open, participatory, and fair to the participants. In addition, the outcome of AR should support the participants' interests so that the knowledge produced increases their ability to control their own situation. We summarize this double meaning of democratization by referring to AR as *cogenerative research.*[1]

Central to the effort to democratize research is changing the roles of the researched and the researcher. Democracy in inquiry cannot be promoted unless the local participants, however selected, are enabled to take charge of the meaning construction process. At the same time, trained researchers cannot make sense of local social life without secure communication links to these local participants. The dynamic tension between insider and outsider knowledge is the basis for this cogenerative process.

In AR, we believe that the whole can be greater than the sum of the parts. The outside researcher is assisted enormously in learning things she or he does not know or immediately perceive through dialogue with insiders and through experiencing and understanding actions. The insiders reformulate and revalue their own knowledge in response to queries from the outsider. Both sides gain understanding from their interactions. And both sides have a complex web of intentions and interpretations of the structures and processes they are engaged in. These two can be made available, at least in part, to each other through the cogenerative process.

Trustworthiness

A key challenge in any social research centers on claims about the trustworthiness of the results. AR holds that validity and reliability can emerge only from a discursive process where participants and researchers negotiate the meanings created by their experiences during the research process. Thus, AR affirms that communication processes themselves are a vital component in creating trustworthy knowledge, linking AR directly to pragmatism and democratic theory, as we point out in Chapter 5, "An Epistemological Foundation for Action Research." Accordingly, a central design challenge in any AR process is structuring arenas for communication that will effectively support an open and inclusive meaning construction process. Cogenerative learning is not merely a methodology or a set of techniques; it is a way of framing an AR process that aims to clarify social positions, communication processes, learning, and action options.

AR Takes Time

Any AR process builds on communications and actions between involved parties. From the research literature and from everyday experience, we all know that engaging in mutually interesting dialogues demands time for learning about each other and the creation of a language that is mutually accessible. AR processes accordingly demand time investments in the form of sustained communications and interactions that shape a common ground of understanding. There are no meaningful "drive-by," one-shot AR processes. Any AR approach that promises quick results should be treated with suspicion.

One Size Does Not Fit All in AR

As important as the cogenerative approach is, it is not a blueprint for designing an AR process. The knowledge produced in AR is linked to the actual context of the work. Methodological approaches are chosen to fit the problem focus of a particular context. The cogenerative view thus is a framework for thinking through how to choose appropriate methods and actions, not a recipe. It is fully and necessarily compatible with the deployment of a wide variety of research techniques and agendas.

The design of these communicative arenas and the use of particular group processes must always result from an assessment of the particular situation. Thus, where a neighborhood has an overriding common interest in economic and social survival, techniques based on consensus building might be appropriate. The use of a search conference methodology (see Chapter 9, "Pragmatic Action Research") might be helpful. By contrast, in a situation where opposing groups have manifest and latent conflicts, for example, regarding the use of natural resources, a conflict-bridging strategy might be more useful. A skillful AR practitioner must be able to read and make sense of specific situations and use this insight to suggest ways to design the AR process.

We are emphatic in rejecting a one-size-fits-all approach to AR. Doing AR means engaging in a process of mutual action and reflection. The skillful professional practitioner must continually reflect on experiences from the field, seeking what is necessary to keep a change process moving and tracking what is being learned. This is reflection-in-action and on-action (these terms are Donald Schön's, see Chapter 11, "Action Science and Organizational Learning"), and it is a core feature of the praxis of AR.

OUR COGENERATIVE AR MODEL

AR can be thought of as a process consisting of at least two analytically distinct phases. The first involves the clarification of an initial research question, whereas the second involves the initiation and continuation of a social change and meaning construction process. This does not mean that the problem definition process is ever final; in fact, a good sign of the learning taking place in an AR project is when the initial questions are reshaped to include newly discovered dimensions.

We can visualize the cogenerative model as shown in Figure 7.1.

The cogenerative model identifies two main groups of actors. The insiders are the focal point of every AR project. They are the "owners" of the problem, but they are not homogeneous, egalitarian, or in any way an ideal group. They simply "own" the problem. Outsiders are the professional researchers who seek to facilitate a colearning process

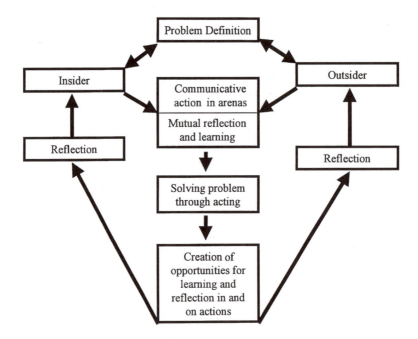

Figure 7.1. The Cogenerative Action Research Model

aimed at solving local problems. Insiders and outsiders are both equal and different. They are different because most insiders have to live directly with the results of any change activity in a project, whereas most outsiders can leave. Another difference is the insiders have the central influence on what the focus of the research activity should be.

Problem Definition

The question to be researched must be of major importance to the participants or the process will go nowhere. Once it is established, we can gain additional leverage by using relevant bodies of professional knowledge in the field, as in the case of the organizational culture literature in the Mondragón project (see Chapter 3, "Action Research Cases From Practice I").

We have argued that an AR process deals with solving pertinent problems for the participants. In this respect, the whole research process emerges from demands arising outside the academy. This contrasts with conventional social science, where research problems are defined as much by developments within the disciplines as by external social forces. Yet AR professionals do not just blindly accept any problem formulation forwarded by the local participants. We view the problem definition process as the first step in a mutual learning process between insiders and outsiders. To facilitate a process where insider knowledge is clarified in relation to outsider professional knowledge, communication procedures must permit the development of a mutually agreed-on problem focus. These procedures include rules of democratic dialogue, which involve openness, mutual support, and shared "air time." A first working definition of the problem under study comes out of a discourse where knowledge held by insiders and outsiders cogenerates a new, mutual understanding through their communication with each other.

Communication Arenas

Central to the cogenerative process is its ability to create room for learning processes resulting in meanings that participants trust. To this end, the ground for communication between the groups of actors must be properly configured. This is what we refer to in Figure 7.1 as the arena. Arenas simply are locations where the involved actors encounter each other in a material setting for the purpose of carrying on AR. They can involve a meeting between two and more people, a team building session, a search conference, a task force meeting, a leadership group meeting, or a public community meeting. The key point is that an arena allows communicative actions to take place.

Thus, a major challenge in any AR project is to design adequate arenas for communication about problems of major import to the local participants. Arenas must be designed to match the needs at issue. If the challenge is to engage a whole organization in an organizational development process, it might be good to gather everyone in a large room to work out the plans for a new project. Dealing with conflicts between managers might better be addressed in a leadership group format. Selecting and structuring proper arenas depends on the professional skills and experience of the facilitator.

In arenas, communication between insiders and outsiders can produce learning and open up a process of reflection for the involved parties. These discussions and reflections are the engine for an upward learning spiral. The initial problem focus suggests a design for an arena for discourse. The subsequent communication produces understandings that help move toward problem solutions, creating new experiences to reflect on for both the insiders and the professional researchers.

The feedback loops are similar for both insiders and outsiders, but the interests and effects of the communication can be quite different. For insiders, it might be central to improve their action-knowledge capabilities, whereas the outsiders may, through the reflection process, produce meaning (publications or insights) for the research community. Both of these reflective processes are then fed back into the communicative process, shaping the arenas for new dialogues aimed at either redefining the initial problem statement or improving the local problem-solving capacity. Cycles like this continue throughout the life of a project.

Communicative Actions in Arenas

The discourses that take place in these arenas are inherently unbalanced. The insiders have a grounded understanding of local conditions far beyond what any outsider ever can gain, unless he or she settles in that specific local community or organization to live. Likewise, the outside researcher brings with him or her skills and perspectives often not present in the local context, including knowledge about how to design and run learning and reflection processes. The asymmetry in skills and local knowledge can be an important force in cogenerating new understandings. The parties engage each other to make sense out of the situation. The democratic ideals of AR research mandate a process, however, whereby the outsider gradually lets go of control so that the insiders can learn how to control and guide their own developmental processes. These ideals also aim to develop the insiders' capacities for sustaining more complex internal dialogues with a more diverse set of participants than would have been the case without this value commitment.

This asymmetrical situation (Markova & Foppa, 1991) thus becomes the root of complex social exchanges. The outsider designs training sessions that make transfer of knowledge possible and uses his or her influence to direct the developmental process. The professional researcher necessarily exercises power. Though the outsider does not have a formal position in the local organizational hierarchy, she or he exerts influence through participant expectations that she or he play a major role in designing and managing the change processes. Dealing honestly and openly with the power those expectations grant to the researcher is a central challenge in AR change processes because it has a powerful effect on the development of local learning processes and is power that is easy to abuse.

At the beginning of a research process, the outsider makes decisions and teaches and trains local participants on topics that both consider important. At the same time, the outsider is responsible for encouraging insiders to control the developmental process. Though the professional researcher's obligation to let go of the group near the end is difficult, this is easier than the collaborative development of the local participants' capability to control and direct the ongoing developmental process according to their own interests. For participants to become active players in a change process, they must exercise power. The initially asymmetrical situation between insiders and outsiders can be balanced only by the transfer of skills and knowledge from the professional researcher to the participants and the transfer of information and skills from the local participants to the outside researcher. In the end, though, the process must be taken over by the participants. The AR process cannot fulfill its democratic obligations unless the main thrust of the process is toward increasing the participants' control over knowledge production and action. Standard training in conventional social science research and the whole academic reward system focus strongly on control over both the design and the execution of research activities, treating them as a hallmark of professional competence.

The struggle to solve important local problems shapes the ground for new understandings, hence the double feedback loops in Figure 7.1. That is to say that, through actions taken as a result of the cogenerative processes, the participants learn new things about the problems they are facing, often revising their understandings in fundamental ways. The outcomes of this collective process action and reflection support the creation of new shared understandings. The larger this shared ground is, the more fruitful the communication has been and the greater the likelihood is that further insights can be developed through reflection and actions based on this shared knowledge. This in turn can open up new ways of formulating the AR problems, and thus result in ongoing learning for all parties.

Model Monopoly

A major challenge in AR is to find a good first question that is at least partly shared among the involved parties, particularly at the outset. There are several obstacles to overcome. The conventional training of academic researchers generally makes them experienced debaters with lots of practice in managing conceptual models. This can create a situation of communicative domination that undermines the cogenerative process. This situation has been called "model monopoly" by Bråthen (1973). He identifies and analyzes situations where one side dominates and, through skills in communication and the handling of certain kinds of conceptual models, constantly increase the distance between insiders and outsiders. In addition, the professional's social prestige and years of formal training may convince people to accept a particular point of view too easily. When this happens, it is a serious threat to the AR process because it distracts attention from local points of view, which are central to the initiation of any AR process. Skilled action researchers develop the ability to help articulate and make sense of local models and are sure they are well articulated in the communicative process.

Insider Monopoly

Another important trap in the initial problem formulation phase is getting locked into the initial insider formulation. This is a pseudo-democratic position based on the assumption that the participants are always right. Believing this creates another kind of constrained situation. In this case, the value of outside knowledge is rejected. We believe the best possible understandings are those negotiated between professional researchers and participants who search together for the best arguments and understandings of a situation. This is a dialogical process, with arguments shifting back and forth in productive tension.

How Good Is Good Enough?

We want to be careful not to overstate the case and make it appear that transcendentally high standards must be met in AR. It is possible and often necessary to start a project with an initially quite limited problem statement and without all the relevant parties at the table. The key is in designing and sustaining a process where important reflections can emerge through communication and some good practical problem solving. Over time, the initial problem can be refined and reformulated, just as hypotheses are reformulated and refined in laboratory science (see Chapter 4, "Scientific Methods and Action Research"), and the composition of the initial group can be changed to reflect the full set of problem owners more adequately. But iteration of this process is limited by the resources, energy, and other elements of the situation in which AR is taking place.

Maintaining Differences

The insiders and outsiders are considered to be equal in integrity because both are expected to behave in accordance with their backgrounds and knowledge base. They have an equal right to be heard. It is important that the AR professional not try to play the game of pretending to become an insider. A professional researcher will always be an outsider situated in an institutional and professional setting that creates particular demands on the professional praxis and ethical standards of behavior. The cogenerative challenge in this unbalanced situation is to take advantage of the differences between the parties. Together, insiders and outsiders can create the ground for new learning for all participants, their differences being one of the main contributions they bring to the process.

When Is It Research?

AR is not just participatory action; it is also research. Doing good things for communities and organizations is laudable, but is not a sufficient justification for calling a process AR. It can be called data gathering, social action, or doing good, depending on the situation. For a process to be called AR, it must be systematic and oriented around posing questions whose answers require the gathering and analysis of data and the generation of interpretations directly tested in the field of action.

These research questions can be of different sorts. Research can refer to the production of knowledge (in the form of papers, reports, books, and PhD theses) that communicate insights to an audience beyond the coresearchers in a particular project. That is, AR can contribute to social science learning.

AR can also refer to untangling and interpreting the complexities of a particular set of local conditions that lie at the center of the project. Whether it is the former kind of generalizing research activity or a more particular and local kind of research, it is not AR unless the knowledge is expressed, analyzed, and tested in action by the participants.

Another difference between AR and most conventional social science is that, in AR, the research activity is based on long-term and personal engagement with a case through living with and acting to solve practical problems. The personal experiences the professional action researcher acquires differentiate this research process radically from single-shot interventions and standard social science research.

Publications

Conventional research publications can result from AR when the researcher learns something of relatively little interest to the local participants but that may address a major issue in the research literature. We believe, however, that even these conventional research results are formulated on a much more solid basis than most conventional social science results because of the long-term engagement and shared understandings developed with insiders in AR.

Communications to the scientific community can be produced jointly by insiders and outsiders in AR projects (see the Mondragón case in Chapter 3, "Action Research Cases From Practice I," and Levin, 1988; Levin et al., 1980a, 1980b). Although this process is complex and creates a variety of new issues about authorship, intellectual property, and so on, it is undeniable that insiders and outsiders together can communicate effectively with the professional research community.

Insider's Reflection

Coproducing reports with outside researchers is one way of introducing lay people to the tool of writing as a form of reflective learning. This writing process, which includes most of the tools of scientific reflection (working with data, analysis, and conclusions), can bring new dimensions to local knowledge production. Although this way of structuring the reflection process is no substitute for everyday practical reasoning, it can be a very useful tool for local organizations and communities to have at their disposal. The insiders also enhance their practical reasoning through sharing experiences and learning from the actions they take as members of the AR team. Such processes often run independently of the outside researcher's efforts, and yet are part of the AR process.

NARRATIVITY

The interaction between local knowledge and expert knowledge through a cogenerative process is a core feature of AR. One consequence of this is that most accounts of AR, trying to be true to the process that constructed them, are rendered in narrative form. They often take the form of case studies, with detailed discussions of the processes that the group went through in generating the knowledge that is being communicated and acted on. As a result, most AR follows many of the rhetorical conventions of narrative writing.

This runs directly against the style and wishes of conventional social scientists for whom narrativity (until the all-out attack on positivism by deconstructivists and postmodernists) is supposedly an evil, a source of confusion and co-optation to be overcome. To parody the conventional researchers, it is as if their practice is contained in the following syllogism:

- AR is storytelling.
- Storytelling is not science.
- AR is not science.

This is a widespread view. Most conventional social scientists are, in practice, positivists with a narrow view of what constitutes meaningful professional standards. Their commitment to objectification causes them to go through painful gyrations as they try to speak in nonnarrative forms about things they learned in contextualized discourse. It is sad to watch neophyte social scientists learning how to take their normal speech and writing habits and convert them into what Richard Lanham (1992) calls "the official style": "It is hypothesized that . . ." "The dependent variable is scalar while the independent variable is . . ." "The hypothesis is confirmed at the .001 level." The passive voice dominates. Verbs are weak and the actors are invisible. These conventions not only turn normal speech into "officialese" but alienate the results of the work from all but another group of scientists who have learned to speak and write this way.

By contrast, the AR syllogism is quite different:

- All general laws must apply to all particular cases.
- AR develops detailed stories of particular cases.
- Therefore AR tests the validity of general laws.

AR gains much of its power through narratives because narratives are inherently particular. Though they may fall into broad types, each narrative refers to a specific situation and a specific set of connections between elements (people, organizations, and events). Thus, if the narrative developed in a particular AR project tells a story that is deemed at variance with a major generalization, the major generalization is either wrong or must somehow be modified to cover the case.

For example, the dominant generalization among economic theorists is that cooperatives cannot compete successfully with noncooperative businesses. The study of Mondragón (Greenwood et al., 1992) demonstrates that the cooperatives are considerably more successful than their direct competitors. Subsequent events have amply confirmed this. Thus, the narrative of Mondragón means that the generalization about the noncompetitiveness of cooperatives, as stated, is wrong—it is invalid!

Not long ago, this would have seemed an outrageous, wooly minded approach and would have been dismissed. But the conventional social sciences have been undergoing a variety of crises of their own making. Most of the general public has lost faith in most of what passes for academic social science, finding it unintelligible, self-serving, and, where it is understandable, either banal or wrong. The dream that the social sciences were building an edifice like that of the basic sciences is a thing of the past, living among the outdated practitioners and the conservative granting agencies that support nonthreatening social research.

Over the past 15 years, a renewed appreciation of narrativity has developed through the recognition that, like all human action, social research is a set of socially constructed understandings built out of discourse structures. These discourse structures have narrative properties, and these narrative properties themselves must be analyzed to understand how the structures of the discourses themselves create local meanings, become hegemonic, or seek to persuade.

Specifically in AR, these issues have been broached repeatedly by Gustavsen (1992) and Johannesen (1996) in their appeal to Wittgenstein and the linguistic turn as the necessary basis for AR. These issues have been further developed by Stephen Toulmin (Toulmin & Gustavsen, 1996) in his integration of this linguistic turn, with his own analysis of social research as a form of *phronesis* or clinical knowledge. This phronetic knowledge is intrinsically context bound, narrative in form, and linked to action contexts. Thus, this form of narrative analysis underlines the linkage between AR, narrative, and clinical knowledge aimed at creating meaningful change.

CONCLUSIONS

These considerations bring us full circle. We began with local knowledge, which is largely narrative in form and expressed through action in context. We built a view of the cogenerative research process that characterizes AR when it is practiced, and we closed with a defense of narrativity as a reliable and meaningful form of knowledge with the power to force all generalizations to the test.

What, then, do conventional social scientists have to fear from AR? Only that their theories will have to meet the test of analysis in which local knowledge and action play a definitive role. This is not good news for them because it undermines both their epistemological project and their comfortable social distance from the world they study.

For us, this is the attractiveness of AR. This form of research most closely approximates the epistemology and methodology of a social science that links the local and cosmopolitan discourses in a reasoned framework that remains open to testing and modification through social action. AR is the high road to warrants for action and an authentic social science.

Note

1. One significant source of vagueness in our discussion here is just who the participants are and who they represent. That an AR process is participatory and cogenerative does not solve local issues of inclusion, hierarchy, gender oppression, and so on. When an AR process is begun, some local community or organizational group of stakeholders opens up a set of issues to be examined. Often, it takes the AR professional a long time to discover who these people are, how they were selected, who is not present, and how their actions may affect larger local collectives. This is inevitable. AR is not a silver bullet producing democracy everywhere in its wake. The obligation of the AR professional is to attempt to discover who is present and who is not, to understand the effect of this on the process and the actions stemming from it, and to advocate regularly for discussions about inclusion and for greater inclusiveness. Of course, the scope of such actions cannot be known in advance.

PART 3

Varieties of Action Research Praxis: Liberating Human Potential

To open this part, we return to the presentation of cases, this time four cases drawn from our practice to show more about action research (AR) under different conditions and to emphasize the complexity and necessary open-endedness of AR practices. Following this, we provide a systematic presentation of our own approach to AR. Then we complete the book with a series of chapters on some of the major varieties of AR, using our approach as a point of reference for comparisons and contrasts. We cover southern participatory AR, feminist research, action science, organizational learning, human inquiry, cooperative inquiry, action inquiry, education-based approaches to AR, participatory evaluation, and participatory rural appraisal.

8

Action Research Cases
From Practice II

As in Chapter 3, " Action Research Cases From Practice I,"
our purpose here is to provide the reader with examples
from our own practice to return the rather abstract
discussions of the previous section to the concrete levels
on which AR takes place. In this chapter, we present four
short cases, some successful and some not. As cogenerated projects, they do not fall under the unilateral control
of the professional researcher, and so they often follow
circuitous paths and occasionally fall radically short of their
initial goals. Though the reader now knows that AR projects
do not have predetermined courses of development or fixed
outcomes, understanding what this means experientially
for the AR practitioner is important.

◄o►

THE BUNT PROGRAM

In the late 1980s, the Norwegian Research Council decided to
launch a program in support of business development with a particular
focus on small and medium-sized enterprises (SMEs). The main idea was

to create a program supporting business development through new technology, and the abbreviation for the Norwegian name is BUNT. The program trained consultants to do strategic analysis in participating companies, which would then lead to concrete development plans for the companies. The program operated from 1989 to 1992 with a total budget of 80,000,000 Norwegian crowns (U.S. $12,000,000).

BUNT taught consultants how to do strategic analysis with an emphasis on new technology in business development. A total of 120 consultants were trained, with the idea that they would disseminate the approach to strategic thinking to the participating companies. The training program was quite extensive, involving three off-sites where trainees had to learn the strategic tools and had hands-on experience working with a company doing a strategic analysis. The teachers responsible for the training program mentored this hands-on work. No consultants were allowed to become participants in the program unless they had gone through the training, and each consultant had to pay the expenses for the training himself or herself.

To assess the value of this approach, the Norwegian Research Council commissioned a combined research evaluation of BUNT to evaluate the program from its initiation through its final results. Evaluation studies did not have a long history in Norway and, consequently, there was no obvious Norwegian institution to take it on. Eventually the Norwegian University of Science and Technology was contacted, mainly because Morten Levin's research group there had received many contracts from the research council over the years and had developed a reputation. Levin's group had never explicitly worked as evaluators, however.

Levin's group identified two major goals as the conditions of taking on the assignment. The group wanted to apply AR to the process and create a program to train PhD students in AR parallel with it. In the negotiations with the research council, the group based its position on rather fragmentary knowledge of evaluation. It proposed to integrate formative evaluation (evaluation while a program was operating) with summative evaluation (evaluation at a program's end) through applying AR methodologies. In taking this approach, the argument was that BUNT would continually produce results that would be used to improve the ongoing operation of the program. The research questions guiding summative evaluation related to issues of technology transfer and business development.

Fortunately, the manager responsible for BUNT wanted this kind of useful on-line knowledge and had the clear expectation that the evaluators should support him with knowledge relevant to the ongoing improvement of his program. In other words, he viewed BUNT as a learning organization. At the same time, other stakeholders in the public and political domain wanted a summative evaluation to give them an objective measure of how the BUNT program had performed.

At the beginning, the consultants participating in BUNT had no clear sense of how evaluation would be of use to them. Over the course of the program, they came to appreciate the value of the evaluation work as a way of getting feedback on their own work. They learned to use this to set their own standards for good consulting practices. The involved companies never expressed any clear position one way or the other on the evaluation results.

The evaluation and research team consisted of three experienced researchers and six PhD students. Morten Levin was the project director and was formally responsible for the PhD program at the Norwegian University of Science and Technology. The two other senior researchers collaborating with Levin in managing the evaluation program, Haakon Finne and Tore Nilssen, came from the Institute for Social Research in Industry, a research institute closely linked to the university in Trondheim. Six students were brought into the program in 1989 and worked on their PhDs until the last student defended his dissertation in 1994 (Elvemo, 1994; Fossen, 1994; Gjersvik, 1993; Klev, 1993; Rolfsen, 1993; Torvatn, 1993). The intellectual roots of this evaluation team included considerable experience in AR in industrial and local community settings and professional training in a combination of sociology and engineering. The PhD group, whose major academic focus was organization and management studies, consisted of postgraduate students with a first degree in engineering.

In designing the PhD program, the team leaders designed a program of study (amounting to 1 full year of course work) that covered both important international texts around the organization-technology interface and key AR texts. Given the freedom available in the university, doing this did not provoke resistance, and the evaluation grant provided enough resources to invite foreign scholars to teach, thereby creating an international intellectual environment in the program. Because skills in conducting AR cannot be learned in the classroom, the program assigned each student to one of the senior members of the program in a mentoring relationship.

The first evaluation task was to participate in and evaluate the BUNT consultant training program. A pair of the PhD students followed each cohort of consultants in training through the program. In this way, the evaluators were able to provide immediate feedback to BUNT on training at the end of the training program. This formative evaluation focused on issues of general pedagogy, the performance of individual teachers, and the content of the lectures.

The evaluations were given as oral feedback to the teaching staff and the managers of BUNT. These evaluations were reasonably successful because the team identified issues in ways that resonated with the teachers and managers and because the evaluations placed a strong emphasis on being concrete and specific. When there were disagreements, it was possible to refer to concrete observations as a way of discussing them. The students played an important role in this work because they participated in all the activities and took extensive notes. The feedback sessions were planned with the students as active partners.

A crisis in the evaluation work occurred when the senior researchers delivered a summative evaluation report at the conclusion of the training program. They had written a 100-page report based on their interpretation and judgement of the data from the training courses (Levin & Nilssen, 1990a). Given the experiences to that point with BUNT, they expected fruitful and challenging discussions, but the expectation was completely wrong. At the beginning of the meeting with BUNT leaders, the program manager bluntly stated that the report was not worth the paper it was written on. The conclusions were contested and the data were not accepted; the whole report was seen as an attack on the program and as far too academic. It became clear to the evaluation team that it had not succeeded in engaging the management of the program in an authentic dialogue. Despite various attempts during the meeting to get back on track, this developed into a major crisis, and the meeting ended with the evaluators fearing that the contract would be terminated.

The evaluation report itself was certainly of good academic quality. No one ever disputed the data and conclusions developed from the analysis. The evaluators had managed to achieve high validity but very little credibility. BUNT management could not identify with the conclusions and could not see how the report would be helpful in improving the performance of BUNT.

Despite this, the evaluation team was not thrown out of the program. There were too many other stakeholders involved, adding up to a complex set of interests surrounding the events. Still, the atmosphere was not particularly friendly. The evaluation team agreed to write an addendum to the report that focused on concrete and practical conclusions and recommendations for the "further development of the program" (Levin & Nilssen, 1990b). These suggestions were very directive and concrete, and were applauded by the management. Little by little, the relationship improved and greater trust and mutual respect developed.

Still, this incident came as a shock. Despite the fact that the evaluation team leaders were experienced action researchers, they had failed to create an arena for mutual learning. Their understanding of the evaluation process was poor, and they had not paid enough attention to or planned for processes involving BUNT management in mutual interpretation and learning about what the data could tell. Instead, they had done a conventional academic analysis, well crafted but useless to local actors. As professional researchers, the evaluation team members had invested a lot of energy and professional wisdom in making sense of the data, but this very process closed down their ability to remain open to other interpretations.

This was a turning point for the evaluators' engagement in the program. They never again made these mistakes. The simple solution to the problem was to engage the stakeholders in the BUNT program from the very beginning of the analysis process. In reflecting on what was learned, the evaluation team leaders named the evaluation practice emerging from this experience *trailing research* (Finne, Levin, & Nilssen, 1995). The main conclusions about what was learned from the

BUNT experience regarding efforts to combine formative and summative evaluations are summarized in the following five points:

- Keep a constant focus on learning processes.

- Clarify roles and expectations.

- Create arenas for dialogues.

- Focus jointly on the issues to investigate.

- Create research consistent with conventional validity claims, but open up the results to discussion before reaching conclusions.

All members of the PhD group successfully defended their theses, and the last candidate graduated in 1994. To a reasonable degree, the program succeeded in building a bridge between a formal degree program and acquiring skills in AR. Two of the students took leaves of absence from the program for a year while they worked as evaluators for another program aimed at support for very small businesses. After graduating later, this pair continued working on trailing research. Most of the graduates now work as action researchers.

The trailing research concept was adopted by a number of European Union projects related to business development (Finne, Levin, & Nilssen, 1995), and the Norwegian Research Council now has a mandatory policy to evaluate all programs it funds. Some of the biggest programs are evaluated using the trailing research method.

Many lessons can be drawn from this project. Probably the most important arose from learning how to handle the crisis created by the first report. Rather than avoiding conflicts, as the evaluation team had done, it is better to run AR projects by confronting and managing as conflicts occur. The team also learned how difficult it is to balance the need for open communication with the evaluators' need to avoid being co-opted. Retaining integrity as researchers is always a major concern, but in AR it cannot be achieved by trying to remain distant from the participants. The solution in this project was to develop a strong identity and open communications among all the members of the evaluation team. The team members often discussed problems related to the management of BUNT within the group and sought collective judgements regarding what would be professionally and ethically right to do in particular situations. These discussions were valuable because they gave the action researchers in the field a source of support. This strategy apparently resulted in BUNT management gaining respect for the evaluators as professionals. As trust grew between the evaluators and BUNT management, more difficult issues were addressed openly and critically.

AR AND COMMUNITY DEVELOPMENT IN SPAIN'S LA MANCHA REGION[1]

To give the reader a flavor of the kinds of processes that AR involves and the unexpected turns such processes take, we here recount briefly an AR project that Greenwood collaborated in. It took place in the town of Herencia (Ciudad Real), and was a project that made a systematic start at AR in important community issues. It ended with the 1994 local elections, which shifted the majority in the municipal government from the Spanish Socialist Worker's Party (PSOE) to the Popular Party (PP). Thus, it is not a success story. It is not a failure either. The project trained a large number of people in AR techniques, helped bring about dialogue among some parties in the community who were not in clear communication before, and opened up the vista of collaborative social change in a deeply divided community with an uncertain future.

Herencia is a town of about 8,000 in the north central area of the province of Ciudad Real. A settlement dating from the 13th century, it was founded by the Military Order of Saint John of Jerusalem. Herencia is a Mediterranean "agro-town," meaning that it is a relatively large and compact settlement with a radial street plan and houses whose exterior walls create unbroken solid walls facing the street but have inner courtyards and patios. The large size and compact settlement pattern gives towns such as these an urban feel. Though agriculture is dispersed over the surrounding landscape, everyone lives together in the town, creating a dense population and an intense face-to-face social life typically associated with cities.

Situated in the heart of the "route of Don Quixote," and part of the royal sheep walks (*Cañadas Reales de la Mesta*), Herencia, until the 19th century, exported raw wool and blankets. Now Herencia cultivates grapes, olives, wheat, barley, and rye; raises sheep; and prepares wine, olive oil, and cheese. The no-longer-functioning seven windmills sitting on the hills overlooking the town are reminders of a time when La Mancha was a major grain and flour producer and exporter. Now the town has a number of nonagricultural businesses, including a number of small light industrial manufacturing plants. A great many women take in sewing as a way of supplementing income.

Though enterprising and hardworking, the *herencianos* have struggled against the long-term decline of agriculture, a decline sped up enormously by the interventions of European Union policies. The high quality of Spanish oil and wine and the quality and price of other Spanish agricultural commodities evidently terrifies Spain's competitors in France, England, and Germany, and these countries have done all they can within the framework of the European Union to undermine the competitive position of Spanish agriculture.

Whether one agrees with this perception or not, the plain fact for Herencia is that the absence of jobs and a secure future has created a situation in which all families in the town have to face the possibility of parents reaching old age after their children have had to leave to seek employment in the urban industrial centers of Spain. In this sense, *herencianos* of all classes and political ideologies have a problem in common: job creation for their children. This problem lay at the center of the project.

No project like this springs up without warning. The path by which it began was circuitous. Greenwood's wife, Pilar Fernández-Cañadas, was born in Herencia. She and her sisters were the first women in their generation to be sent to university from the town, and she is the first to have received a PhD. Greenwood met her in college in the United States; they married in Spain, but have lived for most of the last 34 years in the United States. She always kept up some ties with her hometown, however, where her parents maintain a residence.

During the Spanish civil war, Herencia had been a "red" town and was rapidly collectivized. There were many deaths on both sides. People living there now remember that members of their families were engaged in these activities against each other. In the 1980s, Herencia elected its first socialist mayor in generations, José Roselló López, a man of vision and energy who decided that the only way to move the town ahead was through building alliances across the social and ideological divides within the town to develop projects for the common good. Roselló began slowly establishing contacts with people from all the different social groups around the theme of common town pride. In the case of Pilar Fernández-Cañadas Greenwood, he began sending the program for the annual town festival and for the celebration of Carnival to her, along with a letter of greeting. When he learned more about her, he requested that she contribute an essay for a monograph on the history of the town to celebrate its 750th anniversary in 1989. Through actions like these, he drew her, and many others, into a dialogue about the town and its future. When the Greenwoods visited the town, they paid him a courtesy visit and began to talk more concretely about doing something for the town.

As Greenwood began to understand the problems of the town and its complex social history (having first visited it in 1964), he started to think that a community AR project might be possible and would support the mayor's efforts already under way to link people across social divisions and create more economic opportunities locally. He wrote a proposal for an AR project to be carried out under local management that would involve representatives from all stakeholder groups, and delivered it to the mayor. Almost in the blink of an eye, the mayor acted on the proposal. He engaged one of the town councilmembers, Tomás Berrio, a specialist in adult education who was aware of some of the AR writing on this subject. Roselló and Berrio converted the proposal into a larger document, including their own understanding of AR, and proposed an AR project for the town with Greenwood acting as the facilitator. Greenwood offered to contribute his time gratis during a sabbatical leave from Cornell University. The mayor presented this project to the town council, and it was approved, though with limited funding.

Roselló immediately began seeking other funds to support the effort, eventually involving the Center for Continuing Teacher Education (CEP), the provincial government, the National Distance Education University (UNED), and the administration of the Autonomous Community of Castille and La Mancha. Using contacts developed over 25 years of work in Spain, Greenwood set up a scientific committee with some of the best-known anthropologists in Spain. Backed by the mayor, the scientific committee, and Greenwood's professional credentials as a senior professor at a well-known U.S. university, the initiators went together to possible funders, presented the idea, and were received warmly. Indeed, the reactions of the various agencies were of excitement and interest in this kind of unique initiative.

At the same time, Greenwood began the process of developing a working group in the community to start the process. As an outsider, he knew that it was very important to start with a good and respected group of people, but did not know the community well enough to make an informed choice. Roselló reasoned that one of the best and most socially and politically diverse resources of a community is the schoolteachers. They are also the ones providing educational opportunities to local children, which often result in those students having to leave Herencia to find more challenging jobs elsewhere. So they too had a strong stake in creating more high-quality and demanding jobs in the town. Roselló convened a diverse group of teachers from all levels of the local school system to act as the initial steering group.

This group began meeting immediately and prepared a plan of work. It decided that one of the ways to build AR capacity for local problem solving was by teaching the community about AR. So the group organized a short course on AR that involved an intensive week of lectures and discussions, followed by a search conference and then a couple of days of debriefing. It also got this short course certified for teacher credit by the CEP and the UNED. About 25 people attended the course, including the entire steering group. Other members of the community, including some university students, accompanied them. The course was held in the local high school, which is named for a widely respected local teacher who influenced a number of generations in Herencia after the Civil War. The participants read about AR together and debated the theory and methods. A subset of this group staffed the search conference that was held over the weekend between the 2 weeks of the short course. During the second week, the class as a whole examined the results of the search conference. Grades were given, and the teachers received continuing education credit for their participation.

Simultaneously the ad hoc steering group was meeting to plan the overall process of the project. The centerpiece of the project, by now called the Herencia Project, was to be a search conference. Search conferences are described in Chapter 9, "Pragmatic Action Research." They serve the purpose of developing a common vision and action plan among a very diverse and even conflicted group of stakeholders.

The search process usually takes 2 to 2 1/2 days. It begins with a search question: in this case, how to create jobs that would maintain the social existence of the town. It involves laying out a collective history, an ideal future, and a probable future. Then the obstacles to the ideal future are assessed, and strategies to overcome them are developed. People form action teams to carry out these strategies after the search is over.

Key to any search process is the representativeness of those brought together. Addressing this problem was part of the mission of the steering group. Together, members spent many days attempting to map the maximum social diversity of the town: gender, age, ideology, occupation, disability, and so on. During this process, the message to the steering group was that, for effective social change, all the relevant stakeholders have to be included, not just the usual people. The social map expanded and contracted a number of times. Eventually, local members put names to each of the categories, selecting people whom they felt embodied clear and different positions and who would be capable of speaking up. Subsequently, the group created an informational bulletin about the process and went to each of the identified people and invited them personally to the search conference, explaining the process to them.

A total of 48 people were invited. Ultimately 46 attended. The search was held at a religious retreat center just outside of town, where the group stayed for 2 nights, separated from the usual tasks and the rhythms of local life. Key to the success of the event was the active participation of a respected retired parish priest, the current parish priest, and the mayor, people who set aside their considerable differences on this occasion to make this event work.

The search produced a number of action teams with different foci. One focused on developing a retirement home for local people. Another centered on supporting and upgrading existing economic development organizations. The ad hoc steering committee was reconstituted to include the new leaders of the action teams and became a formal steering committee. This larger group met occasionally to keep track of the projects and to try to support the developing efforts.

An enormous amount of information was quickly accumulated. With some of the money raised for the project, the AR team set up two computational centers, one in a municipal building and the other in the local high school where the short course had been run. The choice of these two locations embodied the principle that the project belonged to the whole community, not just to one institution. At these locations, the complete records of activities, meetings, and plans of the project were available for anyone to examine. This information was organized using a text-based database called FolioViews, and served as a record of the activities of the project.

A modem connection was also established because Greenwood was not resident in the community for more than a few weeks at a time during the project. Each day, information regarding the project was put into files on the local computer and Greenwood would collect it from his home in upstate New York via modem, analyze it, make comments, and send reflections back as a kind of remote contribution to the ongoing processes. Thus, collaboration even at a distance was possible.

Over a period of months, the project showed both promise and difficulties. The promise was seen in the work of a number of the action teams that had developed very clear, detailed, and well-planned interventions. These teams began to incorporate other people who had not initially participated in the search process but whose expertise was critical to the success of a particular team, always a good sign.

On the negative side, the participants most closely linked to the municipal government did not sufficiently heed Greenwood's constant advice to let the teams move at their own pace and according to their own agendas. This left the damaging impression that the project was the property of a political subsegment of the municipal government rather than a shared property of a more diverse community created at the search conference and that represented many of the differences within Herencia as a whole. Although the role of the municipal government, particularly the socialists, was crucial to the initiation and early stages of the project, the project was far more than theirs by this time.

The necessity of separating the project from the town government was not completely evident to key participants, however. As a result, when municipal and provincial elections overturned the socialists,[2] the project was also stopped. Because the socialists had permitted the project to be too closely associated with them politically, even though much of the ongoing effort in the action teams involved people from across the political and social spectrum, taking the mayor's position away from the PSOE also resulted in the termination of the municipal government's support for the project.

What Can We Learn From the Herencia Project?

It is clear that AR and self-managed community development are possible even in deeply divided, economically threatened communities. A history of conflict and an unpromising future do not condemn a community to passivity in the face of its problems.

Greenwood was impressed by the immense value and complexity of local knowledge as it is mobilized through participatory processes. The 50 or so collaborators in this project had intimate, detailed, and valuable knowledge about the socioeconomic life of their community. This community could be mobilized and was capable of developing plans that rival or better official, expert, outside plans for community development. What were in short supply were facilitation and research skills, but these can be learned much more easily than outsiders can learn the details of local knowledge.

Greenwood's inability to separate the project's public face from a particular political group made this project frustrating. In this, there is a moral for other AR initiatives. Electoral politics are a poor basis on which to build AR precisely because electoral politics are built on the principles of adversarial democracy (Mansbridge, 1983). These are the politics of winners and losers, majorities and minorities, whereas AR and participatory community development are processes designed for the benefit of all. These processes aim to respect the heterogeneity of stakeholders and to treat all interests as worthy of consideration. The goal is not to eliminate differences but to learn to accommodate them.

The problem is that we cannot easily choose where to begin an AR project. Action researchers do not hover over the landscape, landing and starting projects at will. We seek opportunities and partners wherever we find them. In this case, the initiative came from an elected official and members of his political coalition. Without his initiative, there would have been no project. Yet we were also unable to move the initiative quickly enough to a more neutral community turf where it could have transcended the vagaries of electoral politics.

This is a significant problem in any AR situation. One of the reasons that the Norwegian and Swedish AR programs have been so successful is because they are rooted in national agreements between the government, the confederations of employers, and the labor unions. These agreements create the AR consultation organizations, provide funding for them, and make their political neutrality more evident. In this way, action researchers can bring both resources and some independence to the table that places AR projects in a more open local environment.

In Spain, these kinds of open institutional spaces are harder to find. To substitute for them, other kinds of less robust structures have been used: neighborhood associations (Bier, 1980), voluntary collectives for social change (e.g., IOE, see Investigación-Acción Participativa, 1993), regional governmental programs for local development, and so on. For the foreseeable future, AR initiatives in Spain will have to begin opportunistically and then struggle to locate themselves on some common and neutral ground to remain viable.

Finally, because the project was stopped in midstream, was it a failure? It is easy to dismiss what was done. It is also tempting for Greenwood, as an advocate of AR, to try to justify what was done to believe that the group did not waste its time. There are some good arguments to be made about the positive outcomes of this project, however.

Positive Outcomes of the Project

- It showed that social adversaries could not only speak to each other but also could plan and implement activities together.

- It provided training in the skills of participation and facilitation to a large group of teachers, who, among other things, are required by law to comanage their own schools, though without any training to support this mandate.

- It exposed local students and teachers to the concepts of AR and concepts of democracy that go beyond coercive models of consensus.

- It identified an array of problems and specific local initiatives that could address them in a way that the initiatives could be owned by a broad cross-section of the community.

- It brought the dynamism and initiative of this town to the attention of educational officials, provincial officials, and the Autonomous Community government, giving the town a reputation for activism on its own behalf.

Negative Outcomes

- The failure of the project to extract itself from electoral politics led some participants to conclude that participatory change is impossible. They might, therefore, be more demoralized than they were at the outset.

THE INTEGRATION OF PUBLIC SERVICES IN A NORWEGIAN MUNICIPALITY

In the late 1980s, the Norwegian government launched a program for municipal development in which local politicians and administrators were to take a leadership role in modernizing and improving public services. The local initiatives were expected to form around organizational development, leadership training, and other types of change activities. The Institute for Social Research in Industry, the Department of Organization and Work Life at the Norwegian University of Science and Technology, and the regional research organization at Steinkjer received a contract for the research at Steinkjer, a county administrative town 100 miles north of Trondheim with a population of approximately 15,000. Morten Levin, Arne Svarva, and Nils Sletterød cooperated in this work.

The project aimed to develop cooperation between three different public agencies responsible for supporting unemployed youth (Levin, Svarva, & Sletterød, 1990). Two of the agencies, the Work Assistance Administration (a governmental agency to help people get work) and the National Health Administration (a governmental agency responsible for social welfare, health care funding, and public pensions) were governmental offices, whereas the Social Security Office (the municipal office for social welfare) was run by the municipal administration. These three offices dealt with the same clients, but they had different rules and systems for granting aid to them. The idea was to combine the different support activities to develop a unified and broad-based support system. We negotiated an action orientation with both the research council and the municipal authorities, but we had no initial agreement with the agencies we later came to work with. That type of agreement was expected to grow out of our contacts with the local participants.

In the initial phase of the project, the team spent a lot of time getting into position to do the work. Being accepted by the municipal steering committee from each of the administrative offices individually and by the steering committee for the cooperation project took 4 months. After this initial phase, the team worked out a plan to develop a search conference (see Chapter 9, "Pragmatic Action Research") to initiate the process and to mobilize the participants from the different offices. The initial plan was to recommend a 2-day search conference held away from the local administrative building.

These steps were agreed to and a date was set. The team then waited for the local actors to take the necessary steps to develop the search conference, but nothing happened. After several calls from the outside team, the local response was to postpone the search conference for 2 months. Then that was also cancelled, and the outside team learned that the three leaders decided to hold a meeting without outside participation. At that meeting, they decided that they should have the responsibility for the process because they were primarily interested in practical solutions and not in what they perceived as an AR project.

After another 2 months, the outside team was invited to a meeting with the three offices, and the participants' reservations regarding the outside team's role were clarified. First, it became clear that the outsiders were considered the long arm of the national power structure reaching into the municipal administration. Second, the three offices feared that the project would get too much public attention and cause them other problems. Third, the local Social Security Office and National Health Administration were negative because the central agency in Oslo feared an erosion of its influence. Yet, to the outside team's great astonishment, the Work Assistance Administration and the Social Security Office wanted to run a search conference.

The search planning gradually resulted in a process the outside team had never planned for or done before. The time frame of the search conference was shortened to 1 day, and the Minister of Health and Social Security was invited as a key speaker. Half of the day was devoted to the minister, and the search was limited to the afternoon and evening. In the view of the professional researchers, no real search process could take place in these few hours, but the team accepted the design because it saw no other way to get the project on track. As expected, the minisearch conference did not result in clear and concrete plans for action.

After the search conference, the initiative remained in the hands of the three offices. They continued to develop the cooperation effort through conventional negotiation procedures. Included in their work was a study trip to another municipality that had managed successfully to establish the kind of cooperation they were seeking. The outside team was excluded from having any influence on the development of the project from this point on. A year later, the local cooperation effort resulted in the opening of a shared office with the joint responsibility of handling all dimensions of assistance to unemployed youth.

This is a story of an AR project that never got off the ground. Many factors explain this. In this analysis, we leave out the factors linked to the overall decision-making processes in the public sector and the local political processes. We concentrate our reflections on what went wrong in the AR process.

- The outside team never managed to clarify its role as researchers. Instead, the local power brokers expected to be the ones responsible for all changes, excluding all outsiders.

- The team never managed to establish a trusting relationship with actors in the three local offices.

- The team never managed to establish integrity as independent researchers, but was viewed as a puppet for local power brokers.

- The outside team made a fundamental error in permitting the abbreviated search conference to take place. It would have been better to work slowly and carefully within each local office to build momentum for the process.

■ The team did not understand how problematic it would be to initiate a participatory approach to organizational change in the public sector, partly because the team's professional experience was primarily drawn from work in industrial organizations.

The research team concluded that this project never took off because of a failure to engage in a participatory process. As action researchers committed to change processes, members of the team were committed to extensive participation. It therefore made no sense to end up negotiating the team's terms of local engagement only with the mayor, the chief operating office of the local administration, and the three heads of the local offices. In retrospect, the team was astonished at how it made no attempt to engage the employees of the three local offices in the work.

LINKING RESEARCH AND EXTENSION IN CORNELL UNIVERSITY'S SCHOOL OF INDUSTRIAL AND LABOR RELATIONS[3]

During one period in its history, the Programs for Employment and Workplace Systems (PEWS) at the School of Industrial and Labor Relations at Cornell, located in the Extension Division, sought to enhance its connections and reputation among the resident faculty in the academic departments, but was having limited success. Greenwood became involved with PEWS through the efforts of one of its founders, William Foote Whyte. As he participated in discussions at PEWS, Greenwood was struck by the radically different mindsets of the PEWS members and the resident faculty. PEWS members were attracted and driven by the needs of their client organizations, whereas the academic faculty were attracted and driven by the paradigms and the struggle for acceptance within their research community. As a result, a division of labor ensued. Action agents were not expected to write much or to think theoretically, and academic faculty were not expected to write or think in terms of the application of knowledge.

During the period that Greenwood worked with PEWS, he suggested that PEWS try a reconciliation of these positions by attempting to suffuse its client-centered processes with research dimensions. As an AR experiment to develop a model of this approach, PEWS undertook a pilot project at a nearby manufacturing plant. This plant faced problems implementing new manufacturing systems (manufacturing cells, total quality, statistical process control, and just-in-time).

As an experiment to increase PEWS' effectiveness, the participants overlaid the early stages of a typical consultation process with a research perspective. First, PEWS gained access, basic familiarity, and an initial contract with the plant. Well into the process, Greenwood, operating as a professional social researcher, accompanied the PEWS staff to the plant for 2 days as a participant-observer. During that time and in written analysis afterward, he raised questions and pursued the issues raised by his observations. This helped make the intervention process accessible to others not directly involved.

Next, Greenwood and the staff members joined other PEWS members and Jan Irgens Karlsen, who was visiting the School of Industrial and Labor Relations to ferret out the research issues relevant to this plant. This provided an opportunity for the PEWS personnel to inform the others about the plant's problems and to raise questions. The question and answer process refined the issues for all involved. An array of important research questions emerged, along with an inventory of further information about the plant that the PEWS consultants needed.

The process pointed in two directions. First, the consultants to the plant with Greenwood and Karlsen identified the larger theoretical issues that the events in the plant embodied. Two large families of issues emerged: the organizational effect of new manufacturing systems and models of organizational change involved in creating manufacturing cells. These, in turn, raised issues about the larger social meaning of the new manufacturing. They also referred to the difficulties organizations face in modeling organizational change.

Second, they identified what the research literature contained on these issues that could be useful in the plant. This involved forays into the literature on organizational learning, models of organization, and new manufacturing systems.

Third, they suggested that the PEWS staff develop the basic data needed to address these questions via study-action teams composed of plant employees. Experience with such teams has shown that they can become very knowledgeable quickly. They often become a positive part of the change process themselves.

Finally, they organized and collated these research materials. These provided good theoretical and methodological perspectives for the PEWS staff to deploy at the plant. The social research issues were as clear to the AR group as were the client's needs. Comparative research through library and fieldwork on elements of the new manufacturing systems deployed at the plant was possible. This kind of research would have been exciting to the academic faculty both for its research value and its utility in providing materials for teaching. In reality, PEWS and other extension programs constantly face problems at the cutting edge, where their clients live. A body of research built on these experiences could serve as a tracking device for students of industrial society. But the initiative stopped at this point.

What prevented it from going forward? Organizationally, it would have required major changes in both PEWS and the School of Industrial and Labor Relations. The PEWS members would have had to balance their commitments to their clients with the disciplines of research by devoting time to reading, writing, and communicating with resident faculty. Resident faculty would have had to be willing to invest time ferreting out the larger issues in the cases, organizing the relevant literature, and engaging themselves with projects in which action was an element. Although the lack of incentives for academic faculty to do this was clear, it was less clear why action agents did not wish to change the structure they were working in.

Thus, a successful AR model was deployed within the organization, provided uniquely useful results, was replicable in other cases, and was never deployed because of the combined division of labor between academic faculty and extension staff at Cornell University (and elsewhere) and because AR made the job of extension staff both harder and more time-consuming than the standard pattern of behavior. The project disappeared without a trace, despite its apparent success, because the initiators did not have the resources and political clout to take it to the next level.

CONCLUSIONS

Each of these cases shows a different kind of deployment of AR. The issues, methods, successes, and failures of the projects are all very different. We hope this gives the reader more of a sense of the rich variety of AR work. Some of the projects we have presented resulted in solving pertinent practical problems. In the other cases, the AR did not produce tangible results. Of course, we know from the epistemological and methodological discussions in Part 2 that new knowledge develops from both positive and negative outcomes. The unsuccessful results can often be as important for knowledge production as successful ones, even though the universal commitment of AR is to try to create positive outcomes.

Going back to Lewin's slogan, we do not understand the inner structure of a social system until we try to change it. That is not to say we always succeed in changing it in the way we hope. Further, all the cases presented here have produced reflections and writings aimed at understanding and improving AR practice and social theory.

One of the fundamental prerequisites for anyone considering the option of becoming an action researcher is a willingness to live with uncertainty. In AR, there is no way to be sure of an outcome in advance. AR involves taking the risks of a journey into the unknown in a context where the researcher can influence only a minority of the relevant factors. The results produced and the knowledge gained depend on the mutual involvement of local participants and professional researchers. This is also what attracts us to the challenges and beauty of AR processes.

Notes

1. A slightly longer Spanish language version of the case study is in press in the journal *Perspectivas de Gestión,* soon to be published in Barcelona.

2. The PSOE won 5 seats on the town council, the PP won 5, and the IU voted with the PP to turn the town government over to the PP.

3. This case originally was written up and published with two others in Greenwood (1989).

Pragmatic Action Research

Chapters 3, "Action Research Cases From Practice I," and 8, "Action Research Cases From Practice II," present six cases drawn from our action research (AR) experiences. Some are success stories and others are failures. All involve important learning on the part of most of the people involved. Because of the way AR is practiced, knowledge is created even when pertinent solutions to problems cannot be found. Although the cases describe some of our practices, they do not explain how we conceive of our own approach to AR to permit the reader to compare and contrast how we work with the approaches detailed in Chapters 10 through 14. Here we will offer a more systematic presentation of our own approach, which we call *pragmatic AR.*

The reader will have noticed that the example cases involved a wide variety of approaches to AR. In each different context and given a specific problem focus, we developed the AR process differently. Although the lack of a perfect fit between an initial formulation and the development of a project is true in all research and intervention situations, in pragmatic AR, the ongoing and purposive redesigning of the projects while they are in process is a key principle of practice. The image that guides practice is that of the friendly outsider interacting with a diverse and complex group of local problem owners in a complicated conversation that results in the generation and clarification of ideas and options and in actions, but that never results in a single, hard-line consensus to which everyone is subordinated. Following Rorty's (1980) view of neopragmatism, we aim to "keep the conversation going."

In most of the situations we described and in many others we have been involved in, the researchers and the local participants together developed a general understanding of where they were heading and what actions to take, but the researchers always resisted making these into stringent plans. The whole AR process, viewed our way, is an emergent one until the problems have been resolved at least to the satisfaction of the local participants, the finances or energy have been exhausted, or some other event intervenes to change the direction of the process or to end it.

This is not to say that the process lacks either logic or rigor. AR as we have described it takes the shape of a structured and logical set of activities aimed at reaching desired results and testing in action. The direction of an AR project is guided by the learning gained through the process, not by a set of a priori norms or expectations imposed on the situation and actors. As we look across the cases derived from our own experience, we feel that this pragmatic[1] approach has yielded a set of generic characteristics common to most situations. These include the construction of arenas for dialogue, cogenerative research processes, and the use of multiple methods.

☐ Construction of arenas for dialogue: In our work, we strive to construct arenas where participants and researcher(s) can engage in a dialogical relationship. These arenas create the space in which mutual learning takes place.

☐ Cogenerative research: The research process emerges out of joint experiences and from mutual reflections about these experiences shared between participants and researcher(s).

☐ The use of multiple methods: We strongly reject the notion that AR is a particular theory or a specific set of methods. A great many theories and methods developed in the social sciences and humanities can be used in AR processes, if and when the participants decide they are appropriate and gain the requisite skills in deploying them together. What defines AR for us is the combination of research, action, and democratization, not adherence to a specific methodology.

These three elements are the centerpiece of our practice of pragmatic AR. The plans, methods, and cogenerated learning processes depend on judgements made in each concrete research situation by the participants. This is fully consistent with epistemological arguments for AR that we derived from pragmatic philosophy (Chapters 5, 6, and 7). Hence, we believe that AR is best understood and practiced as the use of pragmatic philosophical positions in social research.

Our position creates problems for us in describing our practice in a single chapter. Because our approach is purposely fitted to local conditions, we cannot describe it in narrow terms. Yet the reader needs an introduction to the considerations we take into account and some of the techniques we use. What follows, therefore, is a review of some key concepts and tools that can, and often are, deployed in pragmatic AR processes. Because we have already discussed cogenerative learning and the pragmatic approach to the choice of methods extensively in Chapters 4 through 7, we will concentrate on our approach to the construction of arenas for dialogue here. The materials in Chapters 4 through 7 are directly relevant to understanding our own particular approach to AR, however.

—◄o►—

CONSTRUCTING ARENAS FOR DIALOGUE

For us, the core element in pragmatic AR is to create arenas for cogenerative learning for dialogue. The encounter between participants and researcher is the cornerstone on which mutual learning is built. Because we do not begin with a method defined a priori and we try to match our approach to the local situation and actors, it means our AR processes generally have a slow and highly conversational opening stage. By beginning this way, we differ from most other approaches to AR.

We explicitly believe that our obligations as professional researchers are to assist the group in choosing whatever methods and theories are suitable for the particular process underway. We do not rely on particular recipes that always should be followed because we believe that such recipes mainly serve to lessen the insecurities of the professional researchers. We confront the local problems with all the skills and knowledge we have. What we do not know and skills that we lack can be a detriment to the particular project. Of course, we always wish we were smarter and more skilled. We advocate facing our existential and epistemological uncertainties as professional action researchers directly, however, rather than adhering to a particular set of canonical practices that would lower the demands on us. We think that is a necessary part of our integrity as researchers.

Nevertheless, we do not advocate casting around blindly for a way of working. We believe that in AR central skills revolve around the ability to understand and interpret social and material contexts, to decide on and configure appropriate arenas for discourse, to lead the interaction process, and to assist the participants in testing their knowledge in action. Thus, the action researcher must have the ability to interpret and reason about running cogenerative learning processes involving the active testing of the resulting knowledge.

A central ethical stance in AR is to achieve the goal of a liberating outcome. It is not easy to be precise about what a liberating outcome might look like, but we do not advocate narrowing the concept down to a recipe. In our AR practice, determining what is a liberating outcome is an explicit part of the cogenerated learning.

As a point of departure, it is possible to initiate discussion about liberating outcomes by offering an initial definition as "outcomes where local participants gain greater control over their own situation as a group." We are not referring to personal liberation or individual empowerment of group members, but to the increased capacity of local participants to define and manage their own collective situation.

This kind of liberation is not a quantifiable product. In highly coercive situations, a small gain may be intensely liberating, whereas in a more open situation, major changes may not be experienced as particularly significant by the participants. We believe that the change has to be real and meaningful to the local participants as a group. It is not up to the AR professional to decide if people have experienced a liberating outcome; it is up to us to pose this issue for the AR group and to keep the conversation about it going.

SEARCHING AND SEARCH CONFERENCES

Although we argue strongly for a pragmatic, multimethod approach, and we have employed many different kinds of techniques in our work, one broad and well-defined approach to cogenerative learning is particularly appropriate to our pragmatic approach to AR. It is called *searching*. We will present it *in extenso* here, not because we believe it must be used in every AR situation, but because we think it is a wonderful approach that has proved capable of generating powerful results and because presenting it in detail will give the reader a much more concrete view of our way of thinking about AR.

Searching

Searching is a term that refers to a specific kind of process where participants take part in cogenerative learning. The core idea of searching is to create a situation where ordinary people can engage in structured knowledge generation based on systematic experimentation. Participants are helped to learn by doing and by constantly searching out and trying out new ways of thinking and acting (M. Emery, 1993, p. 192).

Search Conferencing

The search conference is a methodology for participatory planning and design. The aim of search conference techniques is to allow for collective planning and design of actions aimed at solving problems directly relevant to the people involved. It is a collective process of inquiry creating learning options for all those participating.[2]

A search conference is a multiday meeting of a fairly large group of people in some kind of retreat setting. Prior to the event, the planning of a search conference begins with a process of problem identification by a planning group and the careful selection and preparation of participants. Once convened, a search conference proceeds with the participants sharing their view of the history of the situation they find themselves in. Then they identify the problems they are addressing collectively through a creative process resulting in a variety of action plans for solving the problems. In the final stage of the search, participants choose among alternative action plans, making collective decisions about what to work on. Thus, a search conference integrates planning, creative problem solving, and concrete action in the same process. This integration is its most unique feature, and it is a uniquely appropriate methodology for carrying out AR.

Search conferences create many different arenas for dialogue. The structure of the events over the time a search lasts is broadly predetermined, and the process moves along according to its inner logic, though under the continued guidance of a search manager. Search conferences almost never fail to tap participants' energy for identifying and solving their own problems, so long as search facilitation is skillful. We have not so far participated in or been responsible for a search conference that has failed, though we have often seen that the follow-up did not meet expectations. Bringing people together and providing them with the opportunity to think through and plan elements of their own future inevitably releases creative energy that is constructively channeled in the search conference process.

The search conference integrates five processes. First, it creates a discourse aimed at sharing different stakeholders' interpretations of history. Second, it develops a common vision (goals) for the future and what will happen if the future is not addressed creatively. Third, it engages the participants in creative activity, searching for action plans to reach desired goals. Fourth, it facilitates a collective prioritizing among action issues; fifth, it links planning to action groups and specific actions. The outcome of a successful search conference is a set of action issues and plans that participants want to pursue collectively.

Historical Roots

Search conferences emerged from the industrial democracy tradition in the United Kingdom, Scandinavia, and Australia. The theoretical and methodological development of searching goes back to key researchers at the Tavistock Institute in London, Fred Emery and Philip Herbst (see Chapter 2, pp. 20-24). They had very similar professional backgrounds as clinically trained social psychologists, and they worked within the same international research network. One was located in the southern hemisphere and the other in the north, and together they shaped the thinking and the practice of searching in parallel. On the Australian scene, Merrelyn Emery played a crucial role in conceptualizing and developing the search process (M. Emery, 1982, 1993).

Another way of describing how searching developed is to state that it arose from the international networks centered on industrial democracy. A major concern among those working on industrial democracy was how to integrate participatory planning in collective actions for change. The main obstacle in most models of AR at that time was domination of the processes by experts, a problem we allude to in our discussion of Kurt Lewin in Chapter 2, "A History of Action Research." Change processes were often planned and executed by the action researchers, and the real involvement of the participants was limited.

A second issue emerging at the time was a concern about the failure of social innovations to spread effectively to broader groups. Many experiments in local social change had turned out to be successful, but very often these successes were encapsulated at the original site. They did not automatically spread by the sheer virtue of the promising results achieved. This led to a concern with ways to diffuse participative processes to broader strata of society.

Emery and Oeser (1958) first stated these latter concerns in a study on the diffusion of agricultural reforms in Australia. Much later, these issues were followed up in two publications where search conferences emerge as a theme. Herbst's 1980 article in *Human Futures* presents a conceptualization of the search conference approach and communicates experiences from the first search conference in Norway, which took place on an island of Skjervøy in the north (Engelstad & Haugen, 1972; Herbst, 1980). This search became very important because it provided experience with the method to a broad group of researchers at the Work Research Institute in Oslo and because it created positive results in the local community.

In Australia, Fred and Merrelyn Emery's work on searching was first published as a working paper from the Australian National University in 1974. The Herbst and Emery publications became the pivots on which the development of search conferences turned and represented the opening of a line of developments that resulted in the widespread and respected practices of search conferences today (Emery, 1998; Martin, Hemlock, & Rich, 1994; Martin & Rich, 1994; Weisbord, 1992).

The Norwegian Tradition

The general thinking underlying the search conference fit into the Norwegian context of the early 1970s. There was an extended public debate on worker participation in a social democracy. The high-profile AR on industrial democracy created fertile ground for participative approaches to social change. In this context, the thinking underlying search conferences nicely responded to the issues of participative planning and the diffusion of change processes.

For example, by this time, the action researchers at the Work Research Institute in Oslo had abandoned the expert model for sociotechnical change (Elden, 1979) and were experimenting with search conference models to enhance change efforts in multiple companies at the same time. Search conferences fit nicely into this situation and led to the first major attempt to use the technique in the planning effort for the municipality of Skjervøy. Philip Herbst, who was the major Norwegian link to the international networks, heavily influenced this first search. This search focused on the challenges of economic and municipal development and was seen as quite radical in the Norwegian context because it based the developmental activity on fairly broad public participation.

Applying search conferences to local community development projects became one of the major development techniques used in Norway, and searching became a central element in some government-supported local community development programs. At one point, more than 60 municipalities were engaged in community development effort, and search conferences were used to initiate the work. The outcomes were successful enough that the Department of the Interior commissioned the writing of a manual on how to run searches (Brokhaug, Levin, & Nilssen, 1986). Although not everyone followed the suggested blueprint, elements of search methodology became widespread, showing that search conferences were a convincing method for many practitioners.

While the deployment of searching in community settings continued, parallels developed in industrial settings. The search conference was adopted as a tool for initiating change processes in industry. The focus was to use the search process to develop a shared vision of the future, create new action possibilities, and initiate concrete changes in organizational practices. This methodology was successfully adapted to several different industries. In particular, the researchers and consultants connected to the Work Research Institute in Oslo focused a lot of attention on searching as a way of initiating change processes (Hanssen Bauer & Aslaksen, 1991, p. 202). These Norwegian experiences were a major inspiration for the U.S.-based private consultant Marvin Weisbord, who spent part of 1987 learning about searching from Norwegian practitioners. Later he took this knowledge and adapted it in his own particular way for use in U.S. business and public administration.

Australian Experiences

Fred and Merrelyn Emery are central in the development of search conferences in Australia, where search conferences have been widely used. Fred Emery was a key international player in the development of the search conference approach. In the Australian context, his wife, Merrelyn, has played an equally important role, and over the years has written a good deal more about searching than he did.

Many of the challenges faced parallel those in Norway. Developing social change processes and seeing to the diffusion of useful innovations was not very effective in Australia. When they were developed, new democratic work forms tended to remain more or less encapsulated where they were invented. Merrelyn Emery published her important monograph on searching (1982), which develops detailed arguments about participants' learning processes. She also argues for multiple searches as a way of gaining broader public momentum for participative planning. This strategy has been important and is embodied in what came to be called "Searching Australia," an ambitious plan for making searching a nationwide effort at social change (Emery & Emery, 1974).

In 1989, Australian work life researchers organized an international conference called "Work Place Australia." One of the major ingredients in this event was that participants would spend 1 week involved in a search conference. Multiple search conferences (20) were organized, bringing together foreigners and locals. Though we cannot judge the effectiveness of this multiple search program, this effort created international awareness on searching as a methodology for participative design. Indeed, the success of this conference is seen in the subsequent activities of Australian researchers, who routinely travel abroad to train professionals in other countries in search conference techniques. For example, in recent years, Merrelyn Emery has set up a structure in the United States to teach people how to run search conferences.

The U.S. Use of Search Conferences

Searching was first brought to the United States by researchers from the Tavistock Institute. In the early 1980s, both Fred Emery and Eric Trist were affiliated with University of Pennsylvania's Wharton School of Business. During this period, Trist was actively working on a major AR project in Jamestown, New York, and Emery was invited to work with Native American groups in upstate New York. This latter activity resulted in a search focused on the future of the Seneca Indians. Although successful, this search did not immediately generate further explorations of searching.

A more powerful influence in the United States came through Marvin Weisbord's consulting. In one of his books, *Productive Workplaces* (1987), he collects several practical examples of search conferences carried out in a broad range of settings and cultures. Weisbord has created a significant consulting business by focusing his attention on training consultants to do search conferences. Between his training efforts and his writing, he has been the dominant influence in the United States on the development of thinking about search methods.

Although this diffusion might be welcome, it also means that a very particular view of searching has achieved broad currency in the United States. Weisbord's (1992) search conference *modus operandi* is a variant of searching tailored to fit within the given power structures of U.S. businesses. One of the principal ways Weisbord's approach differs from those we have discussed already is that he accepts certain power parameters and agrees to push certain areas of disagreement into the background. Thus, he mainly uses the search as a method for shaping a shared vision and tapping some of the participants' creative capabilities. More fundamental rethinking of organizational design tends to be left aside. There is also little emphasis in his approach on how to sustain the development actions initiated through the search process.

Another stream of activity centered on searching revolves around Cornell University. A program of the Cornell School of Industrial and Labor Relations called Programs for Employment and Work Place Systems, inspired originally by William Foote Whyte, explored searching using connections to Morten Levin and the Norwegian University of Technology and Science in Trondheim (Whyte, 1994, p. 307). Given the directness of the connection, the Cornell approach is quite close to the Norwegian one and embodies a stronger link between the Norwegian tradition and U.S. academia than Weisbord's.

Search Conferences as Structured Change Processes

Although we obviously have our preferences, we emphasize that searching should not be equated with just one method or approach; there is no one right way of running a search conference. Practitioners vary in approach and skills. In addition, good practitioners are constantly developing and altering their own approaches as they learn more about the processes involved and gain more skills. There is no reason to grant any one of the founders of this methodology the control of a correct approach. Although we argue that certain processes are necessary for the arena to be conceptualized as a search conference, we do not agree with M. Emery (1993) that there is only one way of doing search conferences.

There are limits to our flexibility. Co-optation of searching is a real problem. Searching, like Lewinian AR and sociotechnical systems work before it, has become fashionable. Far too many processes are now labeled as search conferences while negating the necessary focus on participatory and liberating social change. This might be a consequence of poor planning or of lack of understanding for what a search actually is. A worse situation is the increasingly frequent use of search conferences to create "magical moments" for the participants by giving them an illusion of participating in real change processes, while the underlying intention of the process is merely to reduce internal pressure for change. To focus this problem more sharply and to provide the reader with a more detailed understanding of search processes, we will now discuss the main elements of a search conference as the approach emerged from our own practice.

When Is a Process a Search?

In our view, six major elements must be present if a group process is to be characterized as a search:

- Creating a shared history and letting every participant understand how the world looks according to other groups of participants

- Creating a shared vision about what is a desirable future or solution to the focal problem of the group

- Creating a view of what would be the probable future if nothing were done; sometimes this perspective might be integrated into the work on desirable future

- Identifying action plans for addressing the focal problem

- Creating a collective prioritization process in which participants choose among alternative action plans

- Initiating concrete change activity and structuring a follow-up process aimed at sharing achievements and learning

These six elements differ in content and structure. Working on developing a history is very different from using the creativity necessary for developing new ideas for action plans. In addition, throughout a search, there is a complex interplay between plenary sessions and small group work that creates a new social structure. Another important aspect of searches is how the fairly strict structure and rules create a ritual process that helps shape valuable arenas for dialogue.

Herbst (1980) illustrates the search process as a dual track. Figure 9.1 conveys an overall conception of the search as a generative and

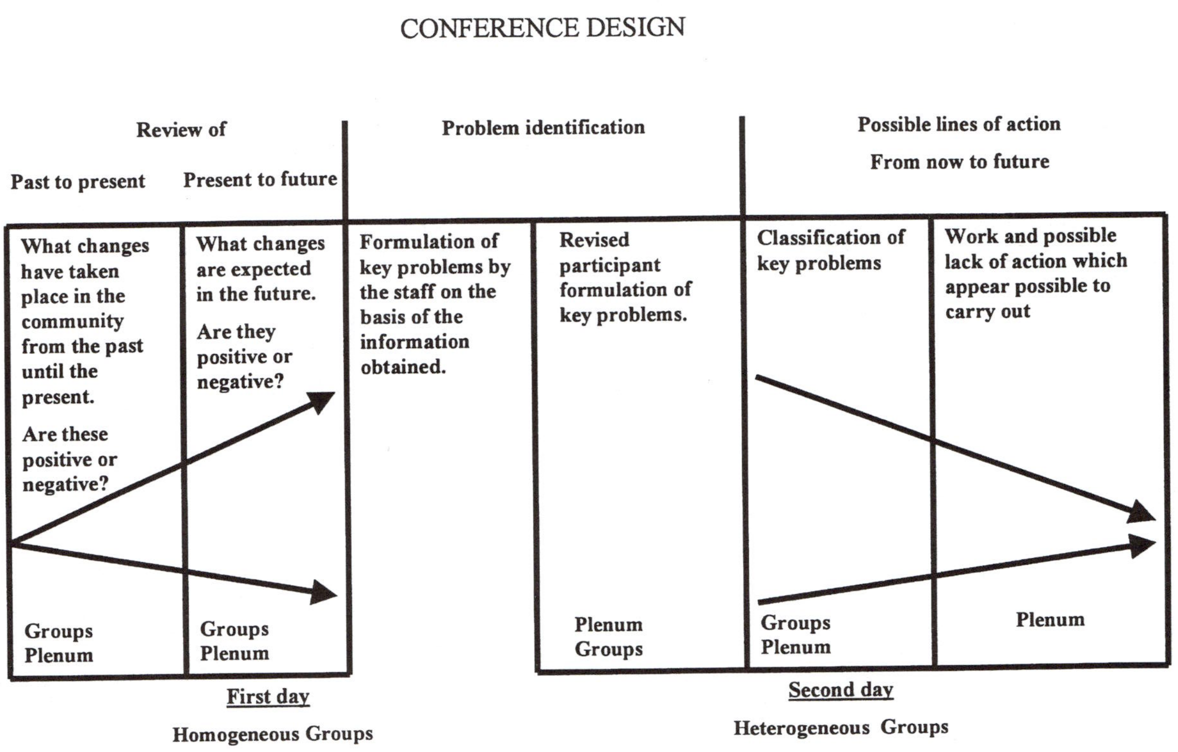

CONFERENCE DESIGN

Figure 9.1. Herbst's Dual Track Search Process

163

creative process (building shared history and visions, generating creative action possibilities, reflecting on the feasibility of action possibilities, and finally working out priorities among the possible action items).

The work process in a search conference involves both plenary presentations and discussions and small group work. These small groups, either homogeneous or mixed in background and interests, are used to prepare ideas and materials for plenary discussions and, thus, to give voice to as many of the participants as possible.

Preparing for the Search

Many roads lead to a search conference. In some cases, the local actors are familiar with search conferences and accordingly know what they are looking for. In this situation, the task for the initiators is to find a facilitator to take on the job. A standard bureaucratic method is simply to call for proposals from various professional search conference managers. We think that searching as a form of AR demands skills and engagement that reach beyond the work styles of most conventional consultants, however.

Another road to a search conference is for an outsider involved in local development work to convince the local actors that a search is appropriate. In this situation, the local actors do not necessarily understand what a search is. The challenge for the outsider is to convey an understanding of the search process and to show that it potentially can help the local actors. Even so, the process of launching a search depends on mutual trust because it is difficult to convey a fair picture of what a search is unless people have experienced one or have seen the positive effects of a search on another group.

Planning and Executing a Search

Commissioning the search. The first step in searching is working with the local actors who want to commission a search. This discussion is important for many reasons. The initial question that motivates local people may not necessarily be the most fundamental one for their group or may not be stated in a way that can lead to a productive search. Because searching is a form of cogenerative learning, ample time must be devoted to discussion with those commissioning the search so that everyone has a clear idea what the process is all about.

Because the process aims to create mutual learning opportunities, the facilitator should challenge the initial problem focus and in turn be challenged by the local definitions of the problem at hand. Through this dialogue, the resulting mutual understanding will provide the definition of the search problem used to plan the actual search conference.

Identifying the participants. The next step is to identify potential participants. For searches, an ideal size is between 20 and 30 persons, but searches have been done successfully with up to 70 participants, and recently some linked searches involving a number of groups concerned with the same issues have been carried out involving hundreds of participants (Robert Rich, 1998, personal communication).

The proper identification of relevant stakeholders is vital. They are identified as a function of the focus of the search. Every effort has to be made to locate individuals and groups that have a legitimate interest or say in the matter under consideration. This is a complex procedure that usually begins with the points of view of those who commissioned the search. But this group is rarely fully representative of the stakeholders. The facilitator must seek to manage the process of inclusion to be certain that as many relevant stakeholder interests as possible are present.

This begins with discussions with those commissioning the search, but quickly the process of finding and inviting relevant participants becomes a form of network analysis. Starting with names and groups provided by the start-up group, each new potential participant contacted is also asked for recommendations about others or other groups who should be invited to the search. Continuing along these lines, an emergent selection of participants is established. Often the scope of those included expands and contracts a few times until a tolerable balance has been achieved.

Inviting the participants. When the facilitator judges that a suitable group of people has been identified, invitations must be made. In our opinion, the best way to do this is to combine the invitation with an interview. This makes sense because the facilitator needs to acquire as much knowledge of the participants, their backgrounds, and their institutional contexts as possible to be an effective search facilitator. This provides an understanding of persons and the situation that permits the facilitator to make knowledge-based decisions regarding the structure and process of the search while it is taking place. At the same time, this invitational interview is valuable as a way of informing participants about what a search conference is. This can both inform and motivate the potential participants. Occasionally, constraints require delegating this task to the planning group. As in everything else, the better prepared the facilitator and participants are, the more likely the search will be successful.

Logistical support. We will not go into detail here about the material support structures for searches, but a good setting and logistical support are critically important. The search depends on a group learning about itself, and so the setting must be at least somewhat retreat-like, permitting the participants to separate themselves from their daily lives briefly and focus on each other and the problem at hand intensively. It is important to find a locale that has a big enough room for plenary discussions. The room needs to be large enough for the participants to move freely around, and the walls should be filled with flip charts displaying the work in progress. The setting must also contain ample small group working spaces. An area to collect and maintain materials is important as well.

In preparing a search, close cooperation with a group of local participants is a prerequisite. This creates a very good basis for inviting members or the whole planning group to serve as cofacilitators. This has the effect of training local people to handle future searches by themselves, but it has also an important democratic effect by giving local people a say in decisions regarding the design of the conference.

The environment should be as free as possible from the ordinary daily demands the participants face. Finding an off-site location is invaluable. This creates the opportunity for people to get to know each other socially during the moments the search itself is not running, and it creates a distance from everyday life that enhances the opportunities for reflection and concentration on the issues of the search.

Stages in a Search Conference

A typical search process takes about 2 days, though the length of time is flexible. The argument for using this much time is that searches depend on collective learning processes, processes that do not move fast. A shorter search might too easily fall into the trap of becoming a quick fix and violate the basic aims of creating a sustainable learning process.

The search begins with a plenary on shared history, followed by sessions on the ideal and probable futures. This usually ends the first day. The second day begins with the development of action strategies, the creation of task forces, and the search ends with the planning of future meetings.

Creating a Shared History

The first step in searching is to create a shared history. This is not to say that a unified understanding of the group's historical roots must exist. Rather, the focus is that all participants should be aware of the other actors' understanding of the relevant history. The core idea is to show how multifaceted and heterogeneous the history is; this is obvious after all points of view have been heard. Most groups at a search already have a history together, but the search-generated history is different because it actively seeks out the experiences and views that are often overlooked or actively suppressed in everyday life.

One common way to initiate the search is to have a well-respected member of the group draw up a kind of broad-view historical sketch. Then each group of participants is given the opportunity to work out its own version of the history. These are combined in plenary sessions until together the whole group has developed a more heterogeneous position that satisfies it as a whole.

Another way to develop a shared history is based on the creative use of drawing and writing. In the plenary room, a wall area is covered with paper to write and draw on. It can be a line of separate sheets or a long sheet of butcher-block paper (Martin & Rich, 1994). On this surface, a very rough timeline is drawn, starting on the left with an initiating point and continuing up to the present. Participants are then given the opportunity to add drawings or events anywhere they have something to contribute. After this, the whole group listens as each person who has added something explains it. Through this approach, participants can learn and build on each other's interpretation of history, and the whole process creates a new cogenerated history.

Creating a Shared Vision

The general aim of this part of the search process is to create a shared position about a desirable and feasible future. This is built from the contrast between an ideal future and a probable one.

An ideal future can be a vision of how the local community or organization should look by the end of the next decade. The core issues here are to have the participants surface their views and share their sense of what a desirable future is. This is again a collective process, where participants engage in a discourse using both small groups and plenaries to create a sort of consensus. What often emerges is a general agreement that allows room for individual interpretations and actions.

Although absolute consensus is not necessary or desired, there must be a tolerable level of mutual understanding and agreement. A search conference can produce useful results only where there is a minimum common understanding and consensus on goals. Martin (1997) argues a harder line in seeing that strong differences about the ideal future make it less likely that a search conference will produce practical results.

One way to carry out the process of defining the ideal future is to start with small, relatively homogeneous groups and to ask each to identify 5 or 10 important goals to reach on the search issue. Each group then presents its view in plenary, and this creates the basis for a discussion among all the participants. The search facilitator must see to it that the plenary discussion gradually focuses on issues that participants can agree on. This working consensus is important because it will be the reference point for the later action teams.

The probable future is arrived at by the same technique. The groups are asked to develop their sense of what will happen if they do not take action to improve their future. This part of the process is sensitive because the negative view of the future is usually easier to articulate and often corresponds to the participants' worst fears. We think groups must deal openly with these fears because naming their worst fears contributes to the sense of the need for real change.

Once the search group has identified the probable future, the kind of bubbling energy that is often associated with the history and ideal future seems to evaporate. This reality check is part of the process, and the facilitator should do nothing to make it easier or more tolerable.

Indeed, we believe that it is important for each participant to experience directly the implications of not taking action. This is the basis for making a subsequent commitment to action. To reinforce this, usually the day ends at this point, with the participants left to their own ruminations about the ideal and probable futures.

Identifying Action Plans

Given an overall understanding of desirable goals and the results of no action, the next day begins with the development of action ideas and strategies that support the attainment of valued goals. This process builds on the creative capacity of the participants. It is important to encourage participants to let their creative capacity come out in the open. Too often in everyday life, we experience very low demands on our personal creativity; in a search, it is a good investment to devote plenty of time to encouraging this kind of creativity.

To do this, certain rules must be observed. Criticism of the ideas of others is not permitted. Participants may ask each other for clarification, but all ideas are treated as worthy of consideration. No one is permitted to dominate the airtime or to shut others down. The facilitator must be alert to gender, age, and ideological differences and try to keep the dialogue as open as possible. One very good way to encourage creativity at this point is to set up small groups with participants who differ in experience and position in the local community or organization. Members work on developing strategies and action plans that are subsequently presented in plenary session. In the plenary, the participants are encouraged not to criticize the ideas presented, though they are free to ask for clarification.

Prioritizing Ideas

If the creative process has worked, by this time the assembled group has generated many options for action from which to choose. All these aim to reach the ideal future. It is in the nature of the creative process leading up to this, however, that these ideas are not in any particular order. To be worked with in the large group, they must be ordered in some way. We believe this is a task for the search facilitators.

Often, in the structure of a search, the first day is coming to an end at this point. Facilitators can use the late evening to work on creating categories of action items that can be grouped together. This is a very important task because it shapes the ground for the prioritization process. This is one of the key skills the facilitator brings to the process. Facilitators must have the ability to understand the local culture, to be intellectually capable of distinguishing between alternatives, and to understand similarities. Although the facilitator's synthesis is never final, it provides the basis for the next day's prioritization process.

The next day begins with the presentation of the facilitator's organization of action items. After questions of clarification and modification have been addressed, an open plenary discussion ensues to create some understanding of how diverse the participants' views are. If common core issues easily emerge, the move toward setting priorities will be straightforward. If no clear and unified view emerges in the plenary, it then makes sense to redivide the participants into small groups to work on the issues. Each group, for instance, might be given the task of developing a list of the three to five most desirable action issues. This will then be presented in plenary, and the group as a whole can see if a possible road to making collective decisions has emerged.

Concrete Change Activity Through Volunteer Action Teams

The final stage of the search is the creation of action teams responsible for addressing the agreed-on action issues. This is the acid test of the prioritization process. Here participants vote with their feet by signing up on sheets where the key action items have been listed. Usually, some of the issues identified by the participants as important will not attract any sign-ups. Although reflecting on these is worthwhile, the purpose of a search is to define not an ideal world of action but a world in which people are willing to commit to concrete actions to solve problems. There are always more plans than energy or courage to deal with them.

To conclude the search conference, the newly created action teams have a brief planning session. Each develops a plan for the first part of their work. This plan should integrate a specification of the goals for the group, a detailed schedule including concrete meeting dates, and the selection of a temporary convenor of the group

The participants as a group also must commit to specific general follow-up meetings. An ideal situation is to have the process, including the search conference itself, last for a year. General follow-up meetings every 2 to 3 months keep track of the development process by allowing participants to share the results of the different task forces. This can lead to increased learning opportunities for everyone, creating collective ownership and control over the change effort.

Once again, we want to reinforce the point that search practices can vary considerably. The length of the phases, the numbers of facilitators and participants, the configurations of small groups, the degree of emphasis on the rules of discussion all differ because facilitators differ or because the same facilitator skillfully adjusts the approach to the developing dynamics of particular groups. Thus, searching is not a recipe but a highly skilled, cogenerative AR process. Efforts to treat it as a recipe result in ineffective action and processes that are misrepresented as participatory.

CONCLUSIONS

Search conferences are only one of the methods that can be used in pragmatic AR processes. Many of the other dimensions of our approach are presented in Chapters 4 through 7. Of course, the whole toolkit of social research is available, if a community or organization cogenerates a need for social research methods. Quantitative methods, qualitative methods, mixed methods, particular techniques (T groups, group dynamics exercises, simulations, force field analyses, variance matrix analysis, participatory design workshops, role-playing, scripting, narrating) can be effective, but are appropriate only if they are deployed within the context of a collaboratively defined set of objectives and if the local participants are helped to deploy them and to analyze the results critically. The core of the pragmatic AR approach is to respect the combined research, action, and democratization goals of AR and to keep the conversation going with the participants. This also one of the lessons emerging from the review of the six cases presented in Chapters 3 and 8. As powerful and valuable as we think searching is, and as good as other tools can be in particular contexts, we doubt that pragmatic AR can be used to mediate situations where some of the participants are committed to the elimination of some of the possible approaches. If the AR facilitator is not observant or skilled enough, a pragmatic AR process can be turned into a playground for the powerful and can further inhibit democratization.

Notes

1. We are using the term *pragmatic* in two ways. We intend it to refer to the philosophical traditions of pragmatism and neopragmatism discussed in Part 2, but we also intend to evoke the ordinary language meaning of pragmatic, which is practical or practically useful.

2. It is important to point out that the use of the term *search conference* has become conventional in the field but is quite misleading. In ordinary speech, we understand conferences to be conventionally planned and preprogrammed activities with speakers and listeners. Search conferences center on the active involvement of and control by participants. Although we wish the terminology were different, it is not.

CHAPTER

10

Empowerment and Liberation
*Southern Participatory Action Research and
Contemporary Feminist Analyses*

In this chapter, we blend the presentation of southern[1] participatory action research (PAR) and contemporary feminism because the approaches share a number of common issues. But they are not the same, nor do they coexist without strong crosscurrents. For example, some feminists have been appropriately critical of southern PAR's androcentrism (Maguire, 1996). We think that bringing the two approaches together is useful, however, because they share a number of major underlying features centering on the analysis of political economy and praxis. More important, we believe that feminism is mainly responsible for resurrecting a concern with southern PAR in particular and with action research (AR) in general. The concerted, anti-canonical, antipositivist feminist critique of contemporary social science provided the opening for the reinitiation of debates about AR in general. Feminism revitalized the politics associated with southern PAR, and this effort has grown into a general reconsideration of AR.

This is not all good news from the point of view of some feminists, who see AR as parasitical on their efforts, viewing the discussion of AR as an appropriation or, worse, a co-optation of their efforts. Although this reaction is understandable, particularly when AR practitioners announce ideas and agendas derived from feminism without realizing or recognizing the source, we do not accept this view. On the other hand, some southern PAR practitioners see feminism largely as a "northern" white woman's movement that co-opts and softens the social transformation that necessarily requires solidarity among the poor. We do not think the politics of either AR or feminism are well served by combat among practitioners, which distracts attention from the shared goals of fundamental social change. We signal southern PAR and feminism's contributions to the many streams making up AR, and believe both groups would profit from a more sustained encounter with the methods and practices of other kinds of AR practitioners.

The diversity and heterogeneity of approaches to participation are nowhere more evident than in these AR analysis-intervention approaches centering on political economy and praxis. This is a rich and differentiated set of discourses and practices directly relevant to AR as a whole. In a single chapter, we cannot reference more than a handful of the approaches. By making a selection, we offend those not mentioned, and we risk caricaturing those we do discuss. The alternative would be worse, however, because it would continue the historical pattern of mutual ignorance and *ad hominem* critique among northern, southern, and feminist action researchers.

◄O►

PARTICIPATORY RESEARCH AND PARTICIPATORY AR

We begin with an analysis of *participatory research* (PR) and *participatory action research* (PAR), a set of theories and practices that came into existence as a critique and practice of liberation set in the context of a model of class struggle as practiced primarily in poor countries and with impoverished groups in rich countries. Criss-crossing them and extending into other areas of theory and practice in both poor and rich countries are a variety of feminist analyses, including feminist approaches to poverty and oppression.

The writers and schools mentioned here do not form a neat set. These approaches differ substantially in their views of power, social stratification, and poverty. But they do share a set of fundamental disagreements with conventional and hegemonic approaches to development and the rationalization of organizational structures. All these approaches are built on a sharply political analysis of power relations and the affirmation that significant social change occurs only if power has changed hands and reduced the oppression. Simply getting along better or mediating conflicts is not enough to constitute sustainable social change.

Terminology is always complex, and nowhere more than here. *Southern* is an ambiguous distinction that has clearer moral content than geographical referents. In invoking the south, this group of practitioners symbolizes its alignment with the poor and oppressed of the world, wherever they are found. There are also terminological problems with *participatory action research* and *participatory research*. For some, these terms are different. For others, they are two names for the same general kinds of practice. For still others, it is necessary to add the term *southern* to distinguish these practices from what has, unfortunately we think, been called participatory action research in the north, forms of practice that many believe to be co-opted and collaborationist with power holders.[2] We have held on to the adjective southern in this chapter mainly to emphasize the explicit political intentions of these forms of practice and to show our respect for these political agendas.

Democratization as Liberation

For many thinkers in industrialized countries, democratization is an ongoing process that furthers the inclusion of groups in self-determining political processes (i.e., a standard liberal view). Others in the north and many in poor countries view the liberation of oppressed people as the sine qua non of democratization, however. Rather than seeing poverty as the result of a lack of inclusion, insufficient education, and inadequate infrastructure, these thinker-actors see poverty as the systemic outcome of the oppression of many by wealthy and powerful domestic and international elites. Their view of the world rests on the belief that inequalities and injustices will not vanish simply because a group of people decides it wants something better or because a well-intentioned outsider comes in to encourage change.

From the southern vantage point, international development projects, whatever marginal changes they may create in poor countries and poor regions, are not the road to meaningful social change. The only serious answer to poverty and oppression is a fundamental alteration in the distribution of power. This sharp and unshakable political focus characterizes southern PAR approaches and, ultimately, links them closely to radical feminism.

These approaches rest on varieties of neo-Marxist views of the world, stressing class conflict, the role of modes of production, the commodization of labor, and the depredations of international capitalism. These are key elements in explaining and maintaining the poverty of most countries in Latin America and Africa, parts of Asia, and the miserably poor parts of most rich, capitalist countries. They also explain the current increasing gap between rich and poor in rich countries.

A logical consequence of these views is that southern PAR approaches usually begin with a study of the distribution of wealth and the consequent distribution of exposure to risk. Existing public institutions are distrusted and generally viewed as protectors of an unjust order, unless a detailed analysis of the case shows otherwise. The suspect institutions include schools and universities, churches, governments and governmental agencies, most intergovernmental international development programs, and businesses.

Thus, work in this approach proceeds from an external analysis of the conditions of poverty and oppression to the design of interventions in local settings. This local intervention often (but not always) begins as a kind of mobilization effort, with the outsiders playing the role of consciousness raisers and catalysts for local discussions. Sometimes, this takes the form of the outsider coming in to support insiders who have already begun to take these steps. In other cases, the outsider arrives with the agenda of provoking and organizing change.

The work involves the external agent in preliminary analyses of the causes of the local situation that are fed back to local people to create the space and appetite for their own analysis of the causes of their situation. From this analysis, plans of action are derived. In some situations, southern PAR takes the form of adult education or literacy programs where the instruction centers on discussion and analysis of the conditions leading to local poverty and oppression. There are many other paths to follow, including working with nongovernmental organizations, churches, and many different kinds of local actors.

Unlike standard revolutionary praxis or orthodox labor organizing tactics, southern PAR values and relies much more on the knowledge, analyses, and efforts of local people. Rather than treating them only as victims (though their victimization is not denied), southern PAR practitioners build their work on respect for the integrity and resiliency of local people and their culture. Their premise is that local knowledge of the situation is authentic, detailed, and valuable, an idea that many external organizers, who are sure they know what is good for the "people," routinely ignore. Southern PAR processes begin with a challenge that is initially addressed by bringing groups of local people together to discuss and analyze their situation. From these analyses emerge agendas for research and social change, but these agendas are the joint product of the outsider and the local people.

This focus on local knowledge is essential to southern PAR. Although local knowledge is occasionally treated romantically in this approach, the underlying aim is to promote respect for it and, through this, to level the relationship between the outside agents and local people in a way that opens them up to collaborative efforts. The fact that knowledge is local and grows out of intense personal experiences makes it respectable and encourages outsiders to listen to what it says and to try to build on what it offers. Put another way, this approach to local knowledge credits the poor and oppressed with having intelligence and analytical capabilities that are generally ignored. Thus, it necessarily explains their poverty, not in terms of their ignorance or laziness, but in terms of their oppression. In this regard, the approach is very much in line with the many other approaches to AR discussed in this book.

Building from this local knowledge and the interaction between the outsider's knowledge and local people's frames of reference, a dialogue begins that can transform the views of both. The outsider's view is necessarily abstract and often wrong about a number of the concrete impediments to local action. The insider's view is often so concrete (and occasionally homogenized by local activists) that it seems to offer only an explanation for poverty but no scope for action. The dialogue between the two perspectives can create a shared sense of locations where practical interventions are possible.

When this point is reached, the analysis often gives way to a focus on research. The outsider and the local people share some frames of reference about the problems faced and can assess and mobilize their resources for confronting them. Because ignorance (backed up by impoverishment) is one of the strongest weapons in oppressive systems, this phase frequently involves training local people in certain research methods and helping them gain confidence in their ability to investigate together the sources of their problems. They often must gather, analyze, and present evidence that supports their claims against the wishes of powerful business and political interests. Research is a weapon in this struggle.

Research training is never abstracted from the context. In the tradition of adult education, the focus of training is the concrete and immediate problems that people face. Sometimes literacy training is an element in this process. In other situations, local people become social researchers by using tape recorders and video cameras to document what they are doing. No matter what the form, the message is the same. Local people are intelligent, capable of rational analysis of their situation, and able to conduct research aimed at improving their conditions. Research gives them a new voice to use in their struggles.

Throughout this process, the outside expert plays a mixed role as instigator, process manager, advocate for groups not yet fully included, trainer in research methods, and, often, chronicler of the activities. This is a complex, high-profile role that contains many built-in conflicts. As an educated person with the wealth to move around at will, this individual is necessarily seen as a representative of a category of outsiders with whom experience has generally been negative and oppressive. Even when this barrier is overcome to some degree, there are still behavioral routines to be dealt with: behaviors of obeisance to educated outsiders (linked with hiding information about local situations), hostility to these outsiders, lack of confidence in local abilities, local power arrangements that are threatened by these new coalitions, racism, and so on.

As the chronicler of the process, the outsider often is in the position to influence unduly how the process is conceptualized and presented externally. If the insiders are at risk for attempting to change an oppressive system, the outsider may be viewed by authorities as a troublemaker, revolutionary, or even terrorist. The process is complex, often uneven, and occasionally dangerous.

Despite these difficulties, there is much to show for efforts that have been conducted in this way. One of the most important and well-known practitioners is Orlando Fals Borda. Building on his own commitments as an intellectual and an academic on the side of democratization and social justice, Fals Borda moved out of the university system into direct action in rural communities in Latin America. Fals Borda has provided a public record of both his thinking and some of the many projects he and his colleagues have engaged in (Fals Borda & Rahman, 1991; Hall, Gillette, & Tandon, 1982; Park, Brydon-Miller, Hall, & Jackson, 1993). Not only do his writings document a theory of practice and a set of cases of interventions that have had desirable effects, but he has taken the attempt further by linking his own views and experiences to those of other practitioners working in Latin America, Asia, and Africa. As a result, through Fals Borda one can gain a view of the practice of liberation-oriented PAR that is applied to the lives of the poor.

Other practitioners who have written effectively for a general audience on these issues are L. David Brown and Rajesh Tandon (1993). They attempt to clarify in a helpful way the value of some distinctions between orthodox research, participatory research, and PAR, and they base their analysis on long familiarity with concrete situations of poverty and oppression around the world. Hall, Gillette, and Tandon (1982), Freire (1970), Park, Brydon-Miller, Hall, and Jackson (1993), and Gabarrón and Hernández (1994) can all be read with profit. Some of these approaches are discussed in more detail in Chapter 13, "Educational Strategies."

North-South Co-Optation

The reader should be aware of the problematic relationships among southern and northern practitioners. The recent rapid resurgence of AR in the north has caused many southern activists to worry legitimately about co-optation of their perspectives in the north for the purpose of obscuring and blunting democratic initiatives. This is not an idle concern. We have all witnessed the co-optation of what were originally left-wing critiques and methods by oppressive forces (e.g., participatory development, sustainable development, human rights, and feminism, all of which have been relentlessly subjected to efforts at co-optation and domestication).

For example, in the private sector in industrialized countries, one way of achieving the currently fashionable goal of total quality management is by involving the work force more fully in the life of the business. This is often framed as increasing participation, and recently, some conventional organizational development consultants have begun calling their work PAR. In most cases, participation means only that workers and other subordinates take on greater and broader responsibilities while gaining little or no greater control over decision making. Often, their share of the profits is not increased. Under these conditions, allusions to participation and to AR are inauthentic because they are not built on an intention to democratize society and increase social justice. One of the greatest benefits to northern practitioners arising from interactions with southern practitioners is to make us more alert to the processes of co-optation.

Having acknowledged the value of the southern perspective, though, we do not accept an equation between work in the north and co-optation and work in the south and freedom from it. If we believed that all AR in the north was necessarily co-opted, we would not be AR practitioners. Our own experience is that AR in core sectors of industrialized societies can engage issues of participation and democratization as seriously as they are engaged in the south. In these cases, the strategies differ to a degree (reflecting different levels of literacy and poverty), the issues are focused differently (advocacy, public awareness, use of existing institutions for new ends), and often the results involve ameliorative rather than revolutionary change. Still, the social changes are real, and the analyses of power relations and oppression are not dissimilar. Being oppressed by a wealthy group of executives, even if the worker has a tolerable standard of living, is still being oppressed. To ignore or deny the rights of these oppressed people simply because there are poorer people elsewhere in the world would be callous.

Situations of oppression in parts of the south are terrifyingly bad in many cases. Poverty and oppression under conditions of profound governmental corruption, the use of a national military to oppress local communities, the interests of foreign and domestic capital in maintaining a cheap labor force, ongoing colonialism, illiteracy, and starvation all make the problems of the north appear less severe. But the racially oppressed, the homeless, the drug addicted, the abused, and the illiterate in the north are oppressed, as are the workers in factories run by executives who use participation as a cover-up for speed-ups, downsizing, and union busting, as are middle managers who are being replaced with cheaper labor that is more easily manipulated. Oppression is oppression everywhere it is found, south or north.

FEMINIST ANALYSES OF INEQUALITY AND DEVELOPMENT

In our teaching experience over the last decade, after we have laid out the basic perspectives of AR, female students ask about the relationship between feminism and AR. They correctly perceive that feminist views deal with many of the same issues found in AR: a critique of positivism, an analysis of power relations, a respect for the knowledge of the "silenced," a critique of canonical positions, and a focus on transformative praxis. They also voice fears that AR is co-opting the analyses of feminism without attribution and possibly without sufficient reformist intentions. These concerns merit attention. Without a meaningful alliance between feminists and action researchers, neither group is very likely to succeed

Feminism and AR are not competing frameworks. AR and feminism share underlying ethical and political commitments to democracy and social justice. And it is important to remember that AR is not a theory but an approach to praxis that uses any and all tools that the coresearchers find helpful. As we have said repeatedly, we view AR as a pragmatic combination of analyses and methods for linking elements of participation, action, and research in concrete situations. We don't need fewer and purer tools, but more and more diverse approaches to meet the endless challenges of inequality and oppression.

By the same token, AR should not seek to domesticate feminism or to make polite gestures of incorporation. This is not about the politics of professional inclusion. It is about figuring out how to create a better world. AR should continue to grow, as it has in the past, by learning from feminism's profound and detailed analyses of gendered oppression and efforts at gender liberation. The critiques of positivism, essential-ism, oppression, and the separation of theory and practice that have been central to feminism are essential to AR as well.

Elements of Feminism That Are Particularly Important in AR

Most feminists begin by viewing oppression as the usual state of affairs and build their praxis on the belief that the status quo must be overturned in favor of a more liberating set of conditions. Feminists have long struggled to gain recognition for their issues, to persuade a larger segment of the world population that the rights of women are routinely trampled on and that the essentialized gendering of human beings is a form of oppression. Feminists affirm that democratic social change is necessary for these evils to be corrected, not just polite conversations about being better people.

In our view, feminists have done more than anyone else in the past two decades to undermine the authoritarian paradigm built into con-ventional social science and social programs. A good review of this contribution can be found in Iris Young's (1990) *Justice and the Politics of Difference*. Young persuasively links oppression to the welfare state, the distributive justice paradigm, and positivist social science in a way that is uniquely informed by feminism but is also directly applicable to the struggle of AR to overcome the ideological suppression of AR by conventional social research.

The feminist critique of the notion of value-free research has been devastating because feminists have been able to reveal repeatedly how such value-free research generally embodies gender-specific values (Fox Keller, 1985; Lather, 1991). It is a short step from this notion to the general notion that value-free research covers up all kinds of oppressive social arrangements under the mask of an impartial, scientific ideology, an essential component of AR.

Feminist approaches also stress the value of diversity. In focusing on the conditions of the underrepresentation of women, they reveal the white, male, middle-class center of gravity of most social theory and social policy. They have demonstrated this as effectively in industrialized countries as they have in poor countries (Sims Feldstein & Poats, 1990).

Neo-Marxism and feminism have also found a useful point of contact in their focus on the actual processes of production. Feminists have worked hard to reveal the unfairly compensated and central role of women in the productive apparatus of society, contributing strongly to the critique of advanced capitalism and its triumphalistic ideologies (Swantz, 1985).

Feminists, dealing routinely with oppression and silencing, have developed a powerful commitment to a view from below, to hearing the voices of the silenced, and to bringing these voices to the table (Mies, 1990). Here the coincidence between feminist analysis with a strong emphasis on life history and local knowledge and AR is self-evident. Both seek to end the silencing of so many, gendered silence in one case and class-based silence in the other.

In poor countries (as well as in industrialized ones), feminists have taken a strongly actor-oriented approach to issues such as environmental protection, welfare services, and development programs. The watchword is *gender-responsible* research, in whatever sector it may be (van den Hombergh, 1993). They have persuasively pointed out that, without systematic attention to gender, the perspectives of women will be ignored in the ordinary course of events. The parallelism between this and the emphasis on local knowledge in AR, based on the experience that without the affirmation of its value, local knowledge will be discarded and oppression will continue in the same vein, is evident.

Thus, for us, the relationship between feminism and AR is complementary. Not surprisingly, we think the benefits flow in both directions. Without the feminist onslaught on the centers of power, we do not believe that the kind of space we occupy as action researchers would exist. At the same time, we think there is scope for both the enhancement of feminist perspectives within AR and the improvement of feminist practice through attention to the many intervention techniques that have been developed in the different AR approaches. Feminists do often engage in AR, but there are only a handful of systematic attempts to link the two perspectives. Among these, we refer briefly to the work of Patricia Maguire, Michelle Fine, and Patti Lather.

Patricia Maguire (1987), in her widely read *Doing Participatory Research: A Feminist Approach,* articulates a combination of feminist agendas, participatory research practice, and the personal experiential dimension of her work. This book speaks better than most to the combination of feminism, participation, and social praxis by using issues from feminism and participation but staying resolutely focused on the social problem Maguire is trying to solve. In subsequent writing,

Maguire (1994, 1996) deepens her critique of a number of kinds of AR practice, arguing effectively that the very notion of participatory research is absurd without the systematic incorporation of feminist perspectives. Though the argument is less developed, she also believes that feminist research must move into the realm of AR to extend its own scope. Thus, Maguire argues for the necessary and productive interdependence of the approaches and issues and persuasively argues for invitations to collaboration across these traditions.

Many others call for some kind of interlinking of feminism and AR. Patti Lather (1991), in *Getting Smart: Feminist Research and Pedagogy With/in the Postmodern,* argues that the principal contributions of feminism have been the critique of positivism, the demonstration that all forms of inquiry are value laden, opening up the possibility of a critical social science, pressing for the politics of empowerment, and rising to the challenges of postmodernism. Her ambitious combination of perspectives strives to get beyond the dilemmas of postpositivism, poststructuralism, and postmodernism through an activist social science. She makes activist research a core element. Lather offers action researchers a wealth of analytical weapons and perspectives.

Other feminist thinkers advocate varying combinations of feminism and AR. Joyappa and Martin (1996) argue for a combination of feminist research and participatory research to storm the barricades of American adult education, and Reinharz (1992) explores the possibilities of what she calls "feminist action research," which links activism and scholarship. The impossibility of having a feminist perspective without a commitment to social change is what links these activists and what links them to AR more generally. In *Disruptive Voices,* Michelle Fine (1992) links feminism, organizational interventions in a variety of organizational systems, and social activism. A number of the examples she provides move feminist research in the direction of cogenerative inquiry aimed at social change.

Many more feminist thinkers deserve mention (e.g., Field Belenky, Clinchy, Goldberger, & Tarule, 1997; Gilligan, 1982), but we hope to have said enough to open up a broader discussion. Even this cursory review suggests the importance of increasing the frequency and detail of communication between feminist researchers and representatives of the many other approaches to AR. We share many agendas, and we think it is clear that AR is not possible without feminist perspectives. In return, action researchers can offer feminists a greater awareness of a variety of intervention and group process techniques developed in the industrial democracy movement, in collaborative inquiry, and elsewhere. These techniques can help harness the feminist commitment to activism to well-known techniques for working collaboratively in groups toward social change goals.

CONCLUSIONS

A great many more approaches to the issues of empowerment and liberation could be mentioned. Our intention is only to say enough to persuade the reader that these perspectives can and should be linked productively and to make this assertion concrete by providing some general outlines of the perspectives that inform southern PAR and feminism. We also hope to have persuaded the reader that there is a south in the north and that approaches to AR informed by southern perspectives are as relevant to the different conditions in the north as they are to the south. Southern perspectives are particularly valuable in reminding northern practitioners of the ever-present dangers of co-optation and triumphalism when participatory language is captured for nonparticipatory purposes. Finally, we argued for an intensification of the discussion about the relationship between feminism and AR as a necessary condition for the success of both.

Notes

1. The term *southern* is widely used and quite ambiguous. It refers to critical, liberationist perspectives and practices aimed at alleviating poverty, exploitation, and oppression every-where. Given the overwhelming poverty of the Third World, this term has been most frequently associated with work done in poor countries. Most southern practitioners recognize that there is a "south" in the "north," that is, in wealthy countries.

2. An example of the kinds of conflicts that bedevil us can be found in Whyte and Whyte's (1991) use of the term *participatory action research* to announce the approach to AR he was developing. Though in the book bearing this title, cases from the developing world are included, the overall politics of the approach are not informed by a liberationist framework, and the prior use of the term *participatory action research* by southern practitioners was not mentioned. This kind of use of language inhibits communication among AR practitioners.

11

Action Science and Organizational Learning

By singling out action science and organizational learning for an extended treatment, we argue for its significance as one line of development of the action research (AR) approach of Lewin and pragmatic philosophy and for its utility in current AR practice. We think action science embodies one of the most significant and systematic attempts to build AR in a way that respects both the need for scientific clarity and practical utility. We are not unbiased proponents, however, as our critique will show. Action science is also important in this book because discussing it permits us to include an approach to AR that has a decidedly psychodynamic emphasis, a component of AR that has been present for at least 50 years.

The principal architects of action science and organizational learning are Chris Argyris and Donald Schön, both prolific writers and renowned teachers. Argyris has written on these themes from many different perspectives over the years (1974, 1980, 1985, 1993; Argyris & Schön, 1978, 1996). We have elected to concentrate on the contents of three major works, *Action Science: Concepts, Methods, and Skills for Research and Intervention* (Argyris, Putnam, & McClain Smith, 1985), a core essay on the action science approach; and two books on organizational learning coauthored with Donald Schön, *Organizational Learning* (1978) and *Organizational Learning II* (1996).[1] The latter two link action science, reflective practice,[2] and organizational learning perspectives.

—◀◦▶—

ACTION SCIENCE

We focus mainly on the book, *Action Science* by Argyris, Robert Putnam, and Diana McClain Smith (1985) because it contains the major ingredients in the approach and we have been able to use the book in the classroom, where it succeeds in making the arguments clear to first-time readers. We believe that the approach deserves an extended presentation because action science is a major strand of development in AR, combining elements from systems theory, psychoanalysis, and organizational behavior perspectives in an overarching approach. It also takes on the issues of scientific knowledge in the practice of social change directly. To date, it is one of the best efforts to deal with the relation between AR and scientific method.

Early on in *Action Science,* the authors state their main objective clearly: "Our focus is on knowledge that can be used to produce action, while at the same time contributing to a theory of action" (p. ix). In so doing, they argue for a link between theory building and theory testing in action as a single repertoire of actions.

Argyris et al. recognize that this has rarely been attempted and attempt to frame an explanation for this failure by discussing what they call the false conflict between "rigor" and "relevance." The authors point to the long-standing institutional habit in the social sciences to assume that what is relevant, what touches the real world in known locations, cannot be by definition the source of rigorous knowledge. They argue that rigor and relevance is a false dichotomy. Referring to Lewin's view that the best way to understand something is to try to change it, they argue that the road to rigor lies through the attempt to apply social theory to social action, a view consistent with the philosophy of AR we have laid out in previous chapters.

Confronting

A key concept and method in action science is *confronting*. Confronting is a process by which social actors are forced to come to terms explicitly with their own defensive reactions to changes and perceived threats by inquiring into the causes of those reactions and analyzing the consequences of giving into them. Though Argyris et al. point out that not all defensive reactions have negative consequences, they strongly believe that defensive behaviors are the key causes for the widespread observation that groups often cycle endlessly between conflicting demands, when the only way forward is to confront and resolve the conflicts.

Theory of Change and Stasis

In Argyris et al.'s view, the aim of action science is to create "an inquiry into how human beings design and implement action in relation to one another. Hence it is a science of practice" (p. 4). But their goals are even more ambitious because they intend to inquire into the

> (1) variables embedded in the status quo that keep it the status quo; (2) the variables involved in changing the status quo and moving toward liberating alternatives; (3) the variables in a science of intervention that will be required if the previous propositions are ever to be tested; and finally (4) the research methodology that will make change possible and simultaneously produce knowledge that meets rigorous tests of disconfirmability. (p. xii)

By means of this effort, Argyris et al. seek to develop a "science of practice" (p. 4) through which individuals and groups can be assisted in "creating and maintaining behavioral worlds conducive to generating valid information [under] conditions in which agents can make free and informed choices and feel internally committed to their choices" (p. 77).

Objectivity

Action science takes on the social science bastion of objectivity directly because Argyris et al. correctly anticipate that the core objections to their formulations will center on this standard positivistic defensive routine. Their response to the objectivity argument is that it is not possible to achieve even the minimal "valid description" (p. xii) until at least some of the defensive routines of the participants have been directly engaged. Because in their view these patterns of defensive behavior can be both functional and dysfunctional, it is not possible to understand behavior until some sorting out of these elements has been undertaken. In other words, empirical description itself is impossible without intervention, a direct attack on the conventional social science position.

Intervention and Science

Argyris et al. argue for intervention as the principal source of meaningful descriptions on the basis of which a science of action can be built. They invert the conventional social science approach to rigor and relevance by arguing that the standard approach to rigor produces irrelevant, untested, and untestable propositions. "We will argue . . . that theory that intends to contribute to practice should have features that differ from those of theory responsible only to the criteria of pure science" (pp. 18-19). In their view, what makes the human sciences unique is that they study a group of people in practice, and the action scientist is a practitioner engaged in parallel processes of practice, reflection, defensiveness, and objectification with these cosubjects (p. 22). In the end, their goal is no less than the following:

> Action science is centrally concerned with the practice of intervention. It is by reflecting on this practice that we hope to contribute to an understanding of how knowledge claims can be tested and justified in practice and of how such inquiry is similar to and different from that of mainstream science. (p. 35)

ESPOUSED THEORY AND THEORY-IN-USE

In developing the argument for action science, Argyris uses concepts and theories developed in a host of previous works, including some written with Donald Schön (Argyris & Schön, 1978, 1996). Among them are espoused theory, theory-in-use, single-loop learning, double-loop learning, and Model I and Model II theories of action. We will develop these notions briefly here because they are fundamental elements in the infrastructure of action science as a form of practice.

The espoused theory/theory-in-use terminology does not refer to newly discovered concepts, but rather names well-known ideas that are important in any kind of competent social research. *Espoused theory* refers to the account actors give of the reasons for their actions. *Theory-in-use* refers to the observer-analyst's inferences about the theory that must underlie the observed actions of the same people if their actions are to be made sense of. Often, espoused theory and theory-in-use do not coincide; occasionally, they are directly at odds with each other.

These are not new distinctions. In anthropology, they have been rendered as the distinction between emic and etic approaches. Historical materialism poses the same issue in terms of ideology and infrastructure as does Gramsci's use of the concept of hegemony. What is new about action science is that the distance between the espoused theory and theory-in-use becomes the focus of attention in a group's inquiry into its own actions as a means to try to move the group to a more liberating dynamic.

Single-loop learning refers to a situation where people or organizations alter their behavior but do nothing to change the behavioral strategies that gave rise to the problematic situation initially. The problem situation is taken as given, and the participants improve their ability to solve specific challenges. The effect is to achieve, possibly, a brief amelioration of a problem, but because the underlying causes are not confronted, the problems return. They persist and regain strength as soon as another dilemma is encountered.

By contrast, *double-loop learning* results from responding to a problem by stepping back and examining alternative larger frames into which the problem can be put. The immediate problem is understood to be the product of a context that itself must be altered. By altering this context, a group can move to a new plane of organizational learning and change. Action science generally views the persistence of single-loop learning as the product of defensive reactions and improper inferences about the motives of others.

The import of the single-loop/double-loop distinction is that it identifies certain kinds of problems as those toward which action science interventions should be aimed. These are "problems that persist despite efforts to solve them . . . [they] are likely to have double-loop issues embedded in them" (Argyris et al., 1985, p. 87).

Linked to these two kinds of learning are theories of action. In what Argyris et al. call *Model I,* the underlying model is based on having unilateral control over others. Few people espouse Model I, but many people practice it. Another theory of action is *Model O(pposite)-1.* This kind of theory of action gives rise to a limited learning system that corrects errors that cannot be hidden and do not threaten the group's underlying norms. Here the center is broad participation, a focus on win-win approaches, and a strong emphasis on expressing feelings while suppressing intellectual analysis.

Counterposed to these are *Model II* theories of action. In Model II, there are "minimally defensive interpersonal and group relationships, high freedom of choice, and high risk taking. The likelihood of double-loop learning is enhanced, and effectiveness should increase over time" (Argyris et al., 1985, p. 102).

Model O(pposite)-II is the same, but the individuals making up a collectivity are acting out Model II theories-in-use. The result is the creation of a *community of inquiry* in which issues and conflicts can be opened up and in which both single- and double-loop learning occurs.

Empirical Testing in Action Science

One of the most interesting features of action science is its strong attention to methods for developing tests of interpretations. The perspective is based on an extensive development of the kinds of concepts used in attributing reasons for people's behaviors, assigning causal responsibility, and achieving intersubjective agreement about the data.

A technique called the *ladder of inference* is used to link subject dialogues, interpretations, and actions into an analyzed interpretation of interactions:

> In action science we deal with this issue with the help of a conceptual device . . . the ladder of inference. This is a schematic representation of the steps by which human beings select from and read into interaction as they make sense of everyday life. (Argyris et al., 1985, p. 57)

In constructing this analysis, the first round is utterances from ordinary speech in a specific situation. Then the observers and participants assign meanings of the utterances (both their own and those of the people they are dealing with). These meanings are then examined and compared, and the inferences used to arrive at the meanings are analyzed. The ladder of inference refers to the connecting links of analysis between the utterance and the interpretation arrived at. Typically, most people make very powerful inferences about the aims of others on the basis of shaky data. The point is to move up and down the ladder together with the actors in the situation being examined, checking how conclusions are drawn, what is paid attention to, and what is ignored. From this, the patterns of behavior leading to a persistence of single-loop learning surface and can be examined.

Note that the ladder of inference is a technique of organizational intervention, not a mere research tool. It is applied because a group has a problem that it has commissioned an action scientist to help it try to solve. Intervention is not at the opposite end of some continuum leading from action to research. Rather, as Argyris et al. put it, "intervention is the action science analogue of experimentation" (p. 64). Without intervention, there is no action science! The Lewin and Dewey inheritance is clear.

A Retrospective Example of Action Science

One of the most outstanding features of Argyris et al. is a fascinating critique of the famous experiments by the U.S. psychologist Stanley Milgram (1974) on the willingness of ordinary people to inflict harm on fellow human beings. By commenting on the Milgram experiments and distinguishing their strategy from Milgram's, Argyris et al. succeed in showing how different a science of action would be from orthodox social science, even on socially relevant subjects.

Milgram used people recruited by an advertisement putatively to teach an experimental subject some word associations. Whenever the subject failed, the teacher was to administer electric shocks, and the shocks increased over the course of the experiment to dangerous levels. In fact, Milgram and the experimental subject were secretly collaborating, and no electric shocks were administered. The "teachers" did not know this, however.

Milgram interviewed the teachers beforehand, and all asserted that they would not knowingly harm a fellow human being. Though Milgram found lots of variation in people's reactions, many people were in fact willing to shock the experimental subject. From this, Milgram concludes, without a clear line to the data, that humans are not intrinsically hostile or aggressive, but rather are weak willed and prone to follow orders by those in authority. As a result of this finding, the work was dubbed the "Eichmann experiments." Milgram reported his findings almost 10 years after completing the work, but made no social intervention other than writing his book.

In commenting on Milgram's (1974) work, Argyris et al. are respectful of his accomplishments, and yet distinguish their approach from his. "In order to reliably describe some phenomenon, one ought to retain its essential features and construct a situation that captures its essence" (p. 111). In Argyris et al.'s view, Milgram did not try to alter the situation and its outcomes. This lost him the possibility of understanding the genesis of the observed behavior. As a result, his experiments could not yield knowledge that might help individuals break out of this dilemma. We never learn of alternatives that might better manage it, and we do not discover the deep structures that maintain it.

Argyris et al.'s Model II approach would have been to alter the parameters of the experiment to change the outcomes. Because what is socially desired is a population in which no one is willing to follow immoral orders, Argyris et al. argue that AR should focus on the disobedient teachers and inquire into the causes of their unwillingness to follow such orders. From this, theories can be developed about the causes of disobedience, and the experiment could be varied to increase the causes of disobedience until the maximum disobedience is achieved. In this way, a Model II inquiry both inquires into the causes of behavior and intervenes directly to promote morally desirable behavior in the research subjects. The distance between this and conventional social science is clear, and the basis of conventional social science itself is revealed to be single-loop, Model I behavior.

Practicing Action Science

Not content simply to lay out abstract theories of action science, Argyris et al. also formulate a number of *rules of practice* that guide their AR. Paralleling these are a series of rules for testing hypotheses, a subject almost never broached in the AR literature. Whatever one thinks of this version of action science, Argyris et al. are correct in making attention to scientific reasoning a higher priority.

Positive Features

There is much that is useful in this framework. Rather than justifying action by using some kind of ethical argument about dealing with social problems, Argyris et al. argue for action science as a better form of scientific inquiry than orthodox science. They also pick up the core of Dewey and Lewin's arguments that it is through action that learning can occur. Thus, in these authors' view, to be scientific, social research must be socially engaged. To put it in the frame that Argyris has long used, the aim of action science is to increase the possibility of unlikely but socially beneficial (liberating) outcomes. They want to achieve this through the deployment of the scientific method. The core logic of their argument is that any social research that is not interventionist cannot be scientific, an argument they make quite effectively in their analysis of the Milgram experiments.

The reverse side of this logic is a less clearly expressed but equally severe judgement of many other action researchers. In Argyris et al.'s view, too many action researchers routinely accept the separation of thought and action that characterizes conventional social science, choosing to justify their work by the urgency of the problems they study or the goodness of the goals they have. More bluntly, the greater part of AR is characterized by foggy epistemologies and incoherent or careless methodologies. By the logic of action science, this is itself a Model I single-loop behavior and will not produce a successful community of inquiry.

A Critique: Psychologism, Defensive Routines, and Intervenor Paternalism

For us, action science takes a very narrow cut of the complexities of human psychology, even though we welcome its analysis of motivation and behavior at this level. In the main, human psychology, as relevant to action, is reduced to the production of defensive routines leading to single-loop outcomes. It does not seem plausible to us that defensiveness is the only major psychological process relevant to these group phenomena. The richness of human motivations, the complex interactions between cultural ideas and the economics and politics of particular situations, and the complex differences among all the participants in a particular situation are not explored if the analysis focuses only on defensiveness.

It is unclear how the action scientists themselves overcome this defensiveness. According to their own view, defensiveness is the "default" form of human action (they describe the Model I responses of individuals as "natural" and "automatic"; Argyris et al., 1985, p. 151). This assumption is quite important because it creates an unexplained gulf between the facilitator and the subject.

Left to their own devices, participants would be unable to redesign the Model I predispositions that lead to repetitive failures. Rather than continue to feel frustrated and hopeless, they might decide that it is impossible to produce Model II action and thereby justify their withdrawal; or they might decide that some Model I strategies are as good as could be expected, and not focus on their counterproductive features. In other words, the defenses that enable people to remain unaware of their theories-in-use in the Model I world would reassert themselves. The task of the interventionist is to help participants begin to redesign their theories-in-use genuinely (Argyris et al., 1985, p. 338).

No justification is ever given for this state of affairs, nor is any explanation provided about the sources of the interventionists' "unnatural" human capacities to overcome these limitations. Argyris et al. appear to be natural-born action researchers in this account.

In speaking of choosing to change, they state that

> although individuals have no choice in their theory-in-use and the OI
> learning system, they can choose to alter their theory-in-use and, hence,
> the organizational learning system and culture. But such changes will not
> occur unless the players are committed. (p. 152)

But why individuals have no choice, what commitment is, and how commitment develops are not discussed.

This view is highly charged politically because it forces us to conclude that action scientists are different kinds of human beings from natural ones. Although this view might be justified through a discussion of the process of people becoming trained to be action scientists, action science does not contain such a discussion. We are left with the action scientist as an unchallenged, self-conscious, and self-contained individual capable of acting on others.

Another way of looking at this problem in action science is to note that the analysis has a strongly dyadic bias. That is to say, although many of the examples occur in group contexts and Model I and Model II refer to group behavior, the predominant image that emerges from a reading of action science is that of a skilled practitioner or teacher confronting a group member and getting that group member to inquire into and change his or her behavior.

We believe that this image of the teacher and student, the therapist and the patient, though having the merit of focusing attention on some of the psychological dimensions of group processes, also incurs significant costs. Until recently in action science, we did not see an analysis of groups as groups. Rather, groups were assumed to function well when all the dyads in them are functioning well. Notions of group structure, political economy, gender differences, ethnicity, and the like have been left out. Groups are portrayed as being constituted of individuals engaged in exchange and as ideally moving toward some kind of rational choice model. In particular, this makes the analysis insensitive to power relationships, including the power this approach bestows on the expert intervenor.

This matters, not because there are no good action scientists; indeed we have both seen marvelous action science practice. Rather, it matters because we think the good practice we see arises, in part, because these practitioners have a more sophisticated social theory than they articulate in their writings and that they practice in a less hierarchical way than the model suggests. Developing a better analysis of these elements is a pending assignment for action science.

These issues of hierarchy matter a great deal because action science proceeds by identifying problems and agreeing when solutions have been found. Thus, the authority to make these decisions is central. Deciding what kind of behavior is appropriate, for instance, is crucial. Yet, for example, in referring to "brittleness" in social relationships, action scientists define it as a "predisposition to express an inappropriately high sense of despair or failure when producing error" (Argyris et al., 1985, p. 156). What is inappropriate and who decides is not discussed; this apparently is a decision to be made by the intervenor. Argyris et al. also speak of "genuine organizational change" without defining what is genuine, again permitting the intervenor the authoritative position of deciding what constitutes change and what does not.

The way in which the ladder of inference is used and the way segments of dialogue are separated for analysis also reveals a highly rule-based vision of culture, a view supported by Argyris et al.'s repeated use of the term *routines* to describe behaviors. Although many schools of thought do this, including componential analysis in anthropology, there are significant limitations to such a view. Behavior is more than rules, just as language is more than grammar. This is particularly important because action science's effort to be scientific requires some sort of notion of "disconfirmation" as part of the approach. But the discussions these authors give of disconfirmation rest heavily on this rule-based view of behavior, giving us little sense of the experiential difficulties of a disconfirmation strategy when the flow of human behavior is viewed in its ethnographic complexity.

History of Science

All of us who are posing critiques of conventional social science approaches must have an explanation about why such conventional social science prevails. If we are right and conventional social science is wrong, then we must explain why it is dominant and we are not. We have already devoted attention to this issue in the present book (see Part 2). We only point out that action science lacks an explanation why the social sciences chose to mimic the natural sciences rather than Dewey and Lewin (Argyris et al., 1985, p. 5) or why there exists what Argyris et al. (1985) call "pernicious separation" of theory and practice (p. 7).

In our view, this inattention to larger issues of social structure and political economy stems from the same dyadic and therapeutic view we commented on above. Action scientists assume that people are misguided and can be brought back to a better view of the matter through high-quality intervention. This ignores the existence of the whole political economy of social research that always moves in the direction of blunting the reformist and democratizing elements in social science for reasons that seem better explained by matters of power than by "defensive routines" of the members of particular groups.

None of these criticisms is unanswerable, and some of them are being addressed by action scientists in recent publications. This framework has gone farther than any other in trying to address some of the methodological and epistemological issues raised by the notion of a science of AR, and deserves close attention for this reason.

ORGANIZATIONAL LEARNING

The long and fruitful collaboration between Chris Argyris and Donald Schön led to a number of books; two of the most important are *Organizational Learning* (1978) and *Organizational Learning II* (1996). Though the term *organizational learning* is now common, Argyris and Schön created it in 1978, at a time when organizational behavior thinking was pointing in very different directions. Now there are hundreds of works and high-profit consulting businesses based on promises about organizational learning (e.g., Senge, 1990).

Many arguments are similar to those presented in relation to action science, but some issues of organizational dynamics are taken up only in these works. Here we deal with the second book, *Organizational Learning II* (1996). It provides an excellent critical overview of the organizational learning literature. The authors offer their own well-grounded and nuanced view of organizational learning, followed by an extended and clear presentation of the basic single-loop, double-loop, Model I, and Model II schemes already discussed.

What is important about this book for the overall action science perspective is that the authors strive hard to get beyond dyadic relationships in which power is not an issue. They discuss organizational politics and show an awareness of the complexities that the symbolic-cultural life of organizations creates not evident in the earlier work (Argyris & Schön, 1978). They also succeed in making inquiry-enhancing intervention a much clearer concept and process than in Argyris et al.

Particularly valuable too is the Afterword by Argyris and Schön, which is built around a robust critique of academic practice, arguing that academics are unlikely to confront theory-practice relationships. We concur with their action science analysis that universities are particularly unlikely to become learning organizations in a meaningful sense.

Few books address the complex issues of action science and organizational learning as effectively as Argyris and Schön. Perhaps only Robert Flood and Norma Romm's (1996) *Diversity Management* shares their epistemological, methodological, and practical ambitions.

Argyris and Schön advance over *Action Science* by showing that they are aware of the need to speak to the issues of organizational culture inherent in organizational learning, an awareness not visible in the earlier work.

Yet this dimension needs more attention, because the treatment of organizational culture remains rather limited and mechanistic in contrast to their dynamic and more differentiated behavioral perspectives. The richness of cultural productivity in organizational contexts and around the kinds of processes Argyris and Schön are attempting to stimulate require greater analytical development. This richness is one of the most enduring experiences of search conferences.

Argyris and Schön also make a number of attempts to get beyond a view of organizations as collectivities of individuals struggling with each other dyadically to a more truly social concept of organizational structure. This is important, but the issue is not well resolved.

The authors show their awareness of criticisms that their perspectives are either blind to power relations or actually reinforce certain kinds of hierarchies in organizations. Nevertheless, the fact that Model I behavior is the default for people in organizations is still treated pretty much as a law of nature rather than as a possible product of particular systems of political economy. This leaves the sources of Model I and Model II still unexplained, just as in Argyris et al. Not explaining the ultimate sources of Model I leaves us without an explanation of why certain individuals (in this case, the authors) are capable of transcending ordinary human limits and then leading others to do so. This opens up legitimations of authority and expertise that deserve more open inquiry. Though the book is clearly in the AR tradition, just like *Action Science, Organizational Learning II* does not speak strongly to the issue of the normative and ethical ends of organizational learning. The clear interest in nondefensive human behavior is positive, but no explicit connection is made between this commitment to democratization. The approach can easily be adopted by conventional consultants for whom participation and democratization are not high priorities.

THE SKILLS REQUIRED FOR ACTION SCIENCE AND ORGANIZATIONAL LEARNING

Good action science practice focuses heavily on group process skills. In the interventions we have observed by some action scientists, we have been impressed by certain skills they develop. For one thing, they are very patient and persistent with the processes. The calm, persistent, clear, and supportive role intervenors play does much to create the space in which the kind of action science inquiry leading to changes in group process can be developed. It is our sense that action science insists that practitioners discipline themselves to wait longer, persist more, and remain calm perhaps more than most other approaches. Perhaps this is part of the therapeutic legacy of this tradition.

Another important feature of action science intervention is the way in which practitioners learn not to feel threatened by silences and vacuums in group processes. Rather than rushing in to fill awkward spaces with sound and action, they keep uncomfortable spaces open longer, confronting the participants with the need to examine their actions in part out of the discomfort caused by the process of standing still.

At every turn, action science practitioners challenge participants to be explicit and to explain their actions, and they repeatedly make explicit their own reactions and explanations as a model for this behavior. This quasi-Socratic intervention often leads participants to make their own analytical breakthroughs rather than allowing them to hide in the interstices of group process. This requires skill in confronting people without silencing them, being strong yet open, sympathetic yet critical, and unusually attentive to the details of speech and action. Again, these are legacies of the therapeutic tradition and are worthy of study and emulation in AR processes.

In conclusion, action science and organizational learning are neither perfect nor wrong. They are bold and clearly articulated attempts to bring AR into direct confrontation with orthodox social science and to pursue a limited social reform agenda. That they have gaps and problems does not make them different from other approaches. They merit close study by action researchers.

Notes

1. In practice, we will deal only with the second of these books because it is a complete revision of the first book, based on their continued practice and the critiques they received.

2. We made the decision not to include a separate chapter on the approach most individually associated with Donald Schön, which he calls *reflective practice* (Schön, 1983, 1987, 1991), mainly because many of the organizational practice elements in this perspective emerge in the coauthored books, and some of the other key elements in the reflective practice approach center on dyadic coaching relationships and not on larger-scale organizational change.

Human Inquiry, Cooperative Inquiry, and Action Inquiry

The terms *human inquiry, cooperative inquiry,* and *action inquiry* refer to (but do not exhaust) approaches and authors, each with a significant genealogy of their own but who have sustained a long and fruitful dialogue with each other. We bring them together here because of some basic commonalities and because they have been interrelated directly through the efforts of Peter Reason at the University of Bath. Reason is a prolific writer (e.g., Reason, 1988, 1994; Reason & Rowan, 1981). The work of this open network of people uses different mixes of elements drawn from psychology, social work, action research (AR), evaluation studies, feminism, and meditation practices. To provide a flavor of the work, we have elected to review the work of three practitioners: Peter Reason, John Heron, and William Torbert.

One of the most striking characteristics of these forms of inquiry is their ongoing trajectory of development through the steady incorporation of a wide variety of perspectives and practices. Peter Reason (1994) nicely defines the central agenda as

> an approach to living based on experience and engagement, on love and respect for the integrity

203

of persons; and on a willingness to rise above
presupposition, to look and to look again, to risk
security in the search for understanding and action
that open possibilities for creative living. (p. 9)

The strong value placed on experience and engagement,
a clear recognition of the emotional and ethical dimensions
of relationships, a desire to have the world of experience
answer back and invalidate preconceptions (against positivism), and a commitment to "creative living" are the key
elements. At the same time, readers will note in this work
that references to concepts from political economy (the
power structure, social class, the establishment, democratization) are infrequent. Instead, the focus is on individual
people and their organizations in their local situations,
people who are attempting to live more creative lives.

—◄o►—

HUMAN INQUIRY

The aims of human inquiry are bold. Reason (1994) lays claim to a
particular epistemology, a methodology that emerges as a consequence
of it, a history of science that backs up the epistemological and methodological claims, and a series of social reform agendas including
democratization, improvement of social services, and the incorporation
of gender perspectives in all dimensions of social change. In this regard,
human inquiry is among the most fully developed and complex combinations of theorization and practice in a combined social psychology-
human relations framework to be found in AR. Its only current limita-
tion is a strong focus on service almost to the exclusion of production
or manufacturing organizations, a focus not inherent to the perspective
but that affects the way frameworks are developed within it.

For our purposes here, we will provide an analysis of human inquiry
through a review of Peter Reason's (1994) most recent book, *Participation in Human Inquiry*. Given the developmental quality of human
inquiry, we think it best to summarize the most recent available state-

ment of the perspective. Also, we believe the book to be a very good overview of the approach.[1]

The basis for this approach (Reason, 1994) is carefully constructed with a framework that insists on the priority of a participatory world-view to match a participatory methodology. In other words, methodology alone is not sufficient to produce the kind of work desired, a point often obscured in other writing. The methods must be couched in a larger vision of the world and human relations that privileges participation as a matter of principle. Only then can the step be taken to transform what would be subjects in orthodox research into coresearchers.

To cope with the problem of the dominant, alienated forms of social inquiry, Reason (1994) tells an unfashionable "grand narrative" about the evolution of human consciousness. His basic notion is that humans move from unconscious participation to a form of alienation created by patriarchalism and seek emancipation in a kind of future participation that has self-awareness and self-reflectiveness, operates in a Batesonian world of pattern and form, involves the conscious use of the imagination, and provides for a very different experience of the self from what is common in gender-divided approaches. The characteristics Reason wants to ground participation in are made clear.

Human inquiry is then set as a discipline in this context, a "method or a training, a set of rules, exercises, or procedures" (Reason, 1994, p. 40) that will lead to this kind of participatory outcome. Reason presents a classification of types of knowledge that he has been working on with colleagues for some time. They are experiential, presentational, practical, and propositional knowledge. This typology successfully calls attention to the diverse set of activities that comes under the heading of knowledge. It also calls attention to the failure of the orthodox social sciences to remember how complex and differentiated knowledge is and how knowledge is built out of sequences and combinations of different kinds of knowing.

The process of human inquiry moves through phases in which particular knowledge forms predominate. In our view, this is one of the most useful parts of Reason's (1994) corpus. AR writing generally offers very few such characterizations to help practitioners portray and understand participatory processes, at least little since the social psychological literature of the 1940s and 1950s.

In human inquiry, the phases begin with coresearchers who are examining a subject together. For Reason (1994), these knowledge forms are mainly propositional, though there is some presentational knowledge present as well. As the process deepens, the coresearchers become cosubjects. At this point, the kinds of knowledge are mainly practical. In the next phase, the cosubjects become immersed in each other's realities, and the knowledge form is mainly experiential. Finally, the cosubjects begin to emerge from the research process together. They review, reframe, and even repudiate some ideas. At this point, the knowledge forms are mainly propositional. But elements of presentational knowledge are used to link the experiential and practical knowledge gained in the process to the propositional knowledge acquired.

Following this, Reason (1994) provides a perfunctory review of the modalities of AR and a history that links AR to the quest for liberation. This is not a strong point of Reason's work.

Human inquiry's dialectical quality is clear, and the constant balancing act that mediates between the legitimate uses of authority, collaboration, and autonomy is visible. Human inquiry is not any one of these, but rather a skill in balancing all three to keep contexts truly open to participation.

An example is the process that gave rise to Reason (1994): a set of exchanges between Reason and the contributing authors about the cases. In the final section of review and reflection, it becomes clear that the reflections grew out of a cycle of interactions between the editor and the case writers in which they heard and responded to Reason's comments, both positively and negatively. The case writers and Reason were cosubjects in a metaprocess of human inquiry that linked the cases into a larger set of lessons.

In his conclusion, Reason (1994) begins by identifying processes, comments interactively with the case writers, and documents both their disagreements and agreements. This ability to admit to and document disagreements is one of the characteristics of human inquiry's approach that lends it a desirable openness. It stands in stark contrast to the positivist mode of writing in which the author's learning process is suppressed and only "revealed truths" are documented, and to some of the writing in AR that makes frameworks seem uncontestable.

Reason (1994) implicitly advocates an approach where the cases begin rather conventionally and then branch out into more experimental and risky forms of participation, an approach that we very much agree with (see Greenwood, Whyte, & Harkavy, 1993). AR is a process, not a thing. Over the course of the process, there are a variety of opportunities to innovate by opening it up to greater collaboration and to the possibility that the partners can become real cosubjects. Just how far the process goes depends on the skills of the practitioner, the situation, the temperament of the cosubjects, and other local factors. What is important is that the process begin somewhere and that the practitioner make a disciplined effort at ever-greater inclusion of the subjects as coresearchers. In the process of revealing this, Reason has much of interest to say about ownership of projects, power relations, and the problems and opportunities of collaboration.

A point that comes through clearly in Reason's (1994) closing essay is that being a good researcher is not enough. To work in human inquiry, the researcher must develop good facilitation skills and have an understanding of group processes. All the formal social science training in the world can be useful but not sufficient. The student of human inquiry must come to terms with group processes, must seek to develop himself or herself as a facilitator and partner, and must continually strive to combine excellence as a researcher with ethical and political commitments as a cosubject with local partners.

Reason (1994) is certainly right to argue for the need for a participatory worldview to match a participatory methodology. Without an appropriate worldview, the methods take us nowhere. He is also a defender of "good stories" as critical elements in this kind of work. For far too long, action researchers have permitted themselves to be coerced by the conventional social researchers who cast aspersions on AR by claiming that we are just telling stories. This criticism is a rear-guard attempt at justifying the masking and jargonizing proclivities of conventional social research. Strong narratives are key to AR and essential to any kind of social science endeavor. Only through the detailed understanding of the real logic of human situations lived and participated in dynamically can we reach for the larger underlying issues and causes that help us account for them.

One of the dominant aims of human inquiry is the transformation of subjects into coresearchers. This is a central tenet of AR in general, but Reason (1994) gives more examples and extends the discussion of these collaborative relationships epistemologically and methodologically more than most other writers. The villain of the piece is the alienation of our society. Reason builds a strong case for the fragmentation of Western epistemology and attempts to root it in a theory of the evolution of human consciousness. Unfortunately, it is both tempting and easy to discount this part because these ideas are far too reminiscent of many 19th and early 20th century pseudoevolutionary treatises that use evolutionary language to construe human history to legitimate a current ideological position (Greenwood, 1985). The stages Reason uses in this process have been repudiated by anthropologists through hundreds of monographic studies of many different kinds of societies. As is often the case with such frameworks, political economy is also ignored.

This pseudo-evolutionism does Reason's (1994) framework a considerable disservice. Yet the point he wants to make requires attention because he is posing the choice between an alienated form of bureaucratic, positivistic, oppressive consciousness (see Herzfeld, 1992) and a kind of collaborative, intersubjective form of inquiry in which the capacities of all thinking beings to conduct research and to transform their situations are given their due credit.

This desired kind of consciousness is appealing because it involves self-awareness and self-reflectiveness, living in a fluid world of complex and dynamic patterns and forms along with the use of the imagination, the emotions, and the intellect together as tools. Human inquiry leads the inquirer not just to conduct research differently but to live in the world as a different kind of person. This goal underlies a great deal of the attractiveness of AR in its many guises, but even that goal is poorly articulated in most written work. By stressing that human inquiry is a discipline and a practice, and that the researcher has the characteristics of a learner, Reason (1994) stresses that AR involves all participants in a process of self-discovery through others.

The distinctions between experiential, presentational, practical, and propositional knowledge are also very useful. The vague assertions in much of the literature about local knowledge or cogenerated knowledge or reflective practice do not make sufficient distinctions for analytical purposes. The phases of the human inquiry process may or may not stand the test of further cases, but these analytical distinctions are still exceptionally useful. In our experience, action researchers often have a very difficult time triangulating the process they are in. By having a sense of phases that can be defined according to the predominance of a particular kind of knowledge, the researcher is given a compass to steer by and a way of continuing to ask interesting questions about what has happened and what the next steps might be.

Crafty behavior is the goal that the researcher strives to achieve. The researcher is not omniscient and certainly not omnipotent, but the researcher has ways of gaining self-awareness and working with cosubjects to generate new mutual understandings and new understandings of the possibilities in particular interventions.

The human inquiry tradition as developed by Reason (1994) and his collaborators contains a great deal of value. Whether or not one agrees with the perspective, the approach contains a systematic epistemological and methodological development and is a good antidote to the intellectual laziness that characterizes too much AR. Often in AR, the justification that the researcher is doing good covers up the researcher's unwillingness or inability to make the intellectual effort needed to think hard about what he or she is doing and how it can be improved.

We hope we have said enough by now to make it clear that human inquiry has a well-argued epistemological position and a workable methodology and provides some good links to the history of Western thought. It attempts to build an integrated system, to develop its behavioral consequences, and to justify itself both intellectually and morally. In this way, it is one of the most ambitious framings of AR currently available.

COOPERATIVE INQUIRY

John Heron is a collaborator and critic of Peter Reason (he set up the New Paradigm Research Group in London in 1978 with Reason and John Rowan). He is also a prolific writer and practitioner in his own right.

Co-Operative Inquiry: Research into the Human Condition (Heron, 1996) is a comprehensive development of an epistemology and methodology for AR. The book begins by disavowing the desire to create yet another orthodoxy. Heron actively seeks to map his approach onto others, including qualitative inquiry in general, and promises to explore the paradigm of inquiry underlying his approach and compare it with others. He tries to live up to these promises, taking an inviting and nonparochial approach to a complex subject.

In cooperative inquiry, the point of departure is *participative reality*, by which Heron (1996) refers to the immanence of mind in nature (reminiscent of Bateson, 1979) and the necessarily cogenerative quality of human knowing. What sets Heron's treatment apart is his distinction between participative reality as an epistemological question from the equally important and powerful political (and ethical) values of participation and human development. These are treated as two dimensions. He does not try to derive one from the other, as is so often done. "The democratization of research management is as much a human rights issue as the democratization of government at national and local levels" (p. 21). His argument for cooperative inquiry links these two meanings of participation, and he systematically defends it against other approaches that he considers more limited. He uses the distinctions between experiential, presentational, practical, and propositional knowing throughout and to good effect; as a good action researcher, he begins the process with experiential knowing.

Heron (1996) also faces the issues of truth and validity squarely, rather than arguing that doing good excuses any imprecision. Heron is a strong believer in the *warrant for action* view of knowledge. One feature of cooperative inquiry that is particularly useful is a clear and concrete emphasis on specific processes and methods. Heron works through the various ways inquiry processes are begun, their phases, and the variety of things that can happen at different points. Though no solution is offered to the dilemmas of coauthorship, Heron confronts this issue forthrightly.

Heron (1996) is particularly attentive to issues of validity, and he makes important contributions to the broader discussion of AR. He connects inquiry cycles, reflection, action, and other elements in the process to an overall view of what constitutes validity in this kind of work. We believe this is the most comprehensive statement of an approach to validity found in AR. Among the validity procedures Heron advocates are research cycling, balancing divergence and convergence in the process, and elements of reflection. The discussion on validity has much in common with the arguments presented in Chapter 5, "An Epistemological Foundation for Action Research." As always in AR, the basis for making claims for validity is whether they warrant action or create workable solutions.

Having taken us this long way, Heron (1996) then returns to the larger worldview that guides cooperative inquiry. He restates his commitment to what he calls an empiricism, but he does so subversively by insisting that empiricism means not prejudging the content of experience. Heron effectively takes on the empiricists in their lair by arguing that their own views of what is empirical are completely inadequate. He closes the work by showing how cooperative inquiry better addresses nearly all the conceptual, empirical, and political dilemmas of conventional social research.

ACTION INQUIRY

Another approach to AR that lies poised between those of Reason and Heron and the action science of Argyris (see Chapter 11, "Action Science and Organizational Learning") is action inquiry as articulated by William Torbert. Although Torbert has developed these ideas in many publications, we refer to a recent and comprehensive statement of his views, *The Power of Balance* (1991; see also Fisher & Torbert, 1995).

This book (Torbert, 1991) opens with a rather quizzical introduction by Donald Schön, who does not ratify many of the things in the book but enjoins us to learn actively from it. Part of the reason for Schön's diffidence may be that Torbert's claims are occasionally extreme, and partly this may be due to the fact that Torbert is occasionally painfully self-revealing in making his points. This tone of self-revelation is not foreign to human inquiry-cooperative inquiry approaches, because they assert that social transformation requires self-transformation. This logically requires a great deal of introspection and a certain kind of openness to the personal that most other approaches seek to hide.

Of the authors discussed in this chapter, Torbert (1991) works hardest at cross-referencing participative change at the individual, group, and larger political levels. Torbert's cases routinely engage power relationships in a direct way that makes his analysis a valuable addition to this general set.

Torbert's (1991) analysis begins with the view that power as ordinarily conceived (i.e., power over others) is far weaker than what he calls the "power of balance," a "self-legitimizing form of power . . . that invites mutuality, that empowers those who respond to this invitation with initiatives of their own, and that generates both productivity and inquiry, both transformation and stability, both freedom and order" (p. 2). The aim of action inquiry is to learn how to exercise this kind of power individually, in groups, and across generations.

Tobert (1991) then distinguishes four kinds of power: unilateral, diplomatic, logistical, and transforming. Blending these four types productively gives rise to the power of balance. This balance comes from what he calls "constructive rationality," which desires to achieve individual rights and fairer social relationships. Thus, the perspective is rooted in a macropolitical vision that is built on a view of group dynamics and individual action, all of which are necessary ingredients in the development of the balance.

Given Torbert's (1991) long experience of teaching in business schools and working in the private sector, most of his examples and his arguments are drawn from these settings. The work contains a long example on curriculum reform in a business school. This stands as one of a very small number of accounts of AR in curriculum change in higher education (for another, see Reynolds, 1994). The work is peppered with shorter analyses of the actions of individuals and groups that often provide vivid illustrations of his key points.

The core practice in action inquiry is what Torbert (1991) calls the creation of liberating structures. Rather than arguing against structure, Torbert argues for structures that lead people to develop themselves and their relationships in an ongoing process of growth, confrontation, and development. In his view, without structure, there is no movement, whereas with coercive structures, there is only resistance. Liberating structures are action inquiry's way out.

Torbert (1991) lists eight essential qualities of liberating structures. First, deliberate irony attempts to move people out of conventional ways of thinking about their organizations. Second, liberating structures must define tasks that, to be completed, must be approached in ways congruent with the broader values of organizational development. Third, they involve premeditated and foretold structural change over time. Fourth, the processes must create ongoing cycles of experiential and empirical research and feedback to the participants. Fifth, leadership can use all available forms of power to achieve these goals. Sixth, the structures are always open to challenge by organizational members. Seventh, the leadership is held accountable to the same values as it espouses the process. Eighth, the leadership aims to ferret out and fix personal and organizational incongruities.

Although these positions echo other frameworks, Torbert's (1991) combination is unique. Torbert is much more attentive to the dilemmas of the exercise of power and leadership. The dimensions arrayed above are played out in a long example of a curriculum reform that Torbert undertook at Southern Methodist University's business school. The vivid retelling, the ethnographic specificity, the tacking back and forth between the organizational story and the personal and existential dimensions of the process, and the macropolitics of the school make this a uniquely valuable case to read. The fits and starts, the uncertainties, the fears, depressions, highs, and errors that necessarily accompany anything so complex as major organizational change are wonderfully retold. These are gradually woven into a larger narrative about Torbert's own trajectory as an educator, husband, friend, and leader. The confessional tone of this writing provides one of the few published accounts of the existential side of AR, a telling reminder that engaged inquiry engages us on all levels, not just as trained professionals.

CONCLUSION

Taken together, these three strands of thought (Heron, 1996; Reason, 1994; Torbert, 1991) give us a broad view of a particular set of related approaches to AR strongly anchored in social psychology, organizational development, and human service work. Peter Reason (1994) offers a grand view of the enterprise combined with short cases and dialogue among practitioners. John Heron (1996) provides a disciplined theoretical and methodological account of a participatory form of inquiry and one of the best arguments on validity we have seen so far. William Torbert (1991) links a micro- and macropolitical framework, leadership issues, and organizational development in AR in a convincing and intelligible way.

We believe that the differences between human inquiry, cooperative inquiry, action inquiry, and other approaches (specifically the industrial democracy movement, participatory AR, action science, and adult education) do make a real difference but do not make elements from each radically incompatible.

Note

1. For the development of this approach, see Reason and Rowan (1981) and Reason (1988).

Educational Strategies

One of the most important and frequent paths leading people into the practice of action research (AR) has been through the field of education in its various guises. Education, as we use the term here, refers to everything from reforms of the formal school system from primary to secondary schools on to universities and postgraduate work. It also includes adult education, either for reskilling people displaced by technological and social changes or for technical education in the latest techniques in rapidly changing fields.

Another form of AR education is the use of consultants who come to organizations for the purpose of imparting techniques and ideas centering on organizational improvement. Unions and many private volunteer organizations (secular and religious) have been actively involved in the development of educational programs on the theory that improvements in knowledge lead to greater self-awareness that, in turn, yields positive social change. Many agencies engage specifically in educational campaigns to increase awareness of particular issues: homelessness, AIDS, drugs, alcoholism, child and spousal abuse. Although taking too broad a focus dilutes the discussion to the point of making it useless, we want the reader to realize that, in AR, educational strategies involve a diverse array of social change efforts.

Educational efforts, formal and nonformal, have been a central field of activity for action researchers during most of this century, and thus the history of the field of education criss-crosses the history of AR at many locations.[1] John Dewey, the putative father of the U.S. public educational system, is an important figure in educationally oriented AR. His notions about the relationships between schools and society, between education and democracy, between learn-ing forms of self-managed inquiry and being free are a powerful reminder of the potential of educational systems to engage in social change. Though Dewey's long and con-stant pursuit of democratizing objectives through the schools yielded very little in the way of meaningful social change (see Westbrook, 1991), many of Dewey's ideas resonated with social change agents. Some trade union organizers saw themselves as educators, as did a host of social reformers concerned with improving the lives of the poor in the U.S. (e.g., Alinsky, 1946; Chávez, 1975; Horton, 1990).

As waves of social change sentiment have come and gone, so too have efforts at educational reform. The labor movement yielded a broad array of educational programs. The aftermath of the Great Depression created commu-nity development and education initiatives. The civil rights era did so as well. The events of 1968 caused a flourish-ing of educational initiatives in the classroom and beyond (Readings, 1996). Every major attempt at societal trans-formation has been accompanied by a set of educational changes aimed at helping people who have been treated as passive objects to become active subjects.

These educational activities are very broadly distrib-uted internationally. The focus on education as a possible vehicle for democratization has overlapped in strategy with southern participatory AR's heavy emphasis on adult edu-cation (see Chapter 10).[2] It is difficult, even artificial, to make a radical separation between adult education and AR in the south. Facing the staggering problems of poor people around the world, poverty created in many cases by the activities of the rich and powerful countries whose educa-tional systems have just been mentioned, southern practi-tioners have developed a strong liberative adult education focus. This is reasonable because most impoverished adults are also poorly educated and not well prepared to take an active role in social change initiatives. Rather than focusing first on childhood education as a point of entry, many AR practitioners have felt it best to focus their resources on the development of skills, competence, self-awareness, and self-confidence among the adults to whom the task of struggling for social change necessarily falls.

Respecting this historical point of departure, this chapter concentrates attention on the rich and diverse literature in adult education, both in poor countries and in the poor areas of industrialized countries. We review a number of education-based interventions, including labor organizing as a form of adult education, trade union education, adult education schools outside the public school system, and the potential role of educational institutions in AR. This discussion necessarily refers to a hetero-geneous set of methods, ideologies, and narratives of practice, but that is just how the field is. This diversity is part of the dynamic energy that has characterized educa-tional strategies for a long time. We are conscious that a variety of AR initiatives in educational institutions within the north are passed over lightly in this chapter, such as the work of Michelle Fine (1992) and Michael Reynolds (1994).

—◄o►—

FOLK HIGH SCHOOLS—THE ORIGIN OF POPULAR EDUCATION

There is good reason to believe that adult education as a distinctive field originated in Denmark with the work of the theologian Grundtvig (1783-1872). He initiated a fierce debate with the theological estab-lishment regarding the scientific analysis of the Bible. His point was that the scriptures should be made sense of by ordinary people through their daily lives in their congregations. From this conflict eventually emerged a conscious effort to create a popular education system where history, theology, and studies of cultural heritage created an integrated and context-bound knowledge system (Nørgaard, 1935). The first "folk" high school was established in 1851, and these schools soon became an important social and political factor in war-ridden Denmark. This popular education movement spread to other Scandinavian countries and was influential farther abroad. The Highlander Folk School in New Market, Tennessee, an institution that Myles Horton founded, was highly influenced by the concept of folk high schools. The Scandinavian folk high school movement is still vital and attracts many students.

TRADE UNION EDUCATION

Education has always been an integral part of trade union development. It has served two purposes. Education is considered important to train members to be efficient agents at the company level, for example, in handling bargaining and negotiating situations. The other main purpose is to educate to raise the level of political consciousness. From very early on in the political struggles of trade unions, educational efforts were taken seriously. Trade unions considered being able to train members to become skillful actors in the company and also in the more general political arena an essential union capacity. This broad educational strategy became very important in the social democratic movements in northern Europe and proved to be a key factor in European politics. To exaggerate the point a bit, the "Eaton" of Norway in the post-World War II era was Sørmarka, the trade union national education facility in Norway. Very few prime ministers and cabinet members came from outside the circles of Sørmarka. In the 1930s, the later prime minister Einar Gerhardsen (1932) wrote a textbook on *Becoming a Union Official,* a book that is still in use.

Trade union education activities involve a combination of practical training for handling union matters on the shop floor and within the larger company, and always involve a strong component of the dissemination of union ideology. These education activities take place in the contradictory context where education for liberation and self-development is dealt with mainly by teaching a specific union ideology.

The conceptual platform for the trade union teaching effort appears to have developed pragmatically, based on specific local experiences. Based on the notion that knowledge is power, trade union education goes beyond this sort of self-evident statement by being linked closely to solving everyday practical problems. The German sociologist Oscar Negt (1977) created a conceptual platform for trade union education. In an introduction to a Danish edition of his work, the translators make the following statements:

> Negt's main interest is to give the working class the possibility, through learning processes, of creating a collective (conscious and unconscious) experience and to give them a political direction . . . [It is important] to take as a point of departure the everyday experiences in the production process, and through information about societal relationships (information that can support the learning process through discussions, materials, analysis, etc.) train the sociological imagination, which means to teach a way of thinking that makes the individual worker capable of understanding the relationships between individual life and the societal development. (p. 7).[3]

For our purposes here, we can accept this platform as an a posteriori synthesis of the conceptual underpinnings of trade union education. It integrated a clear and explicit ideological platform with a practical educational system. In this respect, it has much in common with southern PAR.

POPULAR EDUCATION

The boundaries among adult education, social change efforts, trade union-type consciousness raising, and other initiatives are not easily discerned. The people involved have long been aware of each other and occasionally have worked together. No better example can be found of this than Myles Horton and the Highlander Center.

Myles Horton was a popular educator born in the southern United States in a modest family. He made it through university on a combination of talent and drive. Horton never forgot his origins, and was determined to use education to promote democratic social change. After learning about the Danish folk school movement, Horton decided to set up an education and social change center in the mountains of Tennessee to provide opportunities for local people to meet, reflect, learn, and organize themselves for social change.

Highlander has gone through a number of vicissitudes over the decades, including being attacked by federal agencies and being closed down at the original location, but it is still prospering. It was closely engaged in the civil rights movement, it promoted a quite comprehensive community-based AR project that resulted in the curtailment of many of the most noxious practices of mining companies, and it has become a source of inspiration for generations of social change agents.

Myles Horton was well aware of a wide variety of activist social change traditions, including anarchism, trade union mobilization, civil disobedience, and AR. His own view of the process was remarkably nonauthoritarian. Horton insisted that he could not organize people, that people organized themselves when given a supportive environment and a chance to think for themselves. In this way, Horton set Highlander apart from more leadership-driven change approaches. He venerated local people's experience and capacity for action and communicated this confidence in a way that emboldened generations of change agents.

The story of Highlander is well told both in Horton's biography (Horton, 1990) and in the book he completed with Paolo Freire just before Horton died (Horton & Freire, 1990). Highlander itself continues to be active and is a world center for the promotion of adult education and AR.

POPULAR EDUCATION IN THE SOUTH

Probably the best-known tradition in this field is adult education and social change work in the south. This is an immense field about which numerous books have been written. We have already provided some basic views about it. It is perhaps the best known of all the AR approaches worldwide, and some of its leaders are considered the models of the AR practitioner—Paolo Freire (1970), Budd Hall (1975), Orlando Fals Borda (Fals Borda & Rahman, 1991). Because these practitioners have created effective records of their own thinking and action, they can be read in the original with great profit.

Of course, their broadly similar focus should not obscure their individuality and the uniqueness of the intervention strategies they have developed. Each of them, and their many colleagues worldwide, has a unique voice and perspective to offer. For purposes of this presentation, we will do violence to their individuality to make a compact presentation of the approach.

The points of departure for the popular education approach are resolutely moral and political. The moral point comes first and is never allowed to disappear from view. Humans are entitled to a decent life, free of grinding poverty and political oppression. Humans have a basic dignity and deserve respect as a first principle of all social action.

The political logic that follows from this moral point is simple. Because humans are entitled to be free and have the capacity to manage their own lives effectively, that they do not in so many locations is to be explained. The explanation is oppression backed up by economic power and violence. Thus, the practitioners of this approach build their practices on a strongly Marxist viewpoint. They never lose sight of power and oppression, and they never consider a social change to have occurred until power structures have been overturned and more liberating structures have been put in place.

Along with the many elements of mobilization theories drawn from Marxism and trade union organizing practice, these approaches coincide in privileging local knowledge. The point of departure is that the interests and power of elites make people poor and oppressed, not the poor's own ignorance or lack of ability. Thus, local people in communities and organizations are viewed as having detailed, complex, and valuable knowledge about their situations and the capacity to develop analyses and strategies that can mobilize this knowledge for social change.

The role of the outside expert varies from practitioner to practitioner, but almost always the outsider is a catalyst and facilitator, sometimes pressing, sometimes cautioning, but always trying to convey respect for local people and their rights. This is where the connection to adult education arises because many of these interventions can be understood as forms of adult education and capacity building.

As the AR process continues, people often gain confidence in their own abilities and perceptions, become less willing to submit to authority, and are able to develop organizational strategies to promote social change. In some of these situations, the opponents are simply ignorant or thoughtless. In others, the opponents are truly dangerous and violent.

Thus, such work can range from the development of local organizations that threaten few people to activities that would be defined rightly as insurgency.

Much more could be said about these approaches, but enough has been laid out to encourage those interested to read more of the relevant literature. The focus on local knowledge and its value and the insistence that social change is not a mere matter of adjusting the dials but of changing systems of power are two of the most crucial contributions of the southern AR approach.[4]

ANDRAGOGY: ADULT EDUCATION APPROACHES IN INDUSTRIALIZED COUNTRIES

The general term for adult education in industrialized countries is *andragogy*. Mezirow (1991) defines it the following way: "Andragogy is the professional perspective of adult educators. It has been defined as an organized and sustained effort to assist adults to learn in a way that enhances their capability to function as self-directed learners" (p. 199). On the European continent, andragogy is widely used as a term for adult education, with a number of universities issuing degrees that use this name.

The core of adult education is a view of learning as situated in social, cultural, and material contexts within which individual experiences are transformed into emancipatory actions through critical reflection. Mezirow's (1996) transformation theory

> represents a dialectical synthesis of objectivist learning assumptions of the rational tradition by incorporating the study of nomological regularities and the interpretative learning insights of the cognitive revolution by incorporating the concept of meaning of symbolic interaction. But transformation theory goes beyond the rational tradition to focus on critically reflective emancipatory critique grounded in the very structures of intersubjectivity and communicative competence. (p. 165)

In recent years, the approach has moved much closer to a professional position parallel to AR. Later writings by Mezirow (e.g., 1996) build on Habermas's critique of the scientific tradition and his work on communicative actions. The full step into the world of AR is taken by Wilfred Carr and Stephen Kemmis, both professors of education.

In their book, *Becoming Critical: Education, Knowledge and Action* (1985), they provide an epistemological grounding for AR based on pragmatic philosophy.

A central concept in Western andragogical thinking is the focus on critical reflection and thinking. Brookfield (1987) devotes a whole book to expanding the concept of critical thinking and showing how to facilitate processes that enhance participants' ability to think critically. Brookfield identifies four components in critical thinking:

- Identifying and challenging assumptions is central in critical thinking.
- Challenging the importance of context is crucial to critical thinking.
- Critical thinkers try to imagine and explore alternatives.
- Imagining and exploring alternatives leads to reflective skepticism (p. 7).

An important element in Brookfield's (1986, 1987) work is his focus on the facilitator as a key person in the adult education process. He points to an important contradiction between using power to have students see and reflect on specific issues and then letting go of control over the learning process when the critical thinkers are ready to take over. This contradiction or tension is also discussed in the work of Levin and Martin (1995), where they argue that it is necessary to apply power in a learning situation to be able to gain emancipation.

There are some overlaps and linkages between southern popular education and northern andragogy. Two books, written in a dialogical format, create a reflection on the relationship between the two positions: Myles Horton and Paulo Freire's (1990) *We Make the Road by Walking* and Ira Shor and Paulo Freire's (1987) *A Pedagogy for Liberation*. Both books show how lively and rewarding the relationship between practitioners in the south and the north can be.

REFORMIST EDUCATION PRAXIS IN THE NORTH

Up to this point, we have focused on a variety of strategies that conceive education very broadly. These strategies differ in philosophy, method, and often in politics. Some are hierarchical and controlling; others aim to eliminate hierarchical control systems. Different approaches involve different institutional environments as well. Here, we briefly examine the variety of educational institutions in which AR processes have occurred. Our purpose is to persuade the reader to think of educational strategies in broad terms, beyond the confines of formal educational institutions.

Home Schooling

There is a long tradition of strategies that seek to substitute a privately controlled educational environment for the educational institutions of the state. For example, the home schooling movement has parents or groups of parents cooperating in the process of educating their children outside of public or private schools. Although a variety of ideologies motivates the parents (religious beliefs, demands for higher quality in the curriculum, fears for the safety and health of their children), home schoolers share the notion that education is too important and children are too impressionable for education to be left to strangers. Some believe that formal schooling is a weapon of ideological and class domination. To the extent that they are deeply committed to democratic social change, these people see taking responsibility for the education of their children as a way of struggling against this domination.

Charter Schools

Another approach to primary and secondary education that has gained great momentum in the United States during this decade is the charter school movement. The charter school concept is to end the monopoly of school districts over the provision of education. In more than 20 states in the United States, it is now legally possible to establish schools with unique formats and missions on short-term contracts with school districts. These schools have great freedom to organize as they wish, but they must show that their students perform at least at the standard of the usual schools in the district. They are eligible for local funding just as any other school is, but parents and children are given a choice of schools and learning environments.

Often the founders and teachers develop the school as a social reform project growing out of frustration with the standard school system. The children who come to them often have had bad experiences in the school system. Together, they develop a model of education, administration, and a mission. The results have made believers out of many skeptics, showing that some of the principles of AR (collaborative decision making, respect for stakeholders, value-based decision making) can be put into practice successfully in the school system.[5]

Study Circles

Much more common in Europe than in the Americas, study circles arose in the labor movement as a mechanism for bringing adults together to inquire into the conditions that affect their lives. Study circles are a very common pedagogical approach in trade union education. Many popular education movements in Northern Europe use study circles as a major element in their teaching activities.

The point of study circles is to achieve adult education broadly conceived while focusing on consciousness raising and strategic thinking about specific issues affecting those participating. In one form or another, these kinds of study groups have come and gone in most industrial societies.

Specialized Additive Schools

A host of specialized extrapublic schools has been organized. These include special schools for music, dance, religious instruction, and cultural transmission (e.g., Japanese Saturday schools in many Western countries). Here the focus is additive. These schools intend both to enrich the curriculum and to set the daily public school experience of children in the context of a larger view of the world controlled by parents and teachers.

Corporate Classrooms

One of the most striking features of late capitalism is the emergence of the corporate classroom. The trend is for many companies to create their own training and education systems. Major actors in this field are the multinational consulting firms such as Arthur Andersen and McKinsey and Co. Both have their own training facilities where all newly employed consultants have to go to get an understanding of the corporate culture and to learn the tools of the trade. It seems only natural that these company classrooms spread because this structuring of education closely matches the way these consultants will work as they "educate" and advise their clients. In the United States, it is estimated that more hours of class are taught in classrooms created by and for major private sector corporations than in the 3,000-plus institutions of higher education currently in operation (Eurich, 1985).

Diverse subjects are covered. Many involve technical training and retraining; others involve human relations, management education, accounting practices, self-development, and health care. Increasing numbers of such opportunities are available off-site through advanced information technology to employees.

The corporate classroom has multiple meanings and is open to many possibilities. One meaning is that the formal educational system does such a poor job of preparing employees that further education is necessary for them to function properly in a profitable business. Another view is that the corporate world is so dynamic and challenging that all organizations must become "learning organizations" if they are to compete effectively (Senge, 1990). It is also clear that corporate classrooms can be structured to serve the purposes of socializing and ideologically disciplining employees to the company view of the world.

AR IN NORTHERN HIGHER EDUCATION

The Land-Grant University

One of the most ambitious and well-funded formal educational strategies for democratic social change was the development of the U.S. land-grant university in the 19th century. The basic land-grant system was tied to territorial conditions in the United States. Most states had a certain amount of public land at their disposal. By mandate, the states were to sell some of these public lands and use the proceeds to create a core fund. The income was to be used to build a state university (hence the term *land grant*). Each state was required to have one land-grant university.

As a state university built with public funds, the land-grant university's mission was to be research, education, and public service linked in a putatively seamless web. These universities were to educate the people of the state, to conduct research on subjects of practical interest to the citizens of the state, and to disseminate that knowledge directly to the people of the state. The basic formulation behind the land-grant university is closely linked to AR. It involves a systematic partnership between academic and nonacademic stakeholders, a full dialogue among them about their needs and interests, and collaborative research and testing of the results. Despite this, the land-grant university has not become the source of major AR initiatives.

Though there is little question that such public universities have carried out many of the required services and have prospered mightily,[6] over the years the land-grant universities have become mainly the servants of social power rather than an avenue to the democratization of knowledge. Designed originally as institutions in which faculty would be encouraged and rewarded for their combined intellectual and practical contributions to society, these universities have become internally subdivided into high-status faculty who conduct non- and anti-applied research and extension faculty and other personnel who are much lower in status.

The land-grant universities have routinely supported large farmers and powerful business interests, the substitution of machinery for labor, and other hierarchical efforts. The land-grant concept is an idea hijacked by power, even though the legislative and economic mandate of the system should have supported a far more democratic outcome. Under these conditions, the development of a strongly reformist AR within university walls would not be particularly welcome. And yet, a few reforms manage to be undertaken.

Within the University Attempts at Reform

In Chapter 8, "Action Research Cases From Practice II," we provide an example of an attempt to use AR to reform the internal operations of a unit within a university. More examples can be given. One particularly interesting case is the work by Michael Reynolds undertaken at Cornell (1994). A PhD candidate in education at Cornell, Reynolds was earning his way through graduate school by serving as a teaching assistant in the physics department.

Since the late 1960s, physics had offered one introductory sequence on an autotutorial basis. This means there are no lectures and the learning is self-paced, with the students organizing their studies and using labs and teaching assistants to help them master the material. This concept was still widely accepted at Cornell, but the course had fallen into disrepute. Reynolds decided it might be possible to do an AR project by involving the lead professor, the lecturer in charge, the teaching assistants, and the students in a collaborative study and reform effort.

With money acquired from the associate vice president for academic programs, Reynolds undertook an extensive project in which all dimensions of the course were subjected to close scrutiny and reform. The team found out that the course was overpacked with material because new physics material had been added without any mechanism for eliminating existing material. It also found out that the students were dissatisfied with the textbook, and the team did a collaborative study to select a new one.

After a protracted process, the course was completely revamped. The students did remarkably better on the tests, and their satisfaction with the course was enormously better. Reynolds wrote up the results, shared them with the collaborators who offered criticism, and then requested that they contribute their own reflections to a chapter in the dissertation. They did so and they attended his PhD dissertation defense. From the whole process, we learned that AR is possible in higher education and works very well as a device for curriculum reform. Yet, a proposal to expand this approach to curriculum reform to other courses at Cornell was turned down and nothing further of this sort has been attempted.

This case shows that AR regarding the management and improvement of essential university functions is possible. We also think it is highly desirable. But we know from experience that hierarchical patterns of administration and hermetically sealed departmental fiefdoms make any attempt at such reforms a real battle.

Institutions of Higher Education With
Special Missions Related to AR

A number of institutions develop their educational programs through various combinations of service learning, internships, and co-ops in which work experience and intellectual activity are integrated in the manner that Dewey envisioned. Famous for this are institutions such as Antioch University and Berea College.

SUPPORT GROUPS

Though they might appear to be stretching the notion of education, support groups involve many of the elements of adult education and AR that we have been discussing. Support groups are intentionally created voluntary groups of individuals and families who have been affected by a shared problem: cancer in the family, spousal abuse, substance abuse. The list of support groups is endless.

These groups vary greatly in their organization and philosophies, but they do build on the notion of people coming together to share their dilemmas, solutions, weaknesses, and strengths to help each other come to terms with difficult situations. Often support groups have developed into social change initiatives through the learning acquired in the process. Organizations combating drunk driving, spouse abuse, and many other social issues originated in small support group efforts. A well-documented case that shows the connection between support groups and AR is found in the work by Chessler and Chesney (1995) on support for parents of children with cancer.

NONGOVERNMENTAL ORGANIZATIONS

Nongovernmental organizations (NGOs) in many parts of the world develop and administer extensive educational programs in support of particular kinds of social change of interest to them. Ecological education, agricultural education, sex education, health education, nutrition, and similar themes form the core of the activities of many NGOs.

Though now many NGOs are immense and they are a diverse lot, they generally share a view of international development in which the people, rather than governments and monied interests, are the real agents of change. Historically, NGOs have tended to invest in people so that the people make changes and sustain the changes themselves. This view makes popular education a high priority and constant element in the activities of NGOs.

MISSIONS AND EVANGELIZATION

Whatever else it is, missionization is certainly an educational effort. Missionization is a reality in all the countries of the world, and it is not likely to disappear soon. Stereotypically, missionaries are viewed either as naive do-gooders or as religious fanatics. Though there are plenty who fit this image, recent generations of missionaries are considerably more sophisticated. Some groups are basically popular educators who operate by trying to live out their ideology in local communities, contributing labor and resources to projects of value to the people. Others bring significant resources into communities and use these resources to gather people both for change efforts and for missionization. In some cases, only such religious groups have the courage, political independence, and resources to be in dangerous and divided places. Governments may be punishing the area, afraid of it, or denying the existence of problems. Thus, missionization occasionally reaches those unreached by other means.

A great array of educational strategies accompanies this process, including literacy campaigns, the formation of social groups with particular local or national change projects (see Kurt Ver Beek on the Lenca Indian mobilization in Honduras, 1996), Bible study groups, health clinics, and refugee camps. Some of these organizations promote ideologies of democratization as part of their Christian message.

Although we do not question the legitimacy of their presence, it is important to examine their practices closely. Because one element in missionization is a belief in a final or ultimate truth, there is always the possibility of the imposition of an unwanted framework on local people. When this happens, missionization is inimical to AR. But this is not always the case, and AR practitioners should keep an open mind about missionization, just as they need to be alert to the possibilities for abuse in NGOs, land-grant universities, and everywhere else that democratic interventions are being attempted.

INTERNATIONAL DEVELOPMENT AGENCIES

Some of the most powerful and richest agencies dealing in education are the arms of national governments and international institutions that funnel national funds into development assistance programs. This is an extremely complex topic. These agencies are a dominant force on the same scene where the NGOs and mission organizations operate. We are now speaking of agencies such as the U.S. Agency for International Development, NORAD of Norway, the World Health Organization, the World Bank, and the International Monetary Fund. Built largely on budgets provided by national governments, these agencies support development programs in many countries around the world.

Although it is still fair to say that the bulk of these projects fund large-scale infrastructures, are built from the top down, have generally resulted in only modest improvements in the conditions for the poor, and have not contributed much to democratization, some of the programs have had meaningful local effects. The so-called *green revolution* technologies in the improvement of yields of major food grains have improved the nutritional and health status of people in some world areas. Under the aegis of development programs, thousands of people from poor countries have been sent to Western industrial countries for further education, in some cases to good effect and in others, never to return home at all. These very agencies, in recent years, have been active promoters of techniques such as participatory rural appraisal (with elements of AR), about which we write in Chapter 14, "Participatory Evaluation and Participatory Rural Appraisal." Most now announce their commitment to participatory development strategies, though many of us in AR view these commitments with skepticism because the record of these national efforts is extremely mixed. The funding appropriations that drive them serve national political interests, regardless of the ideological packaging they are given.

One constant feature of these programs over the last 25 years is the assertion that development requires educational and attitudinal change.

A constant feature of the critiques of such programs is their failure to be knowledgeable about local people or to respect local knowledge. Although there is some attempt to improve the record on this, structurally, international development agencies are driven from the top down to meet the goals of the funders, not the local beneficiaries. When these goals are in the interests of local people, there may be room for AR processes. When they are not, AR practitioners necessarily oppose them together with local actors. Of course, distinguishing which kind of situation is which is always a complex judgement call.

Whatever we think of them, these agencies cannot be ignored. They are an important part of the environment of AR and occasionally operate as promoters of action research, as we show in Chapter 14, "Participatory Evaluation and Participatory Rural Appraisal."

CONCLUSION

In many ways, this chapter embodies the overall dilemma of this book: the diversity and complexity of AR approaches. Educational strategies relevant to AR are numerous, diverse, and even contradictory. They range from radical democratization through a variety of organizing techniques to involvement in large formal educational institutions and national and international agencies. To make competent judgements about such efforts is a matter of understanding the details of their operation and not just the general ideological programs. Meaningful AR has been done in all the venues discussed. Profoundly co-opted and repressive work has also been done in all these locations. It is necessary to apply the criteria of AR method, practice, and political-moral goals to any kind of educational initiative to decide its possibilities and its worth. There are no shortcuts.

Notes

1. Because this field has a long history and is reasonably well organized, a number of general books can introduce readers to the major contours. Among some of the most useful general sources are Paolo Freire's (1970) *Pedagogy of the Oppressed*; Budd Hall's (1975) classic article "Participatory Research: An Approach for Change"; the many articles over the years of publication in the journal *Convergence*; Carr and Kemmis' (1985) *Becoming*

Critical; John Elliott's (1991) *Action Research for Educational Change*; and a recent review article by Susan Noffke (1994).

2. We remind the reader that the concepts of south and its opposite, north, are slippery. The south refers to people who are impoverished and oppressed. Because a greater percentage of such people exist in poor countries, the designation south has become a cover term for this, but there are many southern locations in the north, and initiatives such as Highlander were built on the same principles of social and economic justice as we find supporting these change efforts in the south.

3. This is our English translation.

4. For further reading, we recommend Paolo Freire's (1970) *Pedagogy of the Oppressed*; Budd Hall's (1975) classic article "Participatory Research: An Approach for Change"; and Orlando Fals Borda and Mohammed Anisur Rahman (1991) *Action and Knowledge*. To see a mix of these approaches in the south and the north, an excellent source is Peter Park, Mary Brydon-Miller, Budd Hall, and Ted Jackson (1993), *Voices of Change: Participatory Research in the United States and Canada.*

5. An excellent overall review of this movement can be found in Joe Nathan (1996).

6. One need only attend the immense annual meetings of the National Association of State Universities and Land Grant Colleges to see how very successful, at least economically, they have been as institutions.

14

Participatory Evaluation and Participatory Rural Appraisal

Evaluation and auditing processes are a common site of some of the most authoritarian, coercive behavior in organizational life. Private funders, local authorities, governments, and organizational leaders nearly all require evaluations for programs that they fund either to guide or to legitimate their funding decisions or to help them keep activities that they support under their control. Evaluations are often the make-or-break moment in the life of a project and are used as decision support mechanisms by the funder. As a result, evaluation has become a large professional field and a major consulting business.

Being visited by an evaluator, accountant, assessor, accreditation reviewer, or any of the many other figures playing a professional evaluation role is usually experienced as being placed in a subordinate position to a person whose professional role is to review and evaluate you, your program, or your organization "objectively." Nearly all of us have had experiences with such evaluations, and so it should be easy to conjure up the image of the objective, impartial outsider who asks hard questions in what is frequently but not always experienced as a hostile way. Distance is supposed to be crucial in conventional evaluation, and attempts to co-opt an evaluator are to be guarded against (and, of course, often engaged in). Although some evaluators are more skilled than others in managing their relationships with their subjects, conventional evaluation is assumed to center around a potential conflict of interest between the evaluator and the subjects.

The reader will probably have noticed how closely this approach to evaluation parallels the concepts of conventional social science. The notions of objectivity, distance, and the need to avoid bias and co-optation match closely the standard rules for conventional social research with the complex mechanisms of sampling, statistical testing, and the like. In addition, most conventional evaluations take place at the end of a project or at major intervals after some significant project activity has occurred. The purpose of the evaluation is generally to "grade" the performance of the project and its leaders, though, of course, some interim evaluations aim to produce useful information for subsequent phases of the project. One clear assumption is that the subjects should not be trusted to provide either an honest or a good-quality evaluation of themselves and that making use of the evaluation results for immediate and ongoing changes in the project is not a principal goal. Being evaluated this way gives a very good idea what it feels like to be treated as a research subject by a conventional social researcher.

Action research (AR) approaches have made significant contributions to this field by opening up the notion of evaluation to collaborative and participatory approaches, an idea that is just beginning to take hold but that revolutionizes evaluation processes. In this chapter, we discuss two very different and, until now, completely separate groups of approaches that center on issues of evaluation and accounting—participatory evaluation and participatory rural appraisal (PRA). Although these emerged from very different institutional sources and focus on different kinds of processes, both involve the problem owners in the process of generating the basic data on which project design, redesign, and evaluation are constructed. Although our treatment of these subjects is rather brief, these two approaches have generated an immense amount of work in

AR. PRA is especially well funded and, indeed, is in vogue these days in development circles.

◄o►

PARTICIPATORY EVALUATION

Evaluation, as a field of professional work, has been dominated historically by conventional social scientists and accountability thinking. To a high degree, evaluation has focused on measuring and reporting the merits and defects of specific activities, and the outcome of evaluations has taken the form of reports to the authorities who fund the activity or who are responsible for program oversight so that they can document the outcomes of particular activities. Conventional evaluation places little or no emphasis on making a positive effect on a project while it is underway, except in cases of interim evaluations of multiyear projects. Generally, it records outcomes for a particular audience of decision makers.

Programs to fight poverty, to teach the uneducated to read, or to support rural community efforts to survive have all received the scrutiny of evaluators. Such evaluations generally result in reports that are inaccessible to the stakeholders in the programs, either because they are kept confidential or they are written in such a way as to be difficult for most nonprofessionals to understand. Evaluations conducted in this fashion have a negative effect on local participants and their autonomy as intelligent individuals. They have little say in regard to what is evaluated, how it is done, and how to make sense of the results. They simply are treated as the informants for the evaluators—placing them in a passive relationship to the outside and "expert" evaluators. This is because one of the most basic tenets of conventional evaluation is that the essence of evaluation is the professional evaluator's own judgement of the outcome (Scriven, 1995). The cornerstone of the profession, in this view, is to make neutral and objective judgements of the activities under evaluation.

Despite its importance and the degree to which evaluators have been successful in selling consumers of evaluations this view, this is a problematic position for evaluators. The exclusively professional focus and the hierarchical approach make evaluation an activity without practical utility for the programs being evaluated. At best, such evaluations legitimate spending on or terminating projects but do little to help program participants in their daily lives.

In response to this dilemma, recently some evaluators began to develop participative approaches in which the evaluator and the evaluands have created a closer relationship and opened up the possibilities of mutual learning. Patton (1986) was one of the first to point to this different path for evaluation. In his title, *Utilization-Focused Evaluation*, Patton points to the use of the evaluation results to improve projects as an imperative in evaluation work:

> What fundamentally distinguishes utilization-focused evaluation from other approaches is that the evaluator does not alone carry this burden for making choices about the nature, purpose content, and methods of evaluation. These decisions are shared by an identifiable and organized group of intended users. (p. 53)

Basically, Patton (1986) aims to include every stakeholder, as defined by him. They "are people, who have a stake—a vested interest—in evaluation findings" (p. 43).

For any evaluation there are multiple stakeholders—program funders, staff, administrators, clients, and others—with a direct or even indirect interest in program effectiveness. Although much of Patton's (1986) attention is paid to the funders, staff, and administrators, the recipients of the project are included in his thinking and evaluation process. Patton's argument is important in pinpointing how utilization depends on stakeholders' involvement in the evaluation process.

The insight that involvement is necessary for getting the results of evaluations to be used leads to an interest in ways program recipients themselves can deal with evaluation results. These recipients are in a different position from all other stakeholders because they are the actors who potentially should benefit most from the evaluation. Their interest in the program is not the same as the interest of the program staff. They are, in a certain sense, the primary actors in any program, simply because the focus of the activity is to do something about their life situation. No other stakeholder group is in such a position, and so it is a powerful move to focus attention on ways these primary beneficiaries can use the evaluation.

This is where the participatory approach to evaluation makes its appearance. Participatory evaluation aims to create a learning process for the program recipients that will help them in their effort to reach desired goals. Participatory approaches to evaluation purposely muddy the distinction between the program activity and evaluation results because the evaluation aims to make a difference by helping program recipients achieve their goals better. Such an approach often goes even farther and helps to question the definition and ranking of the goals of the program being evaluated.

In an important book on participatory evaluation, Egon Guba and Yvonna Lincoln's (1989) *Fourth Generation Evaluation* introduces a constructivist approach to evaluation, arguing that evaluation is a process of construction and reconstruction of realities. This book is a natural follow-up to their work *Naturalistic Inquiry* (1985), which centers on a thorough development of a postpositivistic methodological stance for the social sciences. *Fourth Generation Evaluation* focuses on carving out an epistemological position for constructivist social science and forwarding a methodological position for researchers who approach the field in a nonpositivistic manner. The underlying theme of Guba and Lincoln's work is to urge social researchers to engage with people directly to make sense of the evaluation process and results. Through this move, participation becomes a central element in debates about contemporary evaluation praxis. As Guba and Lincoln (1989) say, "the major task for the constructivist investigator is to tease out the constructions that various actors in the setting hold and, so far as possible, to bring them into conjunction—a joining—with one another and with whatever other information can be brought to bear on the issues involved" (p. 142).

Patton, Lincoln, and Guba are not the only voices suggesting this approach. Brunner and Guzman's (1989) "Participatory Evaluation: A Tool to Assess Projects and Empower People" is an effort to identify evaluation as "a methodological component of the educational development project that aims at empowering the dominated groups in a society so that they will be able to join the struggle for a just and egalitarian society" (p. 10). Weiss and Greene (1992) and Patti Lather (1991) are other proponents of this approach.

Michelle Fine (1996) summarizes this work in the form of five commitments to participatory evaluation research: building local capacity, evaluation and reform, an ethic of inquiry, evaluation and democratic participation, and rethinking the "products" of evaluation research.

A standard practice in participatory evaluation is to involve the recipients of a program or an activity in the process of interpreting evaluation results. The most conventional way to do this is to discuss the collected data with the local people as a way of making sense of the findings. A more advanced form is to involve participants in the process of designing what to evaluate from the beginning of the project (e.g., decide on the variables), to engage them in the data collection process, and to include them in making sense of the findings.

This participatory process can differ widely among evaluation practitioners. Each evaluator engages the participants in ways that are comfortable for both parties. Some construct meetings, others use group dynamic processes—search conference "look-alikes" have been used—and other participatory techniques.

Participatory evaluation strategies have a lot in common with the complexity, diversity, and specificity of AR approaches in general. Participatory evaluation, though a form of practice in its own right, builds directly on work from AR, and many of the authors refer directly to particular AR works as part of their intellectual repertoire.

Finne et al. (1995) call one recent development *trailing research*. Here participatory approaches to evaluation are merged directly with an AR process. The central idea of this process is to establish a continued engagement with stakeholders throughout the whole program period. The evaluators, jointly with stakeholders, decide on issues to evaluate. Then the research team usually collects relevant data and makes some preliminary analyses, and the stakeholders are involved in the sense-making processes. Out of this mutual learning process emerges redesigned actions implemented in the ongoing program to attain goals or to redirect the program toward new goals.

Although we can clearly see parallels between participatory evaluation and AR more generally, there are some important differences in emphasis. Participatory evaluation emphasizes the participatory dimension as the cornerstone of every move in the process. Most forms of AR have a more developed view of the action orientation and group processes involved in a change project and emphasize a variety of techniques for promoting group actions above and beyond the evaluation part of the process. This is most evident in participatory evaluations that focus on giving a voice to groups that usually are silent but lack a clear focus and strategy about how to channel voices into actions for improving conditions.

By the same token, a good deal of AR has been careless in data gathering and analysis strategies of the sort participatory evaluation excels in. As the field continues to develop, a closer rapprochement between participatory evaluators and other action researchers will be invaluable for both groups.

PARTICIPATORY RURAL APPRAISAL

Linked to a variety of forms of participatory evaluation but occupying a very different institutional position is a collection of approaches that now generally go under the name of participatory rural appraisal (PRA).[1] PRA is an element in overall socioeconomic development programs, mainly in poor countries. These strategies aim to develop more reliable baseline data about problems through involvement of local people in the definition and documentation of those problems. Given the proliferation of worldwide development projects and PRA at present, it is impossible to provide even a partial introduction to the literature. We simply hope to give the reader enough to get started.

There are many organizations where a variety of participatory appraisal strategies are used. Preeminent among them is the Institute for Development Studies at Sussex; the best-known person and most prolific writer in this field is Robert Chambers. We draw heavily on Chambers here,[2] but we remind the readers that related approaches have been developed in many locations, including ISNAR in Holland, the International Potato Center in Peru, in some components of the Cornell Institute for International Agriculture, Food, and Development at Cornell University, and in a number of other locations worldwide. Nevertheless, Chambers is undoubtedly the best synthesizer of what is being learned, is unusually thorough in documenting the work of others, and is remarkably assiduous in the practice of self-criticism. So Chambers's work provides a good point of entry to the practices of a kind of participatory evaluation in what is one of the largest-scale social interventions worldwide: economic development assistance programs for poor countries.

Given the political positions we have taken in this book, it is no surprise that we are not unambiguous supporters of development assistance programs as currently structured and we are dubious about the degree to which meaningful political participation can be built into them. There clearly are many constraints built into the political economy of development that prevent participation from being generated beyond very narrow limits. At the same time, we are fully conscious that more socially ambitious approaches to development through liberation ideologies have generally failed, and that most development work is done precisely in the kinds of agencies that PRA is designed to help. Thus, we believe that PRA deserves a serious look from anyone interested in AR. Until workable alternative approaches to international poverty are developed, PRA embodies one of the most participatory development practices available.

The overall framing of international development work sets a great number of constraints around what can be done and how. International development, mainly an arm of the foreign policy interests of the industrial nations, has created an immense international bureaucracy, professional societies, international institutes, academic fields, journals, book series, and a huge army of practitioners, not a few who have made nice livings by being experts on the world's poor. This multibillion dollar activity gained initial momentum in the 1950s, flourished for a time, and then came under increasingly hostile governmental scrutiny from many sides. Among the donor states, governmental oversight groups began to feel that sending money abroad was a waste of resources, that developing the economies of other countries created harmful competition for national industries, and that it would be better to give money only when it was profitable for the donor nation to do so. Although these views have never fully prevailed, they have created extremely hierarchical systems for designing and evaluating development programs.

In the past 15 years or so, many private voluntary organizations (PVOs) and nongovernmental organizations (NGOs) have entered the development scene as major players. Not constrained by the same nationalistic rationales and politics, these organizations have diversified approaches to development considerably. They are free to be more openly ideological about their goals because they are intentionally created to foment certain kinds of social, economic, and ethical goals. As a result, the present international development scene is a complex patchwork of the big international development projects of nation-states and the activities of PVOs and NGOs. PRA is used in both venues.

To understand why PRA is an important departure from previous practice, it is necessary to have a brief sense of the history of international development work. There have been two major approaches to these issues since the late 1950s—liberal and Marxist—and there have been a number of other more topical concerns that have moved across this landscape as well, including feminism, environmentalism, participation, and international human rights.

The dominant approach to development has been liberal theory. This view is based on a diagnosis of problems of development that treat poverty as an unfortunate and improper outcome of the workings of the world economy that can be corrected by well-targeted actions. A host of theories and methods has supported this generally optimistic line. The predominant paradigm has been that of modernization, in which the problem of poverty is attributed to the unfortunate continuation of a series of traditional and putatively irrational practices that prevent people from doing what is in their best interest. Some theorists have seen this irrationality as a characteristic of uneducated people in general. Others have seen it as the selfish exploitation of the many by a few "traditional" leaders whose positions must be undermined. A wide variety of capital formation theories predominated in the early days of development theory writing arguing that capital formation was the key to successful economic development. Just what that meant differed from theorist to theorist. Often it meant controlling population growth so that per capita income would become higher, or it meant learning how to use and conserve resources better so that the basic productive infrastructure would improve, or it meant an emphasis on education and communication strategies to make "traditional" people into "modern" thinkers.

Technological approaches to development have always been popular with Western industrialized nations. Building dams, roads, and schools and sending tractors, fertilizers, and other technologies have been preferred forms of development assistance and often quite profitable to the donor's employees. More recently, biological technologies such as the green revolution, new varieties of grain seeds and cultivation systems, and integrated pest management have become popular. Generally speaking, these technologies have been developed and often manufactured in the West and then are deployed (or occasionally imposed) on the rest. They have the feature of treating world poverty as a matter to be solved by production technologies rather than by political change and the redistribution of land and capital.

These approaches have been very powerful because governments with lots of money and political clout backed them. National development programs for a whole generation were built on these kinds of notions, as were the agendas of international development agencies such as the International Monetary Fund, the World Bank, and the international agricultural research institutes that have been developing new and more productive varieties of basic food crops. Now PVOs and NGOs have become major players on the scene, adding their particular slant to the development framework.

Counterposed to this development approach has always been a wide variety of political economy theories about the world under development. Many of these are Marxist or neo-Marxist in inspiration and understand the problems of poverty as a constitutive principle of capitalism. The modern world system is unequally developed because the rich countries exploit the poor countries as a source of cheap raw materials, labor, and products. From this vantage point, underdevelopment is a product of capitalism, and international development programs are in fact a cover for political coercion and the maintenance or expansion of the existing order.

This view of the problem leads to very different forms of practice. The principal goal is to break dependency on the powerful and wealthy nations that master the system. Because this is both an extremely risky process and quite unlikely to succeed under current conditions, it has attracted many people ideologically as a way of explaining persistent poverty, but it has not inspired very many revolts. It has influenced the practices of a considerable number of NGOs around the world, however, whose intervention strategies are informed by Marxist analysis and who understand economic development as requiring an intentional democratization of power structures.

Beginning in the early 1970s, other agendas began to find their way into conventional international development thinking. The rising feminist movement developed interpretations of inequality and gender that began to add new dimensions to the problems of development by showing that economic development alone would not decrease male domination of women. Feminist theory also gave a strong impetus to critiques of the liberal international development paradigm in general and supported the development of more participatory epistemological positions.

The environmental movement also had a significant influence. Early development practice did not have a strong sense of the problems of global ecology and strongly emphasized big, energy-intensive infrastructure projects (from which many development agencies and private sector companies derived lots of financial benefits). The emergence of the "small is beautiful" (Schumacher, 1973) and green movements also provided powerful critiques of both the liberal and the Marxist views of development and pressed for more holistic approaches to the complexities of wealth and poverty. This coincided with the emergence of a strong movement for international human rights that went beyond arguments for a tolerable basic standard of living and included the rights to self-determination, freedom from coercion, gender equality, the rights of children and fetuses, and the rights of ethnic groups.

Together, these movements have produced a leavening effect on the macrodevelopment strategies in donor states because they were gradually forced to pay at least lip service to gender, environment, and human rights issues to maintain any kind of ideological legitimacy. This has coincided with events within the wealthy funding countries, which are experiencing their own complex internal dynamics. These days, efficiency, downsizing, participation, and competitiveness are the watchwords of business, and these ideologies have filtered into development agencies. At the same time, on the other end of the political spectrum are increasing attacks on foreign aid as a useless waste of money on people whose poverty is their own fault, an ideology that takes us back to the 1950s. These developments are not surprising in advanced capitalist societies where the distance between the rich and poor yawns wider each year.

Now all the lines have become blurred. Liberal and Marxist approaches were easily distinguished before, but now liberal approaches have appropriated much of the language of Marxist, feminist, and ecological analysis. NGOs have complicated the ideological scene with a huge number of agendas driven by a wide variety of ideologies running from Christian evangelism to the rights of infants and trees. This complex situation has created an environment in which development organizations are forced to restructure themselves, redefine their methods, and try to find new modes of operation. Into this breech, a few development practitioners have inserted more participatory approaches to development.

The Specifics of PRA

Though all major social research is a collaborative endeavor, drawing on the experiences, theories, and expertise of generations of researchers, PRA, like Freire's pedagogy of the oppressed, is strongly associated with the representations of it made by a single practitioner: Robert Chambers. Though by no means the only practitioner, Chambers has developed the most succinct and fully articulated statements of PRA in a series of papers (Chambers, 1994a, 1994b, 1994c), in many training workshops, in colloquia around the world, and now in an excellent book that summarizes the state of the art, *Whose Reality Counts? Putting the First Last* (1997).

In Chambers's account, PRA has its origin in multiple, separate strands of activity. It draws on participatory research (what we have called southern participatory AR). It also draws in elements from the diverse practices of applied or action anthropology, activities that began in the 1950s and continue but that do not have a strong participatory intent. PRA also rests on a variety of traditions of what is loosely called "farming systems research" and includes close observation of local farming practices from a systems perspective and also some notions of on-farm research as a proper modality for the creation of development strategies.

The point of entry for PRA is provided by one of the most bizarre and frustrating dynamics of development programs over the years: the complete lack of baseline data for the development of program strategies and the evaluation of outcomes. A whole generation of interventions was based on presumptions about what was wrong, guesses about how to fix it, and post hoc justifications of the failed strategies. Yet the development establishment resisted baseline research as too expensive, or unnecessary, or impossible. Greenwood himself developed an early (and carefully ignored) position paper (1980) on this subject, arguing that rapid, efficient, and meaningful baseline data could and should be collected.

Over time, the notion that quick baseline studies were necessary and possible developed and, with it, a set of strategies called rapid rural appraisal (RRA) (Belshaw, 1981; Chambers, 1981). RRA was taught at the International Institute for Environment and Development in London, and periodicals such as *RRA Notes* kept track of the developments.

By the mid-1980s, RRA began to criss-cross with a variety of other developments that were popularizing notions of participation in development work, as well as in industrial and service organization restructuring. Before long, a union was forged between RRA and PRA in which RRA was modified to emphasize local knowledge and participation more fully and completely. Although RRA was more expert centered and academically based, PRA gained more momentum through the activities of NGOs worldwide. It stressed local knowledge and training, empowerment, and the development of sustainable initiatives for local self-management. At least in the statement of its aims, PRA sounds very much like many varieties of AR discussed throughout this book.

Unlike many other forms of AR other than participatory evaluation, PRA has a relatively specific set of techniques and methods associated with it. Chambers details these in his papers and book, which should be consulted to get an idea of the multiplicity and flexibility of the methods used. We mention a few here to give the reader a flavor of the approach.

PRA involves a number of interviewing and sampling methods and some specific group and team dynamics approaches. Among the approaches used are participatory mapping and modeling of local communities and problem areas, the picking of key informants as local experts, attempts to identify the different significant local groups and to make contacts with some members of each, having participants help analyze things written about them, the development of timeline and trend analyses with local information, the development of seasonal calendars including crop cycles and labor requirements, and the development of teams and team contracts. Flexibility, attentiveness to the way local people think and react, and a powerful belief in the knowledge systems of local people are the keys to PRA.

Each PRA project is a slightly different mobilization of the techniques depending on the expertise of the outsiders coming in, the capacities available locally, and the problems being examined. Having become massively popular, PRA is now applied in a multitude of situations, including participatory rural appraisal, the development of participatory evaluations of projects, particular topical studies, and as the source of training programs for both community members and outsiders.

PRA sounds many themes familiar from AR. Local knowledge is given pride of place. The behavior of outside experts is carefully controlled to provide space for insiders to make their own choices. The methods are not applied scattershot, and there is a kind of reasonable sequencing in the activity that moves from one kind of knowledge and team dynamics to more complex ones over time. PRA also deals with issues of validity and reliability of data, and it claims to give local people a greater right to define their own situation and act on it.

Issues of power and knowledge are joined directly, at least in Chambers's own practice. The subtitle of his 1997 book, *Putting the First Last*, gives the flavor. The assumption is that the ideas and practices of the rich and powerful will dominate in all situations unless they are intentionally subverted by "handing over the stick" to the local people, by insisting on hearing their views, and by respecting their knowledge. Development professionals are the ones who must change, learn to listen, and then take what they learn to become advocates for local people.

Critiques of PRA abound because of the many problems surrounding its practice. The development establishment has welcomed it as a panacea, without much caring about its participatory dimensions other than the euphonic sound the word *participation* has in moral debates. PRAs are often mandated, but the larger conditions in the agencies that mandate them prejudge the outcome of the work and carry on projects that were already defined without the use of PRA. PRA, though an array of techniques, in the hands of incompetent or insincere practitioners can become an empty formalism, a set of ritual steps to go through rather than a set of tools to be deployed differently as the complexities of local situations become better understood. Of course, this co-opted formalism is not unique to PRA; it is a problem in all forms of AR.

PRA, often sponsored by powerful external agencies, is caught in a contradiction between espousing participatory methods while working within a coercive institutional environment. Feminists have pointed out that many PRAs fail because they do not get to the voiceless members of the community and thus create a false impression of the dynamics of local situations, especially when the outside agents are male and dealing with male local leaders. Some of the best PRA practitioners have taken these criticisms seriously and struggle with these problems.

It seems somewhat surprising that PRA has been so easily co-opted by orthodox development interests. David Mosse (1993) points not to the failure of PRA but to its weaknesses in practice and why it should not be viewed as a panacea. He shows how PRA can unintentionally structure local knowledge to reflect existing social relationships by failing to develop the long-term and subtle sensitivity to local power relationships that an AR project would necessarily develop.

When a PRA team arrives in a community and begins a rapid process of data collection and analysis, it usually does not have the time or inclination to become aware in a detailed, subtle, ethnographic way about the nuances of local power. As a result, the coercion and collusion that dictate the public face of many communities are quite likely to be expressed in the outcomes. PRA is not immune to gender bias for these same reasons because formal representations of knowledge can inhibit women's contribution to its formulation.

At its worst, PRA is an extractive approach to information in which data are gathered for the purposes of the development agency rather than for meeting the espoused intention of having the agency's programs built to suit the needs of the community. Thus, a PRA team may come in, organize a major data gathering effort, organize the data, and leave, designing the intervention in the local community on this basis and calling the process participatory.

Mosse (1993) points out that the participatory language of PRA also can be experienced as oppressive in some situations. When local people ask PRA teams about what should be done and the answer is that "the community should decide," local people can easily experience this as an unwillingness of powerful outsiders to reveal to the local people what their true agenda is. This creates additional insecurity and distrust, whereas in the minds of the PRA team members, they are being open and participatory.

Whatever the problems involved in its deployment, there is a clear relationship between PRA, participatory evaluation more generally, and AR. Local knowledge is valued and is taken as the basis for development program design and implementation. PRA does result in some warrants for action. These approaches also contain a strong critique of urban professionalism as a key element and treat the insider-outsider relationship as a key dimension in the dynamics of the processes.

At the same time, there are dissonances in PRA where it does not match well other forms of AR practice and feminist critiques. PRA is avowedly short-term, whereas AR is generally conceptualized as a long-term relationship between insiders and outsiders. Despite Chambers's own realism about these matters, much writing and practice in PRA are insensitive to power relations, a key element in any AR approach. Though PRA has identified the problem of gender differences as they affect its method, it is clear that PRA has not been sufficiently sensitive to gender relations, and we doubt that such a short-term and rather formalistic approach can overcome these problems.

Paralleling our critique of participatory evaluation, after the initial PRA, the action plans and methodologies to be deployed are much less clearly articulated. PRA, as a short-term intervention, does not contain a clear strategy for sustaining long-term change. Although it does develop local knowledge and teams, it does not appear to be as thoughtful as many AR projects have been about working toward sustainable relationships that will keep innovations from deteriorating back to the original situation.

PRA lacks a clear position with regard to dealing with the intragroup conflicts that it identifies. Local people, when understood properly, have many and often divergent or incompatible interests. PRA is silent on processes that bring these differences together for the purpose of developing an acceptable and fair approach.

We see PRA as an interesting approach and a modestly participatory one. But for now, the agenda for PRA work is still heavily in the hands of the external funders. This opens up the possibility of changing some elements in externally imposed projects, but it does not do so in a very robust way. And by being short-term, PRA is not likely to alter existing power relations to a very significant degree. All that said, PRA is a far better option than previous practices for agencies that are the plainly coercive political arms of foreign governments.

CONCLUSION

Participatory evaluation and PRA are rapidly growing and highly significant developments directly relevant to AR. More dialogue among practitioners is needed to share effectively the diverse kinds of knowledge and experiences they have had and to build more robust approaches for all. The future of AR is intimately tied to what happens in participatory evaluation and PRA, and a strong dialogue among practitioners is essential to the future of all of us.

Notes

1. The terminology and abbreviations are hard to keep up with. PRA emerged out of rapid rural appraisal, which itself arose from a combination of baseline studies, farming systems research, and small farmer focused development initiatives. Recently, the term *PRA* is falling into disfavor and is being replaced by *participatory learning analysis (PLA)*. We use PRA as the terminology for the current chapter.

2. This decision is also dictated by Greenwood's participation in a 2-day workshop on PRA given by Robert Chambers at Cornell University in the spring of 1997.

Conclusion

Elaborate conclusions are not necessary to bring this work to a close. We have made a systematic attempt to define, describe, and justify action research (AR), and we have set this effort into philosophical, methodological, and institutional context. We have presented our own preferred approach and some of the wide variety of other AR approaches important to the field.

—◀o▶—

A great deal has been left out. Many of the approaches have been presented without sufficient nuance. Important contributors to the field have not been mentioned. Complex issues have sometimes received brief treatments. As we said at the beginning, we know that the map is not the territory, but we hope that this mapping has whetted the reader's appetite for AR and that it will serve as a beginning point for a longer itinerary through these approaches.

We do believe that AR can help us build a better and freer society, but we also believe that many social forces are arrayed against AR and its democratizing agenda. We hope to have persuaded some of you to join in the effort to build the strength, quality, and sophistication of AR, and we encourage you to enter into dialogue with us and the colleagues we have discussed in this book as we all seek to democratize research further and, through this, to make ours a more just world.

References

Alinsky, S. (1946). *Reveille for radicals*. Chicago: University of Chicago Press.

Argyris, C. (1974). *Theory in practice*. San Francisco: Jossey-Bass.

Argyris, C. (1980). *Inner contradictions of rigorous research*. New York: Academic Press.

Argyris, C. (1985). *Strategy, change, and defensive routines*. Boston: Pitman.

Argyris, C. (1993). *On organizational learning*. Cambridge, MA: Blackwell.

Argyris, C., Putnam, R., & McClain Smith, D. (1985). *Action science: Concepts, methods, and skills for research and intervention*. San Francisco: Jossey-Bass.

Argyris, C., & Schön, D. (1978). *Organizational learning*. Reading, MA: Addison-Wesley.

Argyris, C., & Schön, D. (1996). *Organizational learning II*. Reading, MA: Addison-Wesley.

Barnes, B. (1977). *Interests and the growth of knowledge*. London: Routledge & Kegan Paul.

Barnes, B., & Shapin, S. (1979). *Natural order*. Beverly Hills, CA: Sage.

Bateson, G. (1979). *Mind and nature: A necessary unity*. New York: Dutton.

Belshaw, D. (1981). A theoretical framework for data-economizing appraisal procedures with applications for rural development planning. *IDS Bulletin, 12*, 12-22.

Berger, P., & Luckmann, T. (1966). *The social construction of reality*. Garden City, NY: Doubleday.

Bier, A. G. (1980). *Crecimiento urbano y participación vecinal*. Madrid: Centro de Investigaciones Sociológicas.

Bradley, K., & Gelb, A. (1983). *Cooperation at work: The Mondragón experience*. London: Heinemann Educational Books.

Bråthen, S. (1973). Model monopoly and communication systems: Theoretical notes on democratization. *Acta Sociologica, 16*(2), 98-107.

Brokhaug, I., Levin, M., & Nilssen, T. (1986). *Tiltaksarbeid på dugnad* [Collective work for community development]. Trondheim: IFIM/ORAL.

Brookfield, S. (1986). *Understanding and facilitating learning: A comprehensive analysis of principles and effective practices*. San Francisco: Jossey-Bass.

Brookfield, S. (1987). *Developing critical thinkers: Challenging adults to explore alternative ways of thinking and acting.* San Francisco: Jossey-Bass.

Brown, L. D., & Tandon, R. (1993). Ideology and political economy in inquiry: Action research and participatory research. *Journal of Applied Behavioral Science, 19*(3), 277-294.

Brunner, I., & Guzman, A. (1989). Participatory evaluation: A tool to assess projects and empower people. In R. F. Conner & M. Hendricks (Eds.), *International innovations in evaluation methodology: New directions for program evaluation.* San Francisco: Jossey-Bass.

Burke, T. (1994). *Dewey's new logic: A reply to Russell.* Chicago: University of Chicago Press.

Carr, W., & Kemmis, S. (1985). *Becoming critical: Education, knowledge and action research.* London: Falmer.

Chambers, R. (1981). Rapid rural appraisal: Rationale and repertoire. *Public Administration and Rural Development, 2*(2), 95-106.

Chambers, R. (1994a). The origins and practice of participatory rural appraisal. *World Development, 22*(7), 953-966.

Chambers, R. (1994b). Participatory rural appraisal (PRA): Analysis of experience. *World Development, 22*(9), 1253-1268.

Chambers, R. (1994c). Participatory rural appraisal (PRA): Challenges, potentials, and paradigms. *World Development, 22*(10), 1437-1454.

Chambers, R. (1997). *Whose reality counts? Putting the first last.* London: Intermediate Technology Publications.

Chávez, C. (1975). *César Chávez: Autobiography of La Causa* (with J. E. Levy). New York: Norton.

Chessler, M., & Chesney, B. (1995). *Cancer and self-help: Bridging the troubled waters of childhood illness.* Madison: University of Wisconsin Press.

Clifford, J., & Marcus, G. (Eds.). (1985). *Writing culture.* Berkeley: University of California Press.

Cummings, T. G., & Worley, C. G. (1993). *Organization development and change.* Minneapolis/St. Paul: West.

Dahl, R. (1989). *Democracy and its critics.* New Haven, CT: Yale University Press.

Davis, L. E., & Taylor, J. C. (1972). *Design of jobs.* Harmondsworth, UK: Penguin.

Deming, W. E. (1983). *Out of the crisis: Quality, productivity, and competitive position.* Cambridge, MA: MIT Center for Advanced Engineering Technology.

Dewey, J. (1900). *The school and society.* Chicago: University of Chicago Press.

Dewey, J. (1902). *The child and the curriculum.* Chicago: University of Chicago Press.

Dewey, J. (1976). *Essays on logical theory, 1902-1903* (A. Boydston, Ed.). Carbondale: Southern Illinois University Press.

Dewey, J. (1991). *The public and its problems.* Athens: Ohio University Press. (Original work published 1927)

Dewey, J. (1991). *Logic: The theory of inquiry.* Carbondale: Southern Illinois University Press.

Diggins, J. (1994). *The promise of pragmatism.* Chicago: University of Chicago Press.

Dreyfus, H. L., & Dreyfus, S. E. (1986). *Mind over machine.* New York: Free Press.

Eikeland, O. (1992). *Erfaring, dialogikk og politikk* [Experience, dialogue and politics]. Oslo: Work Research Institute.

Elden, M. (1979). Three generations of work democracy experiments in Norway. In G. Cooper & E. Mumford (Eds.), *The quality of working life in western Europe*. London: Associated Business Press.

Elden, M., & Levin, M. (1991). Co-generative learning: Bringing participation into action research. In W. F. Whyte (Ed.), *Participatory action research* (pp. 127-142). Newbury Park, CA: Sage.

Elliott, J. (1991). *Action research for educational change*. Buckingham: Open University Press.

Elvemo, J. (1994). *Change agents and change processes*. Doctoral dissertation, Norwegian University of Science and Technology.

Elvemo, J., Grant Matthews, L., Greenwood, D., Martin, A., Strubel, A., & Thomas, L. (1997). Participation, action, and research in classroom. *Studies in Continuing Education, 19*(1), 1-50.

Emery, F., & Emery, M. (1974). *Participative design: Work and community life*. Canberra: Australian National University Centre for Continuing Education.

Emery, F., & Thorsrud, E. (1976). *Democracy at work*. Leiden: Martinus Nijhoff.

Emery, F. E., & Oeser, O. A. (1958). *Information, decision, and action*. Melbourne: Melbourne University Press.

Emery, F. E., & Trist, E. L. (1973). *Towards a social ecology*. London: Plenum.

Emery, M. (1982). *Searching*. Canberra: Australian National University Centre for Continuing Education.

Emery, M. (1993). *Participative design for participative democracy*. Canberra: Australian National University Centre for Continuing Education.

Emery, M. (1998). *Searching*. Amsterdam: John Benjamins.

Engelstad, P. H., & Haugen, R. (1972). *Skjervøy i gar, i dag og i morgen* (Sjervøy, yesterday, today and tomorrow). Oslo: Work Research Institute.

Eurich, N. (1985). *Corporate classrooms: The learning business*. Princeton, NJ: Princeton University Press.

Fals Borda, O., & Rahman, M. A. (Eds.). (1991). *Action and knowledge: Breaking the monopoly with participatory action research*. New York: Apex.

Field Belenky, M., Clinchy, B. M., Goldberger, N. R., & Tarule, J. M. (1997). *Women's ways of knowing*. New York: Basic Books.

Filley, A. C., & House, R. J. (1969). *Managerial process and organizational behavior*. Glenview, IL: Scott, Foresman.

Fine, M. (1992). *Disruptive voices: The possibilities of feminist research*. Ann Arbor: University of Michigan Press.

Fine, M. (1996). *Talking across boundaries: Participatory evaluation research in an urban middle school*. New York: City University of New York.

Finne, H., Levin, M., & Nilssen, T. (1995). Trailing research: A model for useful evaluation, *Evaluation, 1*(1), 11-32.

Fisher, D., & Torbert, W. R. (1995). *Personal and organizational transformations: The true challenge of continual quality improvement*. London: McGraw-Hill.

Flood, R., & Romm, N. (1996). *Diversity management*. Chichester, UK: Wiley.

Fossen, Ø. (1994). *Action research as reflective practice*. Doctoral dissertation, Norwegian University of Science and Technology.

Fox Keller, E. (1985). *Reflections on gender and science*. New Haven: Yale University Press.

Frege, G. (1956). The thought: A logical inquiry, *Mind, 65*, 289-311. (Original work published 1918)

Freire, P. (1970). *The pedagogy of the oppressed* (M. B. Ramos, Trans.). New York: Herder & Herder.

Gabarrón, L. R., & Hernández-Landa, L. (1994). *Investigación participativa*. Madrid: Centro de Investigaciones Sociológicas.

Gadamer, H. G., (1982). *Truth and method* (2nd ed.). New York: Crossroads.

Geertz, C. (1973). *The interpretation of cultures*. New York: Basic Books.

Gerhardsen, E. (1932). *Tillitsmannen* [Becoming a union official]. Oslo: Tiden Forlag.

Gilligan, C. (1982). *In a different voice*. Cambridge, MA: Harvard University Press.

Gjersvik, R. (1993). *The construction of information systems in organizations*. Doctoral dissertation, Norwegian University of Science and Technology.

Greenwood, D. (1980). *Community-level research, local-regional-governmental interaction and development planning: A strategy for baseline studies* (Rural Development Occasional Paper No. 10). Ithaca, NY: Cornell University, Center for International Studies.

Greenwood, D. (1985). *The taming of evolution: The persistence of nonevolutionary views in the study of humans*. Ithaca, NY: Cornell University Press.

Greenwood, D. (1989). Paradigm-centered versus client-centered research: A proposal for linkage. In *Proceedings of the forty second annual meeting, Industrial Relations Research Association* (pp. 273-281). Madison, WI: Industrial Relations Research Association.

Greenwood, D., et al. (1990). *Culturas de Fagor: Estudio antropológico de las cooperativas de Mondragón*. San Sebastian: Editorial Txertoa.

Greenwood, D., et al. (1992). *Industrial democracy as process: Participatory action research in the Fagor Cooperative Group of Mondragón*. Assen-Maastricht: Van Gorcum.

Greenwood, D., & Levin, M. (in press). Action research, science, and the co-optation of Social Research. *Studies in Cultures, Organizations and Societies, 5*(1).

Greenwood, D., Whyte, W. F., & Harkavy, I. (1993). Participatory action research as a process and as a goal. *Human Relations,46*(2), 175-192.

Guba, E. G., & Lincoln, Y. S. (1989). *Fourth generation evaluation*. Newbury Park, CA: Sage.

Gustavsen, B. (1992). *Dialogue and development*. Assen-Maastricht: Van Gorcum.

Habermas, J. (1984). *The theory of communicative action: Reason and the rationality of society* (T. McCarthy, Trans.). Boston: Beacon.

Hall, B. (1975). Participatory research: An approach for change. *Convergence, 8*(2), 24-32.

Hall, B., Gillette, A., & Tandon, R. (Eds.). (1982). *Creating knowledge: A monopoly? Participatory research in development*. New Delhi: Society for Participatory Research in Asia.

Hanssen Bauer, J., & Aslaksen, K. (1991). *Rett sats* [Correct start]. Oslo: SBA.

Herbst, P. (1976). *Alternatives to hierarchies*. Leiden: Martinus Nijhoff.

Herbst, P. (1980, Summer). Community conference design; Skjervøy, today and tomorrow. *Human Futures*(2), 1-6.

Heron, J. (1996). *Co-operative inquiry: Research into the human condition*. London: Sage.

Herzberg, F. (1966). *Work and the nature of man*. Cleveland: World Publishing.

Herzfeld, M. (1992). *The social production of indifference: Exploring the symbolic roots of western bureaucracy*. New York: Berg.

Horton, M. (with J. Kohl & H. Kohl). (1990). *The long haul: An autobiography*. New York: Doubleday.

Horton, M., & Freire, P. (1990). *We make the road by walking: Conversations on education and social change*. Philadelphia: Temple University Press.

Investigación-Acción Participativa. (1993, July-September). *Documentación Social, 93*.

Ishikawa, K. (1976). *Guide to quality control*. Tokyo: Asian Productivity Organization.

Jacob, F. (1982). *The possible and the actual*. Seattle: University of Washington Press.

James, W. (1948). *Essays in pragmatism*. New York: Hafner.

James, W. (1995). *Essays in radical empiricism*. Lincoln: University of Nebraska Press.

Johannesen, K. S. (1996). Action research and epistemology: Some remarks concerning the activity-relatedness and contextuality of human language. *Concepts and Transformation, 1*(2/3), 281-297.

Joyappa, V., & Martin, D. (1996). Exploring alternative research epistemologies for adult education: Participatory research, feminist research and feminist participatory research. *Adult Education Quarterly, 47*(1), 1-14.

Juran, J. M. (1980). *Quality planning and analysis*. New York: McGraw-Hill.

Kasmir, S. (1996). *The myth of Mondragón*. Albany: State University of New York Press.

Klev, R. (1993). *The political construction of a technology transfer program*. Doctoral dissertation, Norwegian University of Science and Technology.

Kuhn, T. (1962). *The structure of scientific revolutions*. Chicago: University of Chicago Press.

Lanham, R. (1992). *Revising prose*. New York: Macmillan.

Lather, P. (1991). *Getting smart: Feminist research and pedagogy with/in the postmodern*. New York: Routledge.

Latour, B. (1987). *Science in action*. Cambridge, MA: Harvard University Press.

Latour, B., & Woolgar, S. (1979). *Laboratory life*. Beverly Hills, CA: Sage.

Levin, M. (1988). *Lokal mobilisering* [Local mobilization]. Trondheim: IFIM.

Levin, M. (1993). Creating networks for rural economic development in Norway. *Human Relations, 46*(2), 193-217.

Levin, M. (1994). Action research and critical systems thinking: Two icons carved out of the same log? *Systems Practice, 7*(1), 25-42.

Levin, M., et al. (1980a). *Teknisk utvikling og arbeidsforhold i aluminiumselektrolyse* [Technical development and quality of working life in aluminum smelting]. Trondheim: IFIM.

Levin, M., et al. (1980b). *Hitterværinger vi kan vil vi?* [Citizens of Hitra we can but will we?]. Trondheim: IFIM.

Levin, M., & Martin, A. (1995). *Power differences in discourse*. Unpublished manuscript.

Levin, M., & Nilssen, T. (1990a). *Evaluering av BUNT-programmets konsulentoppaering* [Evaluation of the BUNT consultant training program]. Trondheim: SUM.

Levin, M., & Nilssen, T. (1990b). *Etter ett år med BUNT fern kritiske faktorer for suksess* [After 1 year with BUNT—Critical factors for success]. Trondheim: SUM.

Levin, M., Svarva, A., & Sletterød, N. A. (1990). *Mens vi venter på* [While we are waiting]. Trondheim: IFIM.

Lewin, K. (1935). *A dynamic theory of personality* (D. Adams & E. Zener, Trans.). New York: McGraw-Hall.

Lewin, K. (1943). Forces behind food habits and methods of change. *Bulletin of the National Research Council, 108*, 35-65.

Lewin, K. (1948). *Resolving social conflicts*. New York: Harper.

Lincoln, Y. S., & Guba, E. G. (1985). *Naturalistic inquiry*. Beverly Hills, CA: Sage.

Lincoln, Y., & Reason, P. (Eds.). (1996). Quality in human inquiry [Special issue]. *Qualitative Inquiry, 2*(1).

Maguire, P. (1987). *Doing participatory research: A feminist approach.* Amherst: University of Massachusetts, Center for International Education.

Maguire, P. (1994). Participatory research from one feminist's perspective: Moving from exposing androcentricism to embracing possible contributions of feminism to participatory research and practice. I. K. de Koning (Ed.), *Proceedings of the international symposium on participatory research in health promotion* (pp. 5-14). Liverpool, UK: Liverpool School of Tropical Medicine, Education Resource Group.

Maguire, P. (1996). Considering more feminist participatory research: What has congruency got to do with it? *Qualitative Inquiry, 2*(1), 106-118.

Mansbridge, J. (1983). *Beyond adversary democracy.* Chicago: University of Chicago Press.

Markova, I., & Foppa, K. (1991). *Asymmetries in dialogue.* Herfordshire, UK: Harvester Wheatsheaf.

Martin, A., Hemlock, N., & Rich, R. (1994). *Saskatchewan highways and transportation traffic safety search conference.* Ithaca, NY: Cornell University Programs for Employment and Workplace Systems.

Martin, A., & Rich, R. (1994). *Seneca Nation of Indians search '94.* Ithaca, NY: Cornell University Programs for Employment and Workplace Systems.

Martin, A. W. (1997). *Search conference methodology and the politics of difference.* Unpublished dissertation proposal, Teachers College, Columbia University.

Maslow, A. H. (1943). A theory of human motivation. *Psychological Review, 50,* 370-396.

Mayo, E. (1933). *The human problems of industrial civilization.* New York: Macmillan.

Mezirow, J. (1991). *Transformative dimensions of adult learning.* San Francisco: Jossey-Bass.

Mezirow, J. (1996). Contemporary paradigms of learning. *Adult Education Quarterly, 46*(3), 158-173.

Mies, M. (1990). Women's studies: Science, violence and responsibility. *Women's Studies International Forum, 13,* 433-441.

Milgram, S. (1974). *Obedience to authority.* New York: Harper & Row.

Miller, J. (1991). *The rise and fall of democracy in early America: 1630-1789.* University Park: Pennsylvania State University Press.

Monden, Y. (1983). *The Toyota production system: A practical approach to production management.* Norcross, GA: Industrial Engineering and Management Press.

Mosse, D. (1993). *Authority, gender and knowledge: Theoretical reflections on the practice of participatory rural appraisal* (ODI Network Paper 44). London: ODI.

Nathan, J. (1996). *Charter schools: Creating hope and opportunity for American education.* San Francisco: Jossey-Bass.

Negt, O. (1977). *Sociologisk fantasi og eksemplarisk indlæring* [Sociological fantasy and exemplary learning]. Roskilde: Roskilde Universitetsforlag.

Nelkin, D. (1982). *The creation controversy.* New York: Norton.

Nelkin, D., & Lindee, M. S. (1995). *The DNA mystique.* New York: Freeman.

Nelkin, D., & Tancredi, L. (1987). *Dangerous diagnostics.* New York: Basic Books.

Noffke, S. (1994). Action research: Towards the next generation. *Educational Action Research, 2*(1), 9-21.

Nørgaard, A. (1935). *Grundtvigianismen* (The Grundtvid way). København: Gyldendal.

Park, P., Brydon-Miller, M., Hall, B., & Jackson, T. (Eds.). (1993). *Voices of change: Participatory research in the United States and Canada.* Westport, CT: Bergin & Garvey.

Parsons, T. (1951). *The social system.* Glencoe, IL: Free Press.

Pateman, C. (1970). *Participation and democratic theory.* Cambridge, UK: Cambridge University Press.

Patton, M. Q. (1986). *Utilization-focused evaluation.* Beverly Hills, CA: Sage.

Peirce, C. (1950). *Philosophy: Selected writings.* New York: Harcourt Brace.

Philips, Ä. (1988). *Eldsjälar* [Burning souls]. Doctoral dissertation, Stockholm School of Economics.

Polanyi, M. (1964). *Personal knowledge.* New York: Harper & Row.

Polanyi, M. (1966). *The tacit dimension.* Gloucester, MA: P. Smith.

Rabinow, P. (1996). *Making PCR.* Chicago: University of Chicago Press.

Rabinow, P., & Sullivan, W. (Eds.). (1987). *Interpretive social science.* Berkeley: University of California Press.

Rapoport, A. (1974). *Conflict in man-made environments.* Harmondsworth, UK: Penguin Books.

Readings, B. (1996). *The university in ruins.* Cambridge, MA: Harvard University Press.

Reason, P. (Ed.). (1988). *Human inquiry in action.* London: Sage.

Reason, P. (Ed.). (1994). *Participation in human inquiry.* London: Sage.

Reason, P., & Rowan, J. (Eds.). (1981). *Human inquiry: A sourcebook of new paradigm research.* Chichester, UK: Wylie.

Reinharz, S. (1992). *Feminist methods in social research.* New York: Oxford University Press.

Reynolds, M. A. (1994). *Democracy in higher education: Participatory action research in the Physics 101-102 curriculum revision project at Cornell University.* Doctoral dissertation, Cornell University.

Rolfsen, M. (1993). *Japanisme: Ideologi og implementering i bilindustrien* [Japanism: Ideology and implementation in the auto industry]. Doctoral dissertation, Norwegian University of Science and Technology.

Rorty, R. (1980). *Philosophy and the mirror of nature.* Princeton, NJ: Princeton University Press.

Russell, B. (1903). *The principles of mathematics.* Cambridge: Cambridge University Press.

Ryle, G. (1949). *The concept of mind.* London: Hutchinson.

Schön, D. A. (1983). *The reflective practitioner.* New York: Basic Books.

Schön, D. A. (1987). *Educating the reflective practitioner.* San Francisco: Jossey-Bass.

Schön, D. A. (Ed.). (1991). *The reflective turn.* New York: Teachers College Press.

Schumacher, E. F. (1973). *Small is beautiful: A study of economics as if people mattered.* New York: Harper & Row.

Schwandt, T. (1997, July). *Towards a new science of action research.* Paper presented at the Tavistock conference "Is Action Research Real Research," London.

Scriven, M. (1995). The logic of evaluation and evaluation practice. *New Directions for Evaluation, 68,* 49-70.

Senge, P. M. (1990). *The fifth discipline: The art and practice of the learning organization.* New York: Doubleday.

Shor, I., & Freire, P. (1987). *A pedagogy for liberation: Dialogues on transforming education.* South Hadley, MA: Bergin & Garvey.

Sims Feldstein, H., & Poats, S. V. (Eds.). (1990). *Working together: Gender analysis in agriculture.* West Hartford, CT: Kumarian.

Skjervheim, H. (1974). *Objektivismen og studiet av mennesket* [Objectivity and the study of man]. Oslo: Gyldendal.

Swantz, M. (1985). *Women in development: A creative role denied? The case of Tanzania.* London: Hurst.

Taylor, C. (1985). *Philosophy and the human sciences*. Cambridge, UK: Cambridge University Press.

Thomas, H., & Logan, C. (1982). *Mondragón: An economic analysis*. London: Allen and Unwin.

Torbert, W. (1991). *The power of balance: Transforming self, society, and scientific inquiry*. Newbury Park, CA: Sage.

Torvatn, H. (1993). *Use of evaluations of Norwegian technology transfer program*. Doctoral dissertation, Norwegian University of Science and Technology.

Toulmin, S. (1996). Concluding methodological reflection: Elitism and democracy among the sciences. In S. Toulmin & B. Gustavsen (Eds.), *Beyond theory* (pp. 203-225). Amsterdam: John Benjamins.

Toulmin, S., & Gustavsen, B. (Eds.). (1996). *Beyond theory*. Amsterdam and Philadelphia: John Benjamins.

Traweek, S. (1992). *Beamtimes and lifetimes*. Cambridge, MA: Harvard University Press.

Trist, E. (1981). *The evolution of socio-technical systems* (Occasional Paper No. 2). Toronto: Ontario Quality of Work Life Council.

Trist, E., & Bamforth, K. W. (1951). Some social and psychological consequences of the longwall method of coal getting. *Human Relations, 4,* 3-38.

Van Eijnatten, F. M. (1993). *The paradigm that changed the work place*. Assen: van Gorcum.

van den Hombergh, H. (1993). *Gender, environment, and development: A guide to the literature*. Utrecht: Institute for Development Research, International Books.

Ver Beek, K. (1996). *The pilgrimage for life, justice and liberty: Insights for development*. Doctoral dissertation, Cornell University.

von Bertalanffy, L. (1966). *Modern theories of development*. London: Oxford University Press.

von Bertalanffy, L. (1968). *General systems theory*. New York: Braziller.

Weber, M. (1958). *The city* (D. Martindale & G. Neuwirth, Trans.). Glencoe, IL: Free Press.

Weisbord, M. (1987). *Productive workplaces: Organizing and managing for meaning and community*. San Francisco: Jossey-Bass.

Weisbord, M. (1992). *Discovering common ground*. San Francisco: Bernett-Koehler.

Weiss, H. B., & Greene, J. C. (1992). An empowerment partnership for family support and education programs and evaluations. *Family Science Review, 5*(1 and 2), 131-149.

Westbrook, R. (1991). *John Dewey and American democracy*. Ithaca, NY: Cornell University Press.

Whyte, W. F. (1994). *Participant observer: An autobiography*. Ithaca, NY: ILR.

Whyte, W. F., & Whyte, K. K. (1991). *Making Mondragón* (2nd ed.). Ithaca, NY: ILR.

Wittgenstein, L. (1953). *Philosophical investigations*. London: Blackwell.

Womack, J. P., et al. (1990). *The machine that changed the world*. New York: Rawson Associates.

Young, I. M. (1990). *Justice and the politics of difference*. Princeton, NJ: Princeton University Press.

Zabusky, S. (1995). *Launching Europe*. Princeton, NJ: Princeton University Press.

Author Index

Subject Index

About the Authors

Davydd J. Greenwood is the Goldwin Smith Professor of Anthropology at Cornell University and Corresponding Member of the Spanish Royal Academy of Moral and Political Sciences. His work centers on action research, political economy, and the Basque Country. He previously held the John S. Knight Professorship of International Studies and the position of Director of the Mario Einaudi Center for International Studies at Cornell University. Greenwood has been at Cornell University since 1970. He serves on the editorial boards of *Dialogues on Work and Innovations, Concepts and Transformation, Systemic Practice and Action Research, Action Research International,* and the *Revista de Antropología Aplicada.* He is also a participant in the Norwegian Enterprise 2000 Program and served on the staff of the Scandinavian Action Research Development Program. His books include *Unrewarding Wealth: The Commercialization and Collapse of Agriculture in a Spanish Basque Town*; *Nature, Culture, and Human History*; *The Taming of Evolution: The Persistence of Nonevolutionary Views in the Study of Humans*; *Las Culturas de Fagor*; and *Industrial Democracy as Process: Participatory Action Research in the Fagor Cooperative Group of Mondragón.* His action research experience centers on a 2-year project in the Guthrie Clinic in Sayre, Pennsylvania; a 4-year project with the industrial labor-managed cooperatives of Mondragón in the Spanish Basque Country; a

1-year collaborative community social and economic development project in Spain; collaboration in a number of projects with the Program for Employment and Workplace Systems in ILR Extension at Cornell University; and ongoing work with a variety of groups attached to the University of Trondheim.

Morten Levin is Professor at the Department of Sociology and Political Science at the Norwegian University of Science and Technology in Trondheim. Through most of his professional life he has worked as an action researcher. His major research focus has been on the relationship between technology and organization, local community development, participative evaluation, and leadership in participative change processes. He has also been in charge of a PhD program in action research. He has been at the Norwegian University of Science and Technology since 1982. He serves on the editorial boards of *Systemic Practice and Action Research* and *Action Research International.* He served on the staff of the Scandinavian Action Research Development Program. Currently he is leading the Trondheim module of the Enterprise 2000 Program, and leading a joint Norwegian/MIT program granting a degree in Technology Management. He is heading the development of an action research group focusing on participative change processes linked to core technological, economic, and organizational transformations in enterprises.

He has published textbooks in the fields of organization and technology (*Leadership and Technology*), and articles on cogenerative learning, action research, critical systems thinking, technology transfer as a learning and developmental process, developing leadership in technology management, creating transdisciplinary knowledge, and "trailing research."